BARUCH
BEN NERIAH

Studies on Personalities of the Old Testament
James L. Crenshaw, *Series Editor*

BARUCH
BEN NERIAH

From Biblical Scribe to Apocalyptic Seer

J. EDWARD WRIGHT

University of South Carolina Press

Published in Columbia, South Carolina, by the
University of South Carolina Press

Manufactured in the United States of America

07 06 05 04 03 5 4 3 2 1

Library of Congress Cataloging-in-Publication Data

Wright, J. Edward.
    Baruch ben Neriah : from biblical scribe to apocalyptic seer / J. Edward Wright.
        p. cm. — (Studies on personalities of the Old Testament)
    Includes bibliographical references and index.
        ISBN 1-57003-479-6 (cloth : alk. paper)
    1. Baruch ben Neriah. 2. Bible. O.T.—Criticism, interpretation, etc.
3. Apocryphal literature (Old Testament)—Criticism, interpretation, etc.
4. Apocalyptic literature—History and criticism. 5. Christian literature,
Early—History and criticism. I. Title. II. Series.
    BS580.B36 W75 2003
    221.9'2—dc21   2002013486

In memory of my beloved parents
James E. and Virginia L. Wright

Contents

Series Editor's Preface

Critical study of the Bible in its ancient Near Eastern setting has stimulated interest in the individuals who shaped the course of history and whom events singled out as tragic or heroic figures. Rolf Rendtorff's *Men of the Old Testament* (1968) focuses on the lives of important biblical figures as a means of illuminating history, particularly the sacred dimension that permeates Israel's convictions about its God. Fleming James's *Personalities of the Old Testament* (1939) addresses another issue, that of individuals who function as inspiration for their religious successors in the twentieth century. Studies restricting themselves to a single individual—e.g., Moses, Abraham, Samson, Elijah, David, Saul, Ruth, Jonah, Job, Jeremiah—enable scholars to deal with a host of questions: psychological, literary, theological, sociological, and historical. Some, like Gerhard von Rad's *Moses,* introduce a specific approach to interpreting the Bible, hence provide valuable pedagogic tools.

As a rule, these treatments of isolated figures have not reached the general public. Some were written by outsiders who lacked a knowledge of biblical criticism (Freud on Moses, Jung on Job) and whose conclusions, however provocative, remain problematic. Others were targeted for the guild of professional biblical critics (David Gunn on David and Saul, Phyllis Trible on Ruth, Terence Fretheim and Jonathan Magonet on Jonah). None has succeeded in capturing the imagination of the reading public in the way fictional works like Archibald MacLeish's *J.B.* and Joseph Heller's *God Knows* have done.

It could be argued that the general public would derive little benefit from learning more about the personalities of the Bible. Their conduct, often less then exemplary, reveals a flawed character, and their everyday concerns have nothing to do with our preoccupations from dawn to dusk. To be sure, some individuals transcend their own age, entering the gallery of classical literary figures from time immemorial. But only these rare achievers can justify specific treatments of them. Then why publish additional studies on biblical personalities?

The answer cannot be that we read about biblical figures to learn ancient history, even of the sacred kind, or to discover models for ethical action. But what remains? Perhaps the primary significance of biblical personages is the light they throw on the imaging of deity in biblical times. At the very least, the Bible constitutes human perceptions of deity's relationship with the world and its creatures. Close readings of biblical personalities therefore clarify ancient understandings of God. That is the important datum which we seek—not because we endorse that specific view of deity, but because all such efforts to make sense of reality contribute something worthwhile to the endless quest for knowledge.

JAMES L. CRENSHAW
DUKE DIVINITY SCHOOL

Preface

This study traces the evolution of the depictions of Baruch ben Neriah, the prophet Jeremiah's scribal assistant, from the biblical materials through the early Jewish and Christian texts and traditions that either mention Baruch or were allegedly written by him. It not only shows how biblical and postbiblical literature depicted Baruch, but also highlights how the various depictions of Baruch reveal the leadership models and religious values cherished by the communities that created these many texts and traditions. The book thus combines a literary history of a biblical character with a socioreligious study of several models of early Jewish and Christian religious leadership. More than just a survey of the life and legacy of one individual, this book traces how communities kept the memory of Baruch alive by revitalizing the biblical stories about him and creating new stories to address the pressing social, political, and religious issues of the day.

I hope that this volume will be of value to general readers, college and seminary students, as well as to scholars in the humanities who are interested in late biblical history and in how early Jews and Christians continued to interpret and reshape the biblical stories. The Baruch found in the Hebrew Bible/Old Testament played a very important role in the history of Judaism. He recorded Jeremiah's revelations and sermons, and he assisted the people of Jerusalem in the dark days before, during, and after the destruction of the city by the Babylonians in 586 B.C.E. This examination of Baruch's life and work within the context of ancient scribes and scribal practices will enable us to understand better his unique contributions to history. After all, Baruch is one of the few people known to us who may have actually written parts of the Hebrew Bible as we now have it.

As a result of how various communities depicted him, there exist many images of Baruch. The "Baruchs" of later tradition show us how the early Jewish and Christian communities reshaped Baruch's persona to have him speak afresh to the pressing social and religious issues of their generation. These later texts that were attributed to but certainly not written by Baruch, provide us insight into the problems these communities faced and how they tried to resolve them. Moreover, this reshaping of Baruch's persona allows us to see how these people updated the Bible and its characters in order to make the ancient traditions relevant to new situations. By reinventing Baruch, early Jews and Christians made the biblical stories speak anew to subsequent generations.

I have been fascinated with Baruch ben Neriah and his legacy for years. My interest in Baruch traditions began in the fall of 1988 during a graduate seminar at Harvard Divinity School on *3 Baruch (Greek Apocalypse)* taught by Prof. Michael E. Stone. That intellectually invigorating seminar led to a dissertation on *3 Baruch* and several publications that serve as the foundation for this study.[1] That such a body of research could grow out of one seminar attests to Michael's ability to inspire his students. Through the years as I have tried to draw this material together I have been encouraged and supported by many dear people, and I owe them all a great debt of thanks. I thank first and foremost my wife Keeley and our daughter Angela for their love and support and for all the joy they bring to my life. I thank Michael Stone for introducing me to Baruch and to the study of early Jewish and Christian apocrypha and pseudepigrapha. I thank my colleagues at the University of Arizona, and especially William G. Dever, for the lively academic community I enjoy in Tucson. Ever since I arrived in Tucson, Bill has been the most supportive mentor and friend a person could hope to have, and my life is better for having the good fortune of knowing and working with him. I also thank my colleagues in the national SBL Pseudepigrapha Group and the Judaism in the Greco-Roman Era Group of the SBL Pacific Coast Region for allowing me to present earlier drafts of this material at various meetings throughout the past ten years. Jim Mueller and Randy Chesnutt have been particularly supportive of my work in this regard. One of the benefits I cherish most about life in the Academy is the opportunity to interact with a community of skilled and supportive scholars. I owe my colleagues a great debt of thanks for their support and their constructive criticisms that have made me a better scholar, teacher, and person. Moreover, Prof. James Crenshaw of Duke University, the series editor, and Barry Blose, the editor for religious studies at the University of South Carolina Press, have been unbelievably patient and encouraging. This book would not have seen the light of day had it not been for their support. Finally, I want to express my love and appreciation for my parents, Jim and Virginia Wright, who always stressed the importance of learning as the way to a better life. They were right, as usual.

Abbreviations

AB	Anchor Bible
ABD	*Anchor Bible Dictionary*, ed. D. N. Freedman
ABRL	Anchor Bible Reference Library
ANRW	*Aufstieg und Niedergang der römischen Welt*
AOT	*The Apocryphal Old Testament*, ed. H. F. D. Sparks
APAT	*Die Apokryphen und Pseudepigraphen des Alten Testaments*, ed. E. Kautzsch
APOT	*The Apocrypha and Pseudepigrapha of the Old Testament*, ed. R. H. Charles
ARM	Archives royales de Mari
BA	*Biblical Archaeologist*
BARev	*Biblical Archaeology Review*
BASOR	*Bulletin of the American Schools of Oriental Research*
BO	*Bibliotheca Orientalis*
BZ	*Biblische Zeitschrift*
BZAW	Beihefte zur Zeitschrift für die alttestamentliche Wissenschaft
CAD	*The Assyrian Dictionary of the Oriental Institute of the University of Chicago*
CBQ	*Catholic Biblical Quarterly*
CBQMS	Catholic Biblical Quarterly Monograph Series
ConBOT	Coniectanea Biblica, Old Testament Series
CRBS	*Currents in Research: Biblical Studies*
CRIANT	Compendia rerum iudaicarum ad Novum Testamentum
GAG	*Grundriss der akkadischen Grammatik*, W. von Soden
HAW	Handbuch der Altertumswissenschaft
HSM	Harvard Semitic Monographs
HTR	*Harvard Theological Review*
HUCA	*Hebrew Union College Annual*
ICC	International Critical Commentary
Int	*Interpretation*

JBL	*Journal of Biblical Literature*
JJS	*Journal of Jewish Studies*
JNES	*Journal of Near Eastern Studies*
JSOT	*Journal for the Study of the Old Testament*
JSOTSup	Journal for the Study of the Old Testament— Supplement Series
JSP	*Journal for the Study of the Pseudepigrapha*
OBO	Orbis biblicus et orientalis
OEANE	*Oxford Encyclopedia of Archaeology in the Near East,* ed. E. M. Meyers, et al.
OTL	Old Testament Library
OTP	*The Old Testament Pseudepigrapha,* ed. J. H. Charlesworth
PG	J. Minge, *Patrologia graeca*
RB	*Revue biblique*
SBLDS	Society of Biblical Literature Dissertation Series
SBLSCS	Society of Biblical Literature Septuagint and Cognate Studies
SBT	Studies in Biblical Theology
SC	Sources chrétiennes
SCS	Septuagint and Cognate Studies
TAPS	Transactions of the American Philosophical Society
USQR	*Union Seminary Quarterly Review*
VT	*Vetus Testamentum*
VTSup	Vetus Testamentum, Supplements
WMANT	Wissenschaftliche Monographien zum Alten und Neuen Testament
ZAW	*Zeitschrift für die alttestamentliche Wissenschaft*

BARUCH
BEN NERIAH

Chapter One

THE SCRIBE

Send me a well-trained scribe so that I may have him write down the message that Shamash sent to me for the king.

ARM XXVI.414:32–33

Baruch ben Neriah breaks onto the biblical scene in the book of Jeremiah as a professional scribe working for the prophet Jeremiah. The name Baruch (בָּרוּד, "blessed one") is a shortened form of the name בֶּרֶכְיָהוּ, Berechyahu (cf. Zech 1:7; 1 Chron 6:24, 15:17; 2 Chron 28:12), which means "blessed by Yahweh."[1] From his full name, Baruch son of Neriah, son of Mahseiah, we learn a good deal about his family. Baruch's father Neriah had another son, Seriah (שריה, Jer 51:59, 61), who, like his famous brother, was intimately involved with the work of the prophet Jeremiah. Neriah (נריה) and his father, Mahseiah (מחסיה), themselves do not play active roles in the biblical narratives, although they may have been priests or from a priestly family. Neriah and Mahseiah are known only through the work of their descendants Baruch and Seriah. Baruch came from what appears to have been a prominent family in Jerusalem during the latter years of Judaean independence.

Baruch, Jeremiah, and the Fall of Jerusalem to the Babylonians

Baruch ben Neriah worked as the prophet Jeremiah's scribal assistant. Jeremiah's prophetic career spanned the reigns of five kings (Jer 1:2–3): Josiah (639–309), Jehoahaz II/Shallum (609), Jehoiakim (608–598),

Jehoiachin (598–597), and Zedekiah (597–586). The opening of the book of Jeremiah (Jer 1:2) states that Jeremiah received his prophetic "call" in the thirteenth year of king Josiah's reign, circa 627 B.C.E. The book of Jeremiah purports to be a record of the prophetic activity of Jeremiah the son of Hilkiah who was a priest from the small village of Anathoth just outside of Jerusalem (Jer 1:1). Jeremiah and Baruch lived during the tumultuous years preceding the fall of Jerusalem to the Babylonians in 586 B.C.E.

Josiah came to the throne of Judah in 639 B.C.E. at the age of eight and was likely under the tutelage of courtiers who possessed what has come to be called a "deuteronomistic" ideology.[2] The hallmark of Josiah's rule was an attempt to reform the cult of Yahweh. These reforms traditionally have been designated the "Deuteronomistic Reforms." The designation is obviously inspired by the name of the biblical book and is entirely fitting because the book of Deuteronomy enshrines the religious principles that characterized this aggressively monotheistic reform. These reforms were at least in part inspired by the "book of the Torah" that was allegedly found in the Temple during Josiah's reign (2 Kgs 22:8). Most scholars now think that this "book of the Torah" is none other than the book of Deuteronomy itself, and that it was not found but composed at this time. The Deuteronomistic History (Deuteronomy through 2 Kings) and the book of Jeremiah indicate that Josiah's reforms—if there ever were thoroughgoing cultic reforms in his day—did not succeed.[3] The people persisted, quite naturally, in their longstanding and diverse cultic activities and maintained their devotion to many gods. Much of the biblical material denounces the non-deuteronomistic cultic predilections of the ancient Israelites and Judeans; nevertheless, this remained their standard religious orientation.

During Josiah's reign (639–609) the Babylonians vanquished the mighty Assyrians, transforming the tiny state of Judah from an Assyrian to a Babylonian vassal. The Judaeans initially experienced more autonomy under the Babylonians, but overall their conditions did not markedly improve. Josiah became caught up in regional politics. He and his kingdom were sandwiched between the two great powers of Babylon and Egypt, each of which intended to extend its regional influence in the eastern Mediterranean at the expense of the other.

With the advice of his counselors and prophets, perhaps even including Jeremiah, Josiah decided to reach an accommodation with the Babylonians and to resist Egyptian meddling in his territory. In 609, Pharaoh Necho II was leading his forces through Judah on his way to a showdown with the Babylonians. Josiah rushed out to attack the Egyptian army near Megiddo as it brazenly crossed through his territory. Josiah and the Judaeans were no match for the Egyptians, and Josiah lost his life in the battle. The great king, whom the Deuteronomistic History regards as the greatest of all of Judah's kings, was struck down in his prime.

The people anointed Josiah's son Jehoahaz—Jehoahaz II, also known as Shallum—as Josiah's successor.[4] Jehoahaz adopted a pro-Babylonian stance and ruled for only a few months in 609 B.C.E. before being summarily deposed and taken to Egypt by Pharaoh Necho II. The pharaoh appointed Eliakim (better known as Jehoiakim) king in place of his brother Jehoahaz. That the Egyptians were able to depose a local ruler and replace him with their handpicked successor is indicative of their thorough domination of Judean politics at the time.

Jehoiakim's reign (609–598) saw a pivotal event in the history of the Near East take place—the Battle of Carchemish in 605 B.C.E. The Egyptian and Babylonian forces battled fiercely at this site, upriver from the Syrian town of Aleppo on the Euphrates. The Babylonians, under the leadership of Nebuchadnezzar II, defeated the Egyptians handily, just as they had previously defeated the Assyrians, and this instigated a shift of power in the Near East. Babylon now became the major power and dominated the entire region to the boarders of Egypt.[5] Sensing the shift of fortunes, Jeremiah redesigned his foreign policy and began promoting a pro-Babylonian agenda. He thought that Judah would be wise to submit to the Babylonians. Jeremiah perhaps knew that Babylon was too powerful to stop and that resistance would be futile. Nonetheless, Jehoiakim eventually decided to resist Babylonian hegemony. Having been given the throne by Pharaoh Necho II, Jehoiakim understandably adopted a pro-Egypt policy. Jeremiah, however, was counseling the people to submit to the Babylonians, as they were God's instruments of punishment for the Judeans' religious infidelity. Jeremiah and Jehoiakim thus found themselves on opposite sides of the most pressing political issue of the day. Moreover, according to the deuteronomistic assessment of his life, Jehoiakim "did what was evil in the eyes of Yahweh as his predecessors had done" (2 Kgs 23:37). Eventually, the Babylonians besieged Jerusalem and conquered the entire region (601 B.C.E.). Jehoiakim submitted for three years and then turned once again to his old ally the Egyptians in the hope that they could help him break loose from Babylonian domination. The result of this ill-advised policy was a complete Babylonian rout of Judah. Jehoiakim died and was succeeded by his son Jehoiachin.

Unfortunately for Jehoiachin, the Babylonians made him pay for his father's rebellion. Jehoiachin (also referred to as "Jeconiah" or "Coniah") reigned for only three months following his succession to the throne (598–597).[6] He had to endure a Babylonian siege of Jerusalem, and, after submitting, was taken captive along with many leading citizens of Jerusalem to Babylon (597 B.C.E.). Included in this group, apparently, was the prophet Ezekiel (Ezek 1:1–3). Jehoiachin appears to have lived as a Babylonian prisoner for thirty-seven years before being released by the Babylonian king Amel-Marduk (the "Evil-Merodach" in 2 Kgs 25:27–30), who thereafter treated him with rather more dignity.

The Babylonians then appointed Mattaniah—Jehoiachin's uncle and a son of Josiah—king in Jerusalem (597–587 B.C.E.). Mattaniah took the name Zedekiah upon becoming king. Zedekiah understood the importance of maintaining loyal relations with the Babylonians, and so he apparently visited Babylon in 594–93 with the goal of assuring them of his fidelity (Jer 51:59). Zedekiah's officials, on the other hand, had nationalist and pro-Egypt predilections. So after initially following a pro-Babylonian foreign policy, a policy that Jeremiah certainly favored, Zedekiah conceded to nationalist fervor and entered into a pact with the Egyptians, thereby breaking faith and his treaties with the Babylonians. With Egyptian support he rebelled against the Babylonians in 588, inciting Nebuchadnezzar to respond with all his military might. Jerusalem capitulated after having been besieged for about a year and a half. Zedekiah, fearing for his life, was able to slip past the Babylonian blockade of the city under cover of darkness. Once outside the city, his officers deserted him and he was eventually captured near Jericho. Zedekiah was forced to watch the execution of his family before being himself brutally blinded: the last thing he saw was the slaughter of his family. He was then taken in chains to Babylon. The Babylonians destroyed the city and deported all but the poorest of the poor to Babylon: "Thus Judah went into exile from its land" (2 Kgs 25:21). The Babylonian response was swift and decisive—they vanquished Judah and laid siege to Jerusalem. The siege lasted nearly three years (589–587 B.C.E.) with only brief interruptions.

Baruch and Jeremiah lived during this difficult period in Jewish history. The nation went from being subservient to the Assyrians to being subservient to the Babylonians, with a brief period of Egyptian domination in between. As a prophet, Jeremiah spoke against the social problems of his generation and promoted what he considered the most prudent national and foreign public policies. This drew him into conflict, however, with both the religious and the political powers of his day. Throughout he was assisted by Baruch ben Neriah, a scribe by trade and a loyal supporter of Jeremiah by choice.

Ancient Near Eastern Scribes and Scribalism

The ancient Near Eastern empires—Babylonian, Assyrian, Egyptian, and others—were vast bureaucracies and had schools for training bureaucrats in the skills required by their positions. Especially in Egypt and Mesopotamia, with their terribly complex writing systems, this training would have started at a young age and lasted many years. Even with the introduction of the alphabet with its simplified writing system, these bureaucrats or scribes would have had to learn the other writing systems to an extent in addition to their own country's standard literary forms and official protocols.[7] Still, the invention of the alphabet with its couple dozen consonants made writing and reading easier. W. F. Albright noted this fact decades ago, and although his estimation of the spread of literacy was overly optimistic, his perceptions of the impact of the simplified alphabetic writing system remain trenchant: "Since the forms of the letters are very simple, the 22–letter alphabet could be learned in a day or two by a bright student and in a week or two by the dullest."[8]

How did the scribes who toiled in the Israelite and Judean kingdoms learn their trade? The exact details of the educational system in ancient Israel and Judah remain unclear. Surely they had some system to train scribes and other bureaucrats, a "system" beyond the home for training young people in the basic behavioral, character, and professional skills expected of bureaucrats.[9] Still, scholars disagree over the extent of an organized, professionally led educational system in ancient Israel and Judah.[10] Epigraphic evidence suggests that during at least the late monarchic era people had rudimentary literacy and could write receipts, their names, and even letters. For example, the following inscription in which a superior officer tells an inferior that he needs to use a scribe and the inferior responds with indignation saying that he knows how to write well enough, suggests that literacy was somewhat widespread and depended on one's functional needs:

> Your servant Hosha'yahu has sent to report to my lord Ya'ush: May Yahweh cause my lord to hear a report of peace and well being. And now, please explain the letter that you sent to your servant yesterday, for your servant's heart has been sick since you sent [your letter] to your servant and because my lord says [to me], "you did not understand it! Call a scribe!" As Yahweh lives, [I swear] no one has tried to read a letter to me, ever. And also, every letter that has come to me, [I swear] I have indeed read and could recite it in detail (Lachish Letter III).[11]

The inferior's protest indicates that he thought himself capable of doing his own reading and writing, without recourse to the scribes who would certainly have been readily available for such tasks in service to an army official.

Another possible indicator of at least rudimentary literacy is the inelegant writing evident in some inscriptions. While not all poor calligraphy is the product of untrained hands—since many factors such as age, fatigue, and poor health can influence writing—there exist inscriptions that appear to have been produced by unskilled hands. The inscriptions found at Khirbet el-Qom and Kuntillet Ajrud do not appear to be the work of skilled scribal hands and therefore indicate that some untrained people could at least write brief statements, dedications, or prayers.[12] Also indicative of less than professional inscriptions are several whose scripts are poorly executed.[13]

Apart from the larger issue of education in ancient Israel and Judah, it is clear from the inscriptional evidence that by the late monarchic period there was an increase in at least rudimentary literacy, especially among urbanites.[14] Moreover—and this is more crucial for our interests here—much like elsewhere in the ancient Near East, there must have existed professional schools attached to the royal court where official scribes were educated in scribal techniques and official protocols.[15] While the scholarly debate continues over when such schools first appeared in administrative centers such as Jerusalem and how extensive the training was, it is by all accounts certain that Baruch ben Neriah lived during a time when scribes were being trained in schools as professional administrators. The number of students admitted into such schools must have been of necessity extremely small. These people, like their ancient Near Eastern counterparts, acquired the skills in Hebrew language and in the administrative literature necessary for the professional functioning of the court on the national and international levels. Moreover, many of these people would have been trained in the languages and official protocols of neighboring countries and regional superpowers. For example, although it is much earlier than our time frame, the fourteenth century B.C.E. Amarna Archive, a collection of cuneiform texts from Egypt that contain correspondence mostly between Egypt and its vassals in Syria-Palestine as well as some from other kings in Mesopotamia and Asia Minor, indicates that there were scribes in Syria-Palestine—whose languages are classified as West Semitic—that read and wrote Akkadian, an East Semitic language. However, although these Syro-Palestinian, or "Canaanite," scribes wrote in the language, their Akkadian was somewhat sloven, being highly flavored by their native tongue. These scribes and other bureaucrats were crucial to the effective and efficient running of the government.

The pride with which scribes regarded their position is apparent from texts widely spread from Mesopotamia to Egypt. Consider the following admonitions to Egyptian scribes and those who would become scribes:

> By day write with your fingers;
>   recite by night.
> Befriend the scroll, the palette.
>   It pleases more than wine.
> Writing for him who knows it,
>   is better than all other professions.

It pleases more than bread and beer,
    more than clothing and raiment.
It is worth more than an inheritance in Egypt,
    than a tomb in the west.

Be a scribe, take it to heart,
    That your name become as theirs . . .
Man decays, his corpse is dust,
    All his kin have perished;
But a book makes him remembered,
    Through the mouth of its reciter.[16]

And now the scribe lands on the river-bank and is about to register the harvest-tax. The janitors carry staves and the Nubians rods of palm, and they say, Hand over the corn, though there is none. The cultivator is beaten all over, he is bound and thrown into the well, soused and dipped head downwards. His wife has been beaten in his presence, his children are in fetters. His neighbours abandon them and are fled. So their corn flies away. But the scribe is ahead of everyone. He who works in writing is not taxed; he has no dues to pay. Mark it well.[17]

Scribes fulfilled important roles in the ancient world. They represented a select group within society and performed many duties that enabled both simple and complex societies to function. Their work ranged from the pedantic activity of a notary to the culture-forming work of literati, as Philip Davies has pointed out:

The scribal duties . . . traditionally embraced a range of activities, amounting to a good deal of ideological control: archiving (possession and control of the present), historiography (possession and control of the past), didactic writing (maintenance of social values among the elite), predictive writing (possession and control of the future).[18]

A common feature associated with many ancient Near Eastern documents that would have been produced and preserved by scribes are seals. Seals exist in many forms and evolved through time depending on what kind of documents were being "sealed." For example, ancient cuneiform tablets were often sealed with cylinder seals. These seals were hardened cylinders, inscribed with designs or words, that would be rolled on a wet clay tablet so that they left a permanent impression once the tablet was baked. Another common form of sealing was the stamp seal. This kind of seal was commonly attached to leather or papyrus documents. The document would be rolled and/or folded, wrapped with twine, and then a moist dollop of clay would be affixed to the outside. The scribe would then press an inscribed seal into the clay so that it created an impression whose design was peculiar to the individual scribe. This inscribed dollop of clay is called a bulla. The clay bulla would eventually dry and thus become a hard, permanent attachment to the document. In several cases archaeologists have uncovered bullae that were found in areas that had been burnt. Although the fire completely consumed the documents themselves, the clay bullae survived and were even made more permanent by being baked in the fire.

Seals are mentioned several times in the Hebrew Bible and early Jewish and Christian literature.[19] Archaeologists have unearthed many Hebrew bulla and seals in their excavations. Moreover, many antiquities dealers and collectors have come into possession of many more bullae and seals. While the bullae and seals discovered in controlled excavations are readily dated by their archaeological context, they can also be dated paleographically, or according to the writing style used in the inscription. Bullae and seals that are in the possession of antiquities dealers come primarily from illegal, clandestine excavations— thieves. These seals may not have a verifiable archaeological context, but the inscribed writing can reveal their general date. In fact, there is debate over how reliably we can date unprovenanced seal inscriptions, that is ones that do not come from controlled archaeological contexts. On the one hand some scholars, such as Benjamin Sass, regard the dating of seals to be an almost impossible task. Andrew G. Vaughn has recently focused on the eighth to seventh century B.C.E. seals alone to devise a taxonomy for dating seals of this period. He concludes that based on the seals alone, the seals of the eighth to seventh centuries cannot be dated with any greater precision than approximately one hundred years. Moreover, he urges great caution in attributing inscribed bullae or seals of unknown provenance to specific biblical characters. Larry Herr, on the other hand, is a bit more optimistic about these attributions.[20]

Baruch as a Scribe

Baruch ben Neriah is one of the few biblical personages attested archaeologically. A clay bulla or seal impression whose inscription closely resembles Baruch's name and title in the Bible, "Baruch, the son of Neriyahu, the scribe" (Jer 36:32), was found with other bullae bearing the names and titles of other royal officials of Judah. This bulla would have been attached to a document much like the one mentioned in Jeremiah 32. Nahman Avigad, the premiere authority of his generation on Hebrew inscribed seals, published this bulla which reads: לברכיהו בן גריהו הספר, "belonging to Berekyahu, the son of Nehriyahu, the scribe."[21] At first glance this seems to be a different name, but the biblical name Baruch (ברוך) is simply a hypocoristic or shortened form of the name Berekyahu (ברכיהו). While the scribe's name is Baruch (ברוך) in the Bible, the scribe's father's name is spelled alternatively Neriah (נריה; Jer 32:12,16; 36:4,8; 43:3; 45:1) or Neriyahu (נריהו; Jer 36:14, 32; 43:6) in the book of Jeremiah. The biblical equivalent of Baruch's full name and title as it is written on the bulla appears only in Jeremiah 36:32: Baruch, the son of Neriyahu, the scribe (הספר ברוך בן גריהו). The Baruch bulla was purchased from a Palestinian antiquities dealer and came from some undisclosed location in Judah, obviously the product of unauthorized archaeological digging or looting.

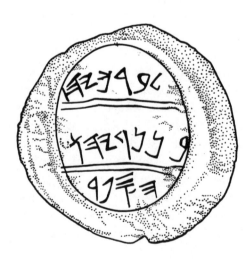

Baruch Seal: "Belonging to Berekyahu, son of Neriyahu, the scribe." Drawing by Katharine Mackay. Used with permission.

The looters were reluctant to disclose where they found it, but since it was part of a much larger cache of bullae, it is almost certain that it came from Jerusalem. Although the exact archaeological context of this bulla cannot be identified, the paleography—how the letters are written—indicates that the seal used to create the Berechyahu bulla was fashioned in the seventh to sixth century B.C.E. Moreover, in this cache was a seal with a name and association that matches a character in the stories of Jeremiah and Baruch: Yerachmeel son of the king (cf. Jer 36:26). This lends some additional likelihood to the possibility that the Baruch bulla, although its modern archaeological origins are obscure or even suspect, is likely related to the famous biblical figure. Baruch appears only in the book of Jeremiah in the Bible, and there he is depicted as a scribe who performs customary scribal duties.[22]

Jeremiah 32—Jeremiah's Land Transaction

Baruch first appears in the book of Jeremiah at 32:12–16 when he witnesses and certifies a land transaction between Jeremiah and his cousin Hanamel. This is a typical duty of an official scribe.[23] Jeremiah reports:

> I wrote out a deed, sealed it, had it witnessed, and then weighed out the silver on scales. I took the deed of purchase—the sealed text and the open one—and gave the deed of purchase to Baruch ben Neriah ben Mahseiah in the presence of Hanamel my kinsman, the witnesses who signed the deed of purchase, and all the Judaeans who were sitting in the prison court. In the presence of all I commanded Baruch, "thus, says Yahweh of Hosts, the God of Israel: 'Take these deeds—this sealed deed of purchase and this open one—and put them into a clay jar so they will last for a long time.' For thus says Yahweh of Hosts, the God of Israel: 'houses, fields, and vineyards will yet again be purchased in this land!'"

This passage seems to refer to a document drawn up on leather or papyrus. One version—the sealed deed—would have been signed by witnesses, folded, and sealed with a bulla; the other—the open deed—summarizing the contents of the official sealed document would have been attached to it. This passage provides a great deal of information regarding the process of creating, verifying, and depositing legal documents. First, the parties contracted a scribe who could draw up a legal document presumably in the correct legal format. This was Baruch's job. Once the participants and witnesses had signed the document, it was either rolled or folded. It was then tied with a string that was wound around it several times. A moist dollop of clay was then applied to the outside of the document on top of the string, and the parties, the scribe, or perhaps another official, impressed into the clay his or her individually designed and inscribed seal, which, when it dried, would be permanently affixed to the document. Although the text suggests that Jeremiah did this work, it is likely that the prophet had Baruch do it, for this was Baruch's profession.[24] When the text reports Jeremiah's words, "I wrote out a deed, sealed it, and had it witnessed," it likely means that Baruch the professional scribe wrote the document, folded or rolled it up, attached a dollop of clay, and then "sealed" (חתם) it by impressing his personal seal on it. The Berekyahu bulla mentioned above was produced by just such a seal. No one would claim, however, that the seal we now have is the same one that was on this deed agreement between Jeremiah and his cousin Hanamel. Baruch was a professional scribe and undoubtedly sealed many documents in the course of his career. Baruch's seal shows Jeremiah's land deed to be an official or otherwise important document. There are many examples of similar documents, such as an early sixth century letter from Arad (Letter 17) which reads as follows:

> To Nahum: now, come to the house of 'Elyashib son of 'Eshyahu, and take from there one (measure of) oil and send it to . . . quickly and seal (חתם) it with your seal (חתמך).[25]

'Elyashib may have been one of the military commanders at Arad. The text suggests that the seal served to indicate that the oil to be transferred was an official item or was sent with official authorization. The inscriptions on many of the Hebrew seals and bullae indicate that they belonged to royal or governmental officials or people with official powers. The following are just some of the titles found on seals/bullae: "servant of the king" (עבד המלך), "son of the king" (בן המלך), "mayor of the city" (שר העיר), "majordomo" (literally, "the one who is over the house"; אשר על הבית), and "scribe" (ספר). Many seals and bullae list just the owner's name and that person's father's name: for example, 'Ashyahu son of Shemaʿyahu.

As it was, Jeremiah's folded, sealed document would have lasted a long time, and everyone involved in this story would have known that, especially Baruch. However, sealing the two copies of the deed in a jar would have made them last even longer: "put them into a clay jar so they will last for a long time" (Jer 32:14). The point Jeremiah makes—and this, too, would have been immediately known to the audience—was that it was going to be a long time before he, Jeremiah, or anyone else would return to Judah from the Babylonian exile to possess and work their own fields (Jer 32:42–44).

Papyrus and leather are not very durable substances even in this arid region. Nonetheless, some papyrus and leather documents that were left in the drier parts of the country, most notably in the Dead Sea and southern Judean Wilderness, have survived. This is most dramatically proven by several of the Dead Sea Scrolls and the Babatra Archive discovered in the caves in the Judean Wilderness. Sealed in clay pots and left in caves in the late first century C.E., the Dead Sea Scrolls were discovered by bedouin and archaeologists nearly 1900 years later. The Babatra Archive was secreted away in another cave during the time of the Bar Kochba revolt (132–135 C.E.). This collection contains papyrus documents that were folded and sealed much like the description in Jeremiah 32.[26]

Jeremiah 36—A Scroll of Disaster

Jeremiah 36 presents Baruch performing another of his official duties as a scribe. Here he records, at Jeremiah's dictation, all the words God had spoken to Jeremiah in the period from the thirteenth year of Josiah (627 B.C.E.) until the fourth year of Jehoiakim (605 B.C.E.) regarding Jerusalem, Judah, and the surrounding nations. The story recounted is one of high drama and suspense. The reader fears for the fate of Jeremiah and especially Baruch as they stand toe-to-toe with the king, opposing Jehoiakim's foreign policy regarding the Babylonians.

> In the fourth year of King Jehoiakim son of Josiah of Judah, this word came to Jeremiah from Yahweh: "Take a scroll and write on it all the words that I have spoken to you against Israel and Judah and all the nations, from the day I spoke to you during the days of Josiah until

today. Perhaps the house of Judah will hear all the disasters that I intend
to do to them, and thus will turn from their evil way so that I may for-
give their iniquity and their sin." Then Jeremiah called Baruch son of
Neriah, and Baruch wrote on a scroll at Jeremiah's dictation all the words
of Yahweh that Jeremiah spoke to him. Then Jeremiah commanded
Baruch, saying, "I am restricted from entering the precincts of Yahweh's
temple. So you must go and read the words of Yahweh from the scroll
that you have written at my dictation in the hearing of the people in the
precincts of Yahweh's temple on a fast day.[27] You must read them also in
the hearing of all the people of Judah who come from their towns. Perhaps their plea will come before Yahweh, and each one will turn from his
or her evil way, for great is the anger and wrath that Yahweh has pro-
nounced against this people." Baruch son of Neriah did all that the
prophet Jeremiah commanded him about reading the words of Yahweh
from the scroll in the precincts of Yahweh's temple.

Now the following took place in the ninth month of the fifth year of
king Jehoiakim son of Josiah of Judah. All the people in Jerusalem and
all the people who came from the towns of Judah to Jerusalem proclaimed a fast before Yahweh. Baruch read the words of Jeremiah from
the scroll in the precincts of Yahweh's temple, in the chamber of
Gemariah son of Shaphan the scribe, in the upper court at the entry of
the New Gate to Yahweh's temple in the hearing of all the people. When
Micaiah son of Gemariah son of Shaphan heard all the words of Yahweh
from the scroll, he went down to the king's house, into the scribe's chamber. All the officials were sitting there: Elishama the scribe, Delaiah son
of Shemaiah, Elnatan son of Achbor, Gemariah son of Shaphan,
Zedekiah son of Hananiah, and all the officials. Micaiah recounted to
them all the words that he had heard Baruch reading from the scroll in
the hearing of the people. Then all the officials sent Jehudi son of Netaniah son of Shelemiah son of Cushi to say to Baruch, "Come, and bring
with you the scroll that you read in the hearing of the people!" So Baruch
son of Neriah grabbed the scroll and came to them. And they said to
him, "Sit down and read it to us!" So Baruch read it to them. When they
had heard all the words, they turned to one another in fear, and then
said to Baruch, "We certainly must report all these words to the king."
They questioned Baruch, "Tell us now, how did you write all these words
at his dictation?" Baruch said to them, "he would dictate all these words to

me, and I would write them with ink on the scroll." Then the officials said to Baruch, "Go and hide, you and Jeremiah, and let no one know your whereabouts." The officials went to the court of the king, leaving the scroll in the chamber of Elishama the scribe, and recounted all the words to the king. The king then sent Jehudi to get the scroll, and he took it from the chamber of Elishama the scribe. Jehudi read it to the king and to all the officials attending the king. The king was sitting in his winter quarters for it was the ninth month, and a fire was burning in the brazier before him. As Jehudi read three or four columns, the king would cut them off with a scribe's knife and throw them into the fire in the brazier, until the entire scroll was consumed in the fire that was in the brazier. Still, neither the king nor any of his servants who heard all these words feared, nor did they tear their garments. Even when Elnatan and Delaiah and Gemariah pleaded with the king not to burn the scroll, he would not listen to them. Then the king commanded Jerahmeel the king's son and Seraiah son of Azriel and Shelemiah son of Abdeel to arrest Baruch the scribe and Jeremiah the prophet. But Yahweh had hidden them.

The word of Yahweh came to Jeremiah after the king had burned the scroll with the words that Baruch wrote at Jeremiah's dictation: "Take another scroll and write on it all the former words that were in the first scroll that King Jehoiakim of Judah burned. And concerning King Jehoiakim of Judah you shall say: 'Thus says Yahweh, you burnt this scroll, saying, "Why have you written in it that the king of Babylon will certainly come and destroy this land, and will cut off from it human beings and animals?" Therefore, thus says Yahweh concerning King Jehoiakim of Judah: "He shall have no one to sit upon the throne of David, and his corpse shall be cast out to the heat by day and the frost by night. I will punish him, his descendants, and his servants for their iniquity. I will bring on them, on the inhabitants of Jerusalem, and on the people of Judah all the evils that I told them. But they did not listen."'" Then Jeremiah took another scroll and gave it to Baruch son of Neriah the scribe, and he wrote on it at Jeremiah's dictation all the words of the scroll that King Jehoiakim of Judah burned in the fire, and many similar words were added to them.

Jeremiah apparently dictated to Baruch all the prophetic messages God had given him as well as his own sermons that were based on those revelations, and Baruch dutifully recorded them (36:17–18). Given the condemnatory nature of most of those revelations and sermons over a twenty-two year period (627–605 B.C.E.), this scroll must have certainly been both impressive and threatening. This story also provides us with a glimpse into the relationship between Jeremiah and Baruch. The telling phrase occurs in the editor's remarks at 36:8: "Baruch son of Neriah did all that the prophet Jeremiah commanded him regarding the reading of the words of Yahweh from the scroll in the temple of Yahweh." The phrase "he did all that God commanded him" and slight variations on it typically describe how righteous people, especially Moses, respond to God's instructions (e.g., Noah in Gen 6:22 and 7:5; Moses in Ex 40:16, Lev 8:4, and Num 27:22; David in 2 Sam 5:25). Similar phraseology indicates how people faithfully follow instructions given by their leaders, and here, too, one of the most common describes how people follow the commands given by God to Moses (e.g., Uriah the priest obeying king Ahaz in 2 Kgs 16:16; Ruth obeying Naomi in Ruth 3:6; people of Israel obeying Moses' commands in Ex 12:28, 50, 39:42, Num 1:54, 9:5, Josh 14:15). The phraseology in Jeremiah 36:8, therefore, suggests that Baruch was loyally obeying Jeremiah's instructions and was not simply fulfilling a task as some hired hand. The rest of the story in Jeremiah 36 indicates how personally involved in Jeremiah's work Baruch actually was. The text states that Jeremiah and Baruch began writing the scroll in the fourth year of Jehoiakim's reign (605 B.C.E.) and that Baruch read the scroll during a fast day in the ninth month of the following year. There was, therefore, at least a nine-month interval between the beginning of the work on the scroll and Baruch's public reading thereof in the temple precincts. It surely took a long time to compose the scroll, but the text gives no explanation for the delay between the initiation of the work and its public presentation. Most of the time was obviously taken up by the labor-intensive work of composition, but the text suggests that Baruch and Jeremiah were also waiting for an appropriate public event at which to present it.

The fateful day came on a day of fasting. The text gives no explicit indication of the reason for this communal fast. Given the historical setting, however, it is not difficult to imagine a likely scenario. As noted above, in 605 the Babylonians defeated the Egyptians at Carchemish.

Baruch sitting attentively at Jeremiah's feet, carefully recording the prophet's words. The nineteenth-century French artist Gustave Doré (1832–1883) composed thousands of drawings and paintings, but is best known for his engraved illustrations of scenes from literary masterpieces. Doré's drawing illustrates one image of the biblical scribe: one who writes everything the prophet says word-for-word. Taken from Gustave Doré, Pictures of the Bible: The Old Testament and the Book of Maccabees *(Cambridge, Mass.: Harbour Press, 1988), 121.*

Nebuchadnezzar, after briefly returning to Babylon to bury his father and replace him as king, followed up the decisive victory at Carchemish with a campaign in 604 down the eastern Mediterranean coast with the intent of pushing the Egyptians out of the region. One of the casualties was the Judean coastal town of Ashkelon (Jer 47:5–7). News of the Babylonian advance and of Ashkelon's fate no doubt produced the kind of anxiety that would cause the people to call a solemn fast day as mentioned in Jeremiah 36:9. On the occasion of such a fast, Baruch read Jeremiah's scroll of disaster (Jer 36:10). Jeremiah had asked Baruch to read the scroll on his behalf because he had been barred from entering the temple precincts and perhaps because, anticipating the response of the country's leaders, he feared for his life (36:5–8). Baruch's willingness is commendable, but it put him in grave danger as well: the people or leaders might just as easily turn against him. Again, this indicates that Baruch was not simply fulfilling his professional duty as a scribe, but was personally committed to promoting Jeremiah's social, political, and religious program. This in turn tells us something of Baruch's personal character. In spite of all the potential dangers, Baruch stepped into one of the ancillary rooms of the temple complex belonging to Germariah the son of Shaphan and read Jeremiah's scroll of disaster (Jer 36:10). Here we learn that Jeremiah had supporters other than Baruch. That Gemariah allowed Baruch to use his room in the temple complex suggests that he was at least somewhat receptive to Jeremiah's religious and geopolitical ideas. Moreover, although nothing is said about the people's reactions, we do learn that one young man—Gemariah's son Micaiah—was startled enough by the reading to rush to a meeting of Jehoiakim's royal officers and report what he had heard. These officers—Elishama, Delaiah, Elnatan, Gemariah, Zedekiah, and others—summoned Baruch into their chambers and told him to read the scroll to them. This took some daring on Baruch's part. He had first risked public ridicule and persecution and was now risking the wrath of the king and his court. Fortunately for Baruch, this group of royal officials was somewhat receptive to Jeremiah's message. They quickly realized that they must report these profound words to King Jehoiakim, for it was their job to keep the king apprised of what was going on among the people and especially to report to him any prophetic messages no matter what the content. Knowing, however, that the contents of this scroll would likely upset Jehoiakim, they hid Jeremiah and Baruch (36:19). They also deposited the scroll for safekeeping in the room of Elishama the scribe, another of the ancillary rooms of the temple complex, before going to the king. All this reveals the drama that was being played out in the public arena during these tumultuous days, and Baruch ben Neriah was right in the middle of the action.

Ancient prophets and their associates functioned in myriad contexts, and this story happens to take place in a royal context. For the most part the Hebrew Bible comprises refined, literary narratives that contain collected and edited prophetic sermons, laments, denunciations, and so on; accounts of the social location of prophetic activity are rare. Still, this passage and 1 Kgs 22 recount prophetic activity as it occurred in the palace precincts. Ancient Israelite prophetic activity was part of a larger world of ancient prophecy, and so other ancient Near Eastern cultures provide examples that help us better understand the various types and social contexts of prophecy. Most notable for biblical scholars have been the records of prophetic activity from Mari.[28] These much earlier texts describe how "prophets"—male or female—received and delivered their prophetic dreams and messages and how the king or other royal officials responded to them.[29] Many of the cases correspond to the situation with Baruch, Jeremiah, and king Jehoiakim: a prophet receives a divine message, discloses it either publicly (i.e., in a temple or in the city gates) or privately to the king, who in turns responds by either accepting, rejecting, or, most often, by seeking further confirmation of the prophecy via other means of divination.[30] These messages often address issues pertaining to the well being of the king or his kingdom.

> Speak to my lord: Thus says Šibtu your maid-servant: the palace is safe. In the temple of Annunītum, on the third day (of the month) Šelibum went into a trance. Thus spoke Annunītum: "Zimri-Lim, they will test you with a revolt. Guard yourself. Put at your side servants, your associates whom you love. Set them so they can guard you. Do not go out by yourself. And the men who test you, I will deliver these men into your hand" (ARM X.7).[31]

In this instance Šibtu, the queen, reviewed the message prior to passing it on to the king, as appears to have been her custom. Thus she, and likely others, serves as a board of review that decides which messages warrant the king's attention. There were surely many instances each week of people claiming to have a message from the gods for the king. Only the most pressing and substantiated of these "prophecies" would have been passed on to the king. Much like this report, Jeremiah's scroll dealt with issues that threatened the well-being of the state and the king. It demanded immediate attention.

> Speak to my lord: Thus says Yarim-Addu your servant: regarding the news about Išme-Dagan going up to Ekallatum about which my lord hears often—he does not in fact go up to Ekallatum! There are rumors about him, and people are lurking around him. An *apilum* of Marduk stood at the gate of the palace and continued to proclaim: "Išme-Dagan will not escape the hand of Marduk! He will bundle straw and he will be chopped!"[32] Thus he continued to proclaim at the gate of the palace, but no one said anything to him. Just then he stood at the gate of Išme-Dagan and continued to proclaim in the assembly of the entire country: "For peace and good relations you go to the *sukkal* of Elam, but instead of good relations you have revealed to the *sukkal* of Elam the secret of Marduk and the city of Babylon. You have exhausted the grain piles and my storehouses and did not return my kindness. And now you want to go to Ekallatum? The one who revealed my secret should not ask me about it . . ." Thus he continued to proclaim in the assembly of the entire country, but no one said anything to him (ARM XXVI.371).[33]

Much like the discussion caused by this prophet's public proclamations, Jeremiah's scroll was presented in a public context and caused quite a stir since it addressed international issues. This unrest threatened the political stability within Jerusalem at a time when foreign armies were poised to destroy the kingdom. Much like the Mari report's implications for international relations, the contents of Jeremiah's scroll clearly warranted the attention of the king. The people of the ancient Near East believed that the gods could and would reveal their intentions and the future to humans. As a result, kings in Israel, Judah, and elsewhere in the ancient Near East took prophetic pronouncements seriously.

Jehoiakim naturally wanted to hear what it was in Jeremiah and Baruch's scroll that had caused such a commotion, so he sent Jehudi, one of his attendants, to retrieve it. Jehudi returned with the scroll that he had retrieved from the room of Elishama the scribe and read it aloud before a gathering of the king and his courtiers. As Jehudi read from Jeremiah's scroll before the court, King Jehoiakim tore it into pieces and tossed the pieces into a fire. The entire scroll was destroyed. Apart from the high drama of the king so shamelessly dismissing a prophet's message, this must have been a very fractious meeting of the royal court. On one side there were the officials Elnatan, Delaiah, and Germariah, who were apparently supportive of Jeremiah's program and who tried to persuade the king not to destroy the scroll but to heed its warnings; on the other side were the king and those who supported his social and geopolitical agenda. The entire religious and geopolitical spectrum of the day was represented in that room and the decision to burn the scroll and ignore its warnings was fateful. The Babylonians conquered Judah and Jehoiakim became a vassal of Nebuchadnezzar. Jehoiakim revolted three years later, and that brought on the first of several deportations of Judaeans to Babylon.

After Jehoiakim burnt the scroll, God told Jeremiah to have Baruch rewrite the scroll adding a few extra words for the recalcitrant king. In this story Baruch twice functions as a scribal assistant—many scholars have referred to him as Jeremiah's "secretary"—who wrote down Jeremiah's sermons, and because of this passage many think that Baruch was the editor of the book of Jeremiah as we now have it.[34] In the end, however, the focus of this chapter is not on scribal activity or court intrigue; it dramatically confirms the reliability of Yahweh's word as given through his prophet. The king may tear and even burn Yahweh's words, but they will endure and will be fulfilled.[35]

This passage is dated precisely: "Then in the fourth year of Jehoiakim, son of Josiah, king of Judah, this word of Yahweh came to Jeremiah" (Jer 36:1). The date would have been circa 605–604 B.C.E. Although they would not destroy Jerusalem for twenty years, the Babylonians, having defeated the Assyrians and Egyptians at Carchemish in 605, were beginning to exert their influence in the region. This brought them into conflict with the Egyptians, who had been vying for dominance over this region with the Assyrians for decades. After the battle at Carchemish, roughly the time of the events recorded in Jeremiah 36, the Babylonians set their sights on the eastern Mediterranean and intended to expand their dominance as far as the

borders of Egypt. After returning from his father Nabopolassar's funeral and being installed as Babylon's new king, Nebuchadnezzar
marched his forces through Syria-Palestine south towards Egypt. In
604 he marched through Judah, destroying Ashkelon (Jer 47:5–7).
Jerusalem itself was spared because Jehoiakim submitted and became a
vassal of Babylon (2 Kgs 24:1). As we will learn later, the heavy Babylonian yoke did not set well on the necks of Jehoiakim and the
Judaeans. They would eventually revolt and bring the might of the
Neo-Babylonian Empire down upon themselves.

Jeremiah's words that Baruch recorded on the scroll described in
chapter 36 were prescient. Jeremiah knew that the Babylonians were
bound to control this region, and he counseled a policy of accommodation and acquiescence. Although the text recounts his having
learned this from divine revelation, anyone who knew what Nabopolassar and his son Nebuchadnezzar had done to the Assyrians at Nineveh in 612 and to the Egyptians at Carchemish in 605 could have
divined what the Babylonians had in store for the states along the eastern Mediterranean coast. King Jehoiakim was brazen enough to tear
Baruch's scroll into pieces and burn them. Jeremiah, likely angered at
the king's actions, instructed Baruch to rewrite the scroll with its predictions of disaster for the country and its inhabitants. To this second
edition of the scroll, however, Jeremiah also added an explicit con-
demnation of the king for his wanton disregard for the "word of Yahweh." Jeremiah even "added many similar words" (Jer 36:32) to this
rewritten scroll. One can only imagine what those "similar words"
were, but given how the king and some of his courtiers treated the
message in Jeremiah's first scroll, I am sure that these were harsh words
indeed.

In this story Baruch functions again as a professional scribe: he
writes down Jeremiah's sermons. Although it was customary for a
scribe to write down what another person needed to record, the fact
that Jeremiah asked Baruch to read his sermon before a public audience suggests that the two had more than a patron/client relationship.
Baruch did this at great personal risk to himself: the scribe was being
associated with the contents of the scroll regardless of the fact that it
came from Jeremiah the prophet. Although the people did not turn
against Baruch as he read the first draft of the scroll in the temple

precincts, some of the royal officials eventually did, and Baruch's life was in jeopardy. His willing association, apart from what he had done for the prophet prior to this, was what engendered the idea that Baruch and Jeremiah were collaborators. It is certainly conceivable that Baruch agreed to proclaim Jeremiah's words, much as Jeremiah did for God, because he agreed with Jeremiah's message. In fact, one biblical definition of a prophet is a person who speaks for another (cf. Ex 7:1–2), and in this sense Baruch is speaking for Jeremiah. Another understanding of the term prophet is "one who is called," and in this sense Baruch was here called by Jeremiah to work on his behalf, again, just as Jeremiah was doing for God.[36] Much as the "word of Yahweh came to Jeremiah" and the prophet proclaimed it, so in a sense did the word of Jeremiah come to Baruch, and he proclaimed it in this context without regard for the consequences. Baruch appears, therefore, to be interested not only in recording but in promoting Jeremiah's religious and geopolitical teachings, teachings that contain divinely revealed, community defining precepts, traditions, and values. In this way Baruch stepped out of a traditional scribal role as detached technician or diplomat to become an active participant in the debates over the country's current crisis.[37] Baruch was prepared not only to record Jeremiah's words, but also to promote the prophet's agenda. Thus Baruch appears already in the biblical text as one committed to taking an active role in guiding the people through difficult times.

Jeremiah 43—Baruch Incites Jeremiah?

In Jeremiah 43:1–7 the Judaeans charge Baruch with inciting Jeremiah to proclaim disaster for those who planned to escape to Egypt in order to avoid exile to Babylon. These people then took Jeremiah and Baruch to Egypt by force.[38] The religious and political tensions evident in Jeremiah 36 continue in chapter 43: will people obey Jeremiah's warnings and submit to Babylon, or will they ignore them and entrust their fate to the Egyptians? This story, then, reveals the actual conflicts that existed within the Judean community at this time.[39]

> When Jeremiah finished speaking to all the people all the words of Yah-
> weh their God, all these words which Yahweh their God had sent him for

them, Azariah son of Hoshaiah, Johanan son of Qareach, and all the other insolent men said to Jeremiah, "You are telling a lie! Yahweh our God did not send you to say, 'Do not go to Egypt to settle there!' Rather, Baruch son of Neriah is inciting you against us, to hand us over to the Babylonians to kill us or take us into exile in Babylon." So Johanan son of Qareach, all the commanders of the forces, and all the people did not obey the voice of Yahweh and remain in the land of Judah. Instead, Johanan son of Qareach and all the commanders of the forces took all the remnant of Judah who had returned from all the nations to which they had been driven to settle in the land of Judah—the men, the women, the little children, the princesses, and everyone whom Nebuzaradan the captain of the guard had left with Gedaliah son of Ahiqam son of Shaphan—and the prophet Jeremiah and Baruch son of Neriah. They came into the land of Egypt because they did not obey the voice of Yahweh. And they came to Tahpanhes.

The events of chapter 43 are part of a larger narrative about the aftermath of the Babylonian conquest of Jerusalem and Judah (Jer 37–44). The question facing the inhabitants of Jerusalem and Judah was, what do we do now? Do we submit to the Babylonians or flee to Egypt as refugees? The people who were contemplating fleeing to Egypt came to Jeremiah and asked him to inquire of Yahweh about their plans (Jer 42:1–6). Although Johanan son of Qareach, one of the leaders of this group, and his associates had pledged to do whatever Jeremiah instructed them to do, when Jeremiah gave them the "word of Yahweh" on this matter, they resolutely refused to obey.

The opening verse of chapter 43 sets the stage; Jeremiah had just finished telling the people "all the words that Yahweh their God had sent him to say to them" (43:1). Jeremiah's message detailed Yahweh's response to their query as to whether they should stay in Judah or flee to Egypt. This response included an unambiguous warning against fleeing to Egypt to avoid the Babylonians: "Do not go to Egypt" (42:19). The people rejected Jeremiah's warnings. In fact, the leaders of the people, Johanan son of Qareach and all his "insolent men," went so far as to accuse Jeremiah of lying and of being incited by Baruch to tell them to remain in Judah (43:2–3). For some reason the narrator suggested that these leaders thought that Baruch wanted them to suffer at the hands of the Babylonians. In fact, their fear was not unjustified. Johanan son of Qareach, one of the leaders here identified by name, was also one of the Judean officers who accompanied Ishmael son of Netaniah on a visit to Gedaliah shortly after the Babylonians had appointed Gedaliah governor of Judah (cf. Jer 40:5–12). This Ishmael was a scion of the royal Davidic family who himself perhaps intended to reestablish the Davidic monarchy. He allied himself with the Ammonites and eventually assassinated Gedaliah (Jer 41:1–3). Johanan, to his credit, warned Gedaliah of Ishmael's murderous intentions and afterwards tried to avenge Gedaliah's murder. Nonetheless, Johanan may have thought that due to his early association with Ishmael the Babylonians may have thought that he was somehow implicated in the assassination. Moreover, despite Gedaliah's assurances that the Babylonians would treat the Judaeans evenhandedly, Johanan probably thought, and correctly so, that the assassination of a Babylonian-appointed governor would bring a forceful response by the Babylonians. To avoid such a response he and his followers intended to flee to Egypt for safety. Jeremiah, based on the revelations he had received from Yahweh, maintained that the only safe place was under the protective umbrella of the Babylonians (42:7–21, 43:7–44:30). Jeremiah, ever the faithful deuteronomistic Yahwist, insisted that obedience to Yahweh's word was the only way to avoid disaster.[40]

But why blame Baruch for the oracle that forbade flight to Egypt? It was Jeremiah who proffered this as an oracle from Yahweh. It could be that while Jeremiah was simply interested in religious issues—that people would obey "the word of the Lord," Baruch had more purely political interests in these events and so somehow "influenced" Jeremiah's message or how it was transmitted.[41] The book of Jeremiah as we now have it is composed of several literary layers. Only the "A" layer, the poetic sayings, is traditionally attributed to the prophet Jeremiah. The "B" (Baruch) and "C" (deuteronomistic discourse) layers were composed by others and only later were attached to the authentically Jeremianic element. The story in chapter 43 is part of the "B" layer, the unit traditionally attributed to Baruch. Therefore, according to Brueggemann's reading of this chapter, Baruch was taking the politically neutral messages of Jeremiah about heeding the divine oracles and infusing them with political import. Baruch, and the politically interested families he represented, used Jeremiah to advance their political agenda vis-à-vis the Babylonians and Egyptians. Given Brueggemann's reconstruction of the setting of this story, it is clear why the "insolent men" leveled their charges against Baruch and not Jeremiah: Baruch was distorting the prophet's message for his and his party's own political gain. Baruch and those of his ilk took Jeremiah's basic religious message of submitting to Babylon as Yahweh's instrument of judgment and transformed it into a rigid political program of unswerving obedience to Babylonian policy in Judah. Still, it is very likely that Baruch was not distorting the message at all, that this was indeed Jeremiah's message. Prophets were, after all, deeply political, and their messages were often designed to influence national policy. Baruch was singled out for blame in this instance because he was intimately involved in the crisis and may have been acting again as Jeremiah's point person in the debates.

Jeremiah 45—A Message of Hope for Baruch

Baruch makes his last appearance in the book of Jeremiah in chapter 45. Here Jeremiah delivers a divine oracle intended personally for Baruch:

> The word which the prophet Jeremiah spoke to Baruch son of Neriah when he wrote these words in a scroll at the dictation of Jeremiah in the fourth year of King Jehoiakim son of Josiah king of Judah: "Thus says Yahweh the God of Israel to you Baruch: You said, 'Woe is me because Yahweh has added grief to my pain. I am weary with my groaning, and I can find no rest.' Thus you shall say to him, 'Thus says Yahweh: Behold, what I have built I am going to tear down, and what I have planted I will uproot—even the whole land. But you, do you seek great things for yourself? Do not seek them, for I am going to bring evil upon all flesh, says Yahweh. Yet I will give you your life as a prize of war in every place wherever you may go.' "

There are actually two contexts for this passage: the historical and the canonical. In the historical context this passage is set in the years 605 or 604 B.C.E., at the time when the Babylonians had soundly defeated the Egyptians at Carchemish. This battle, as mentioned above, was a turning point in the ancient history of the Near East. It marked the time when the Neo-Babylonian Empire came to dominate the entire Near East by supplanting the Assyrians in Mesopotamia and the Egyptians along the eastern littoral of the Mediterranean. Anyone with a basic appreciation for the geopolitics of the Near East at the time knew that the Babylonians would force their will on the states of Syria-Palestine, the region that included the state of Judah. It was only a matter of time. On a more directly personal level, this was also the year when Baruch read Jeremiah's "scroll of disaster" (Jer 36) on the prophet's behalf.

Another way to imagine the context of this passage is according to its canonical position, that is to say, according to its literary context in the Masoretic version of the book of Jeremiah. Although the individual chapters of the book of Jeremiah are obviously not presented in chronological order, the oracle in chapter 45 is awkwardly out of place, coming as it does after a prolonged section on the post-destruction era and immediately prior to the "oracles against the nations" section (46–51). A literary or canonical reading of the text will overlook the dating of the oracle in 45:1 historically to the fourth year of king Jehoiakim, explaining it away as a later, incorrect insertion into the narrative or focusing on its position within the surrounding narrative.[42] In this supposed ahistorical or suprahistorical literary context, this oracle comes after accounts of events connected with the Babylonians' conquest of Judah and their devastation of Jerusalem (Jer 40–45). The Davidic line of monarchs had come to an ignoble end. The city's institutions had been leveled and its leading citizens had been deported to Babylon. These were the darkest days that the kingdom of Judah had ever experienced. The Judaeans witnessed the dismantling of the northern kingdom of Israel by the Assyrians in 722 B.C.E. but they escaped and retained at least some autonomy. Now their country, too, had fallen to a Mesopotamian power. Gone was all the glory of the past, replaced by the ignominy of utter subservience. Moreover, on a more personal level, Baruch and his friend Jeremiah had been forcibly taken to Egypt against what they believed was God's will (Jer 43).

According to either the historical or the literary/canonical reading, how could things be worse? Words fail to describe their grief. One could understand if Baruch and Jeremiah suffered from disillusionment or even depression in these circumstances. On the one hand, the historical context reveals that Jeremiah's prophetic messages left him banished from the temple precincts, putting Baruch in the unenviable position of having to read Jeremiah's "scroll of disaster" to largely unreceptive audiences (36:5–6). Moreover, Jeremiah's "scroll of disaster" had attracted considerable political attention, and both Jeremiah and Baruch were forced into hiding from king Jehoiakim and his supporters, who bitterly resented the prophet's particular religiopolitical agenda with its pro-Babylonian bias. The king sought to arrest Jeremiah and Baruch, but Yahweh had hidden them, quite literally, God knows where. On the other hand, according to an alternate explanation of the larger literary context, Jeremiah, Baruch, and their country had lost everything—their king, their central temple, their artisans and leading citizens, their city, and, ultimately, their personal and national independence. Now they and many of their fellow Judaeans lived as refugees in foreign lands. They escaped their ravaged country with the few possessions they could carry with them. They had nothing. Who wouldn't be depressed?

It is in this context that Baruch sent up his lament: "Woe is me because Yahweh has added grief to my pain. I am weary with my groaning, and I can find no rest" (45:3). Baruch was moved to lament just as Jeremiah had many times in the course of this book (e.g., 4:19; 8:18; 14:17–18; 15:10; 20:7–18). Obviously, Baruch had come to the end of his ability to endure during these difficult days. He had worked indefatigably for Jeremiah, at times even at great personal risk. For what? The king and many others were not heeding Jeremiah's messages, and the overall political situation was deteriorating. It all seemed pointless. He threw his hands up in despair and asked "why?" Given the difficulties Baruch and his supporters faced, it is really quite easy to sympathize with him.

The divine response to Baruch's lament was twofold. First, God told Baruch through Jeremiah that "I am going to tear down what I have built, and uproot what I have planted—even the whole land" (Jer 45:4). Baruch was not mistaken; God intended to bring utter devastation on the land and its inhabitants. There will be no rest and no end to groaning for Baruch or his fellow Judaeans. These words, "what I have *built* I am going to tear down, and what I have *planted* I will

Baruch's anguish. This drawing depicts one of two events: it could be depicting Baruch's personal torment as expressed in Jer 45:3, or his turmoil as he went into hiding and rewrote the scrolls of the words of Yahweh and Jeremiah that king Jehoiakim had burned (Jer 36). Taken from Gustave Doré, Pictures of the Bible: The New Testament and the Apocrypha *(Cambridge, Mass.: Harbour Press, 1988), 87. Although the recent Harbour Press edition of Doré's biblical illustrations relates this drawing to the Book of Baruch 1:3, and the Dover Publications edition (*The Doré Bible Illustrations *[New York: Dover Publications, 1974]) associates it with Book of Baruch 3:14, the many scrolls seen lying next to Baruch suggest that this illustration is instead depicting Baruch amidst the process of copying, rewriting, and editing Jeremiah's sermons (Jer 36). The introduction to the Book of Baruch speaks of only one scroll. Alternately, the image captures the anguish when he cried: "Woe is me because Yahweh has added grief to my pain. I am weary with my groaning, and I can find no rest" (Jer 45:3).*

uproot," Jeremiah borrowed from what appears to have been a popular tradition in his day. In fact, Jeremiah—or more correctly the editors of the book of Jeremiah as we have it—had an affinity for these words and used various collocations of them several times in the book (1:10; 18:7,9; 24:6; 29:5,28; 31:4–5,28; 35:7; 42:10; 45:4). Some of these same words appear in Deuteronomy 6:10–11 where Moses promised that if the people obey Yahweh's commandments, the Almighty would bring them into the land he promised to their ancestor and give them "cites they did not *build* . . . and vineyards and olive groves they did not *plant."* Thus, in Deuteronomistic vocabulary the verbal roots "building" and "planting" are associated with living in the Promised Land under divine protection. The book of Joshua ends with a word-for-word confirmation of Moses' words. Joshua told the people in his farewell speech: Yahweh has given you "land which you did not cultivate, cities which you did not *build* yet have settled, vineyard and olive groves which you did not *plant* yet you eat from them" (Josh 24:13; italics mine).[43] These terms appear in the book of Amos as well. The prophet Amos lived in the northern kingdom of Israel in the middle part of the eighth century B.C.E. and throughout his book he warned of the fall of Israel as a result of its wicked ways: "you have *built* houses of hewn stone, but you will not live in them; you have *planted* luxuriant vineyards, but you will not drink their wine" (Amos 5:11). Yet the end of the book, Amos 9:11–15, completely transforms this image. Several linguistic features and the optimistic tone of Amos 9:11–15 differ significantly from the rest of the book. These and other factors have led many scholars to conclude that this section of the book does not come from the prophet Amos but was appended to the book by a later redactor.[44] If this is the case, then a later anonymous redactor transformed the sense of these terms in order to have the book end on a positive note, pointing out that Yahweh would eventually restore the devastated nation.

> I will restore the fate of my people Israel. They will *build* and inhabit their devastated cities. They will *plant* vineyards and drink their wine, make gardens and eat their fruit. Then I will *plant* them on their own land, and never again will they be *uprooted* from the land which I have given to them, says Yahweh your God (Amos 9:14–15).

This collocation of terms clearly had special meaning to either the prophet Amos or the book's anonymous redactor. While the books of Deuteronomy and Joshua used these terms in relation to the settlement of the land, and Amos applied these terms to the Assyrian crisis, Jeremiah associates the words *build* (בגה), *plant* (נטע), and *uproot* (נתש) with the Babylonian conquest of Judah in 586 B.C.E. Now the results are disastrous: God intends to demolish what he has built and uproot what he has planted. There are no terms that more vividly depict the results of conquest—buildings demolished and the land ravaged.

Still, in spite of the unavoidable calamity, there is hope, for in the second part of this oracle, the positive element in the oracle, God assured Baruch with the following words: "And you, do you seek great things for yourself? Do not seek them; for I am going to bring evil upon all flesh. . . . But I will give you your life as a prize of war in every place wherever you may go." In this part of the oracle Baruch is told not to seek "great things" for himself but to wait for God to deliver him from the present disasters and to give him his life as "prize of war" (שלל) wherever he would go. What "great things" did Baruch seek? A position of political leadership? The prophetic mantle of Jeremiah? It is not entirely clear. The term גדלות, "great things," appears somewhat frequently in the Hebrew Bible. It can refer to the marvels of God's creation (Job 5:9, 9:10, 37:5) or to his power in delivering his people, especially in extracting Israel from slavery in Egypt (Deut 10:21; Ps 71:19, 106:21). Psalm 131:1–2 suggests that thinking about "great things" is somehow inappropriate for mortals, especially the devout.

> O Yahweh, my heart is not lifted up,
>> and my eyes are not elevated too high.
> I do not concern myself with *great things*,
>> and marvels that are beyond me.
> Rather, I have calmed and quieted my soul,
>> like a weaned child with its mother;
>> like the weaned child is my soul with me.

But more telling for Jeremiah 45 is the passage in 2 Kgs where the king asks Gehazi to recount to him the "great things" that Elisha has done: "And the king was talking with Gehazi, the servant of the man of God, and said, 'Recount for me all the great things (גְדֹלוֹת) that Elisha has done'" (2 Kgs 8:4). Gehazi obliged by telling the king of Elisha's miracle in raising a young boy from the dead. In this context גְדֹלוֹת refers to the marvelous deeds of a prophet. The idea that the term refers to things that only divinely empowered people can do appears also in Jeremiah, and this seems determinative for the term's meaning in the Jeremianic corpus. Jeremiah 33:1–3 connects גְדֹלוֹת, "great things," with prophetic activity:

> The word of Yahweh came to Jeremiah a second time while he was still confined in the prison compound. "Thus says Yahweh who makes a plan and enacts it. Yahweh is his name. 'Call on me, and I will answer you. And I will declare to you *great things* (גְדֹלוֹת), secrets you have not known.'"

So, in Jeremiah the term גְדֹלוֹת, *great things*, is associated with prophetic activity, and this suggests that Baruch wished to become a prophet or to receive a revelation of secrets that might explain the present turmoil or reveal the future.[45] For some unstated reason God denied this to Baruch and instead promised to give Baruch his life as a "prize of war" wherever he would go. This is a most enigmatic phrase, one that has always troubled commentators. The term "prize of war" or "war-booty" (שָׁלָל) is rather common in the Hebrew Bible, occurring thirty-seven times. It refers to the plunder that warriors take from those they defeat, items such as livestock, foodstuffs, personal property, prisoners, and so on. The phrase "your life as a prize of war" appears only in Jeremiah. In 21:9 and 38:2 it refers to the people who would heed Yahweh's counsel and therefore submit to the Babylonians. They would escape the coming calamities with their lives. In 39:18 it refers to Ebed-Melech the Cushite, who, like Baruch, was a faithful supporter of Jeremiah and obeyed the word of Yahweh as spoken through the prophet. Moreover, Baruch and Ebed-Melech are the only people who received private oracles from Yahweh through Jeremiah, and both of them are promised to receive their "life as a prize of war" (39:18 and 45:5). Thus, in the book of Jeremiah oracles promising deliverance using this phrase are addressed to righteous people who follow Jeremiah's policies: they obey the word of Yahweh and are prepared to submit to the Babylonians.[46] The intended meaning is that although they would have to endure the terrible events of the Babylonian conquest, they would in the end escape with their lives. They would make it safely though the disaster and survive to continue Jeremiah's mission.

This last scene in the passages involving Baruch has an odd sense to it. Why was such a private, personal oracle of deliverance, like the one to Ebed-Melech in chapter 39, made public by including it in this book? When prophets deliver the word of God, they normally have a public audience, or their messages to individuals have some wider social implications. Baruch's oracle could not be more private, and its inclusion must have some bearing on both the image of Baruch and the purpose of the book. Its presence here suggests that the editor is trying to tell us something about Baruch. Brueggemann and Taylor suggest that the Baruch of chapter 45 represents the "Baruch community" or the righteous Yahwists.[47] Thus, the oracle is not intended solely for Baruch but for all those who follow his religiopolitical agenda. It is an oracle of hope not just for the individual scribe, but for all those Judaeans who were loyal Yahwists and who supported Jeremiah and Baruch's pro-Babylonian agenda: submit to the Babylonians as God's instrument of judgment and you will survive the calamities of conquest.

There may exist yet another explanation for the nature and position of this oracle. Chapter 45 completes the passages in the book of Jeremiah involving Baruch, an admittedly small corpus. Here Baruch is the recipient of a private oracle. In the course of the book of Jeremiah Baruch has developed from a mere recorder of contracts (chapter 32:10–16) to someone who warrants special attention from the Almighty (chapter 45). As the stories in chapters 36 and 43 suggest, Baruch the scribe was more than a mere recorder, a scribe who simply wrote for others. Baruch was actively engaged in promoting Jeremiah's religiopolitical program with its pro-Babylonian agenda as the only proper response to the Babylonian onslaught. This ideology is presented in the book of Jeremiah as "the word of Yahweh" to the people and their leaders, words which were at least in part recorded by Baruch himself. This "word of Yahweh" is ignored only at great personal or national peril, as Baruch and his contemporaries discovered. By the latter portions of the book, therefore, Baruch had become an integral member of the group to which Jeremiah belonged, the deuteronomistic circle of Yahwists who were ultimately responsible for the theological history of ancient Israel we know as the books of Deuteronomy through 2 Kings, as well as portions of the book of Jeremiah and perhaps other works as well. Deuteronomy through 2 Kings, the "Deuteronomistic History," is a theological history whose basic religious tenet is that if you obey the commandments or prophetic word of Yahweh things will go well for you, but if you disobey, harsh punishment awaits. This tenet does not always work out perfectly, however. Although Jeremiah was certainly a faithful deuteronomistic Yahwist, his life was punctuated by crises and persecutions. Baruch, too, suffered as a result of his close association with Jeremiah and his prophecies, but in the end Baruch was favored by a divine promise: he would survive the awful treatment that the Judaeans would endure at the hands of the Babylonians. Baruch was a leading figure in the final, dark days of the Judean monarchy. He was perhaps expected to take Jeremiah's place as a community leader and recipient of divine revelations. While this is only suggested in the Hebrew or Masoretic version of the book of Jeremiah, the Greek or Septuagint version of Jeremiah more clearly indicates that Baruch succeeded Jeremiah as a leader of the people and intermediary between the Almighty and the community.

The Structure of Masoretic Jeremiah

Bernhard Duhm was one of the first scholars to detail the complex compositional history of the book of Jeremiah. He posited a theory, which most scholars have come to espouse, that there are three components of the book: poetry by Jeremiah, Jeremiah biography, and prose discourse added by later redactors. Duhm concluded that it was these later redactors who created the persona of Jeremiah and that this persona was much larger than life.[48] Sigmund Mowinckel took up Duhm's thesis and designated three elements, A (poems), B (biography), and C (prose), respectively.[49] Mowinckel, however, disputed Duhm's claim that there is little if any historicity to the portrayal of Jeremiah in the book. This dispute over the extent of the historical reliability of the portrayals of Jeremiah and even Baruch continues to dominate the scholarly debate over the contents of this book. Although it is clear that the book of Jeremiah had a long and complex compositional history, our concern is with section "B," the biographical material, for it is this material that has customarily been attributed to Baruch ben Neriah. Honestly, we cannot say for certain whether Baruch compiled or wrote this material, but this hypothesis has been adopted by many Jeremiah scholars. Still, the question of who put all this material together into its final form remains.

Recent scholarly focus on the literary form of prophetic books has resulted in an increasing lack of interest in the historical prophet. The prophetic books are now widely viewed as curated artifacts that present us not with a historically reliable depiction of the prophet but with the persona of the prophet that the final editors themselves created. Assessing the historicity of the book of Jeremiah, therefore, has tended to be weighted on either end of the spectrum. For example, on the one extreme, Holladay's and Bright's readings of the book are too historicist.[50] Carroll, at the other extreme, while providing an insightful depiction of the book as largely literary fiction, has too summarily jettisoned the potential historicity of the events narrated in the text.[51] Continuing the perspective initiated by Duhm, for Carroll the editors of the book created the persona of Jeremiah; the historical figure was nothing like the figure depicted in the text.[52] Interestingly, the Baruch stories in Jeremiah have found several archaeological confirmations, and perhaps in some ways uniquely so. Dearman finds that the collocation of scribes' names and references to scribal practices in Jeremiah 36 and their agreement with archaeological data suggest that these were perhaps the people involved in composing this book.

> The point is that not only are there several external agreements between inscriptions and officials in specific instances, but the portraits of their activities are also consistent with the cultural record. It is likely, therefore, that behind the literary portraits of the scribal officials stand real individuals, who were primarily responsible for the contents and shape of the Jeremiah scroll.[53]

Dearman, then, even more so than either McKane or Brueggemann, has found a delicate balance between reading these Baruch stories as history and as literature.[54] Dearman has perhaps gone the furthest in identifying the authors of our Jeremianic corpus, finding them among the scribes who were Jeremiah's disciples and "support group."[55]

The Structure of Greek Jeremiah

Ever since the time of the Christian biblical scholar Origen (circa 185–255 C.E.), it has been clear that the Hebrew and Greek versions of Jeremiah differ significantly: "I discovered many instances [of differences between the Hebrew and Greek texts] in Jeremiah. Actually, in that book I found much transposition and variation in the readings of the prophecies" (Origen, "Letter to Africanus" 4 [PG 11, col. 56]). There are thus two versions of the biblical book of Jeremiah—the Masoretic version found in the Hebrew Bible and the Greek version found in the Septuagint and represented also in fragments of the book of Jeremiah discovered among the Dead Sea Scrolls.[56] The overall structure of the Greek version of Jeremiah differs substantially from the Masoretic version. The Greek version is not simply a revision based on the Masoretic, but represents a different literary tradition of the book.[57] The texts of the Masoretic and Greek versions of Jeremiah differ both in details of structure and in overall length. The Masoretic version is roughly one-sixth longer than the Greek version. It seems likely that these two versions of Jeremiah are not related as parent and child (i.e., original and copy), but that they are dependent on two different, earlier Hebrew texts—they derive from two different Hebrew parents. That is to say, the Greek version is not an abbreviation of the Hebrew Masoretic version, nor is the Hebrew Masoretic version an expansion of the Hebrew text that lies behind the Greek version. These two versions ultimately represent two different Hebrew versions of Jeremiah. This indicates that for ancient Jews the exact shape of this prophetic book had some fluidity. Moreover, it may suggest that even in the early stages of the composition or compilation of the book, there was a dispute among Jeremiah's disciples as to the best way to arrange this material.

The most obvious structural difference between the two versions is the location within the book of the "Oracles Against the Nations" section. In the Masoretic version this collection of oracles appears at the end (46:1–51:58). In the Greek version, however, this collection of oracles is located in the middle of the book, inserted after 25:13. The location of these oracles influences the location of the episodes involving Baruch. In the Masoretic version the Baruch episodes appear in the middle and are followed by the "Oracles Against the Nations," while in the Greek version the Baruch episodes appear at the end of the book after the "Oracles Against the Nations." This arrangement in the Greek version presents a different picture of the relationship between Jeremiah and Baruch than the arrangement in the Masoretic version. Baruch is the last person in the book to receive a divine oracle in Greek Jeremiah (chapter 51).[58] Although the Masoretic text has this same material involving Baruch, albeit at an earlier point in the book (chapter 45), the placement of the oracle for Baruch at the end of Greek Jeremiah suggests that this editor is portraying Baruch as the successor to Jeremiah.[59] This arrangement of the material does not indicate the authorship of the work, but testifies to a belief by the people responsible for this Greek version of Jeremiah that Baruch was Jeremiah's successor.[60]

If Greek Jeremiah represents a more pristine form of the book, then Masoretic Jeremiah represents a rearrangement of the material that, for some reason, does not wish to suggest that Baruch was Jeremiah's successor.[61] Nonetheless, in the Greek version of Jeremiah, there is a clear attempt to portray Baruch as the successor to the prophet Jeremiah. It is this motif that provides at least part of the reason for the increasing prominence of Baruch in later Jewish and Christian texts. While the depiction of Baruch in the Masoretic version of Jeremiah is that of a scribe performing customary scribal duties, the Greek version of Jeremiah suggests that Baruch was Jeremiah's successor.

Recent work on prophecy and prophetic literature suggests that "prophetic" activity has many features, which begin with the reception of the divine message and end with the proclamation of that message to the intended audience.[62] Apart from hearing, speaking or performing the divine word, writing can be considered part of the prophetic repertoire.[63] In this sense Baruch may have been associated very early with prophetic activity because of his "writing" prophecy and his reception of a divine oracle. For the community that created, edited, and cherished Masoretic Jeremiah, the most important social role was that of the prophet, the one who delivered the divine message to the people. For this reason Jeremiah remains the focus of the book from beginning to end. For this community Baruch was simply the one who wrote the divine oracles at Jeremiah's dictation and otherwise assisted the prophet in his work. This is entirely befitting his role as an official scribe (סֹפֵר). That this was Baruch's professional position within late Judaean society is confirmed, as noted above, by the presence of a bulla with his name inscribed on it in a collection of bullae that have the names and titles of other high-ranking officials in Judah. Scribes were valued for their facility for the written word. They served in the royal courts and on the city streets. Baruch, though not a prophet according to the Masoretic version of Jeremiah, was a valued member of the community. From the biblical record it appears that he served Jeremiah faithfully through many difficult years; nevertheless, according to the Masoretic version of the book of Jeremiah, Baruch was not Jeremiah's equal.

Within the community that created, cherished, and transmitted the form of the book of Jeremiah now reflected in the Greek (Septuagint) version, however, Baruch was more than just a scribe, no matter how prominent that profession may have been. For these tradents of Jeremiah traditions, Baruch was also Jeremiah's successor. They viewed Baruch as an intermediary between God and his people. This explains, at least in part, how the depiction of Baruch began to be transformed from that of a scribe into that of a sage and seer throughout the course of the Second Temple period. Some believed, and their sacred texts indicated, that God appointed Baruch to become a leader of the people. But not everyone regarded Baruch as a prophet. Clearly the tradents of the Hebrew Masoretic version of Jeremiah did not. The debate over whether Baruch was a prophet or not continued in rabbinic circles for some time. What is clear is that at least some segments of the Jewish community regarded him as a prophet who succeeded Jeremiah.[64]

Baruch ben Neriah has, for the most part, languished in obscurity in the Jewish and Christian religious imagination for centuries. A closer examination of the Baruch passages in the book of Jeremiah, however, reveals a person who was intimately involved in Judean religious and geopolitical affairs. In reality he did not hide in the shadows but stepped forward to make his mark at great personal risk. In the biblical traditions he has been almost completely eclipsed by the great prophet Jeremiah. Nonetheless, Baruch played a very important role in Jerusalem in the days leading up to and following the Babylonian destruction of the city. Like the biblical prophets, he passes from history without any mention of his death. However, his reputation as a leader of the community flourished in postbiblical literature and tradition.

Chapter Two

THE SAGE

Do not forsake the discourse of the sages,
but devote yourself to their maxims;
for from them you will learn discipline,
and how to serve princes.

Ben Sira 8:8

Every society values some occupations more highly than it does others. The role of a sage was one of the more highly regarded positions in many ancient Near Eastern cultures. Israel was not alone in viewing sages as exceptional people who had much to contribute. This chapter explores the nature of sages and their roles in ancient Near Eastern societies, focusing on their familiarity with ancient lore and their role in perpetuating or revitalizing cultural values.[1] A few postbiblical texts present Baruch as a sage, one thoroughly acquainted with ancient lore and one who promoted the religious and social values of the community. These texts indicate how Baruch's persona was evolving beyond his biblical persona. The Book of Baruch presents Baruch as one who was more than simply a wise man or a skilled scribe. He was one whose "wisdom" was not just technical knowledge or familiarity with ancient lore, for the Book of Baruch redefines "wisdom" as obedience to biblical standards of piety. Wisdom, now characterized as living in accordance with the divine commandments (Torah), is no longer the property of the elite few, but is open to all who will adopt this way of life. Baruch thus became the model Jewish sage. In the Paraleipomena of Jeremiah Baruch takes on the role of community leader during the time that Jeremiah was exiled in Babylon. He is the one for whom God performs miracles and to whom God reveals mysteries. As such, in both the Book of Baruch and the Paraleipomena of Jeremiah Baruch appears as a leader of the Jewish community who models Torah obedience and who receives divine revelation.

The Work and Role of Ancient Sages

As discussed in the previous chapter, scribes, one kind of a sage, fulfilled some of the most important social roles in the ancient Near East. Their learning came from the wisdom handed down from previous generations (Job 15:17–35) and from their professional training. Their literacy was crucial to the smooth functioning of an urban society. They were needed to transact all manner of public and private business, and they served at all levels of society including the royal palace and its archives, the various temples, small businesses, and private individuals. Beyond the scribal profession, ancient sages occupied a variety of roles in society.[2] People whose profession included astrology/ astronomy, magic, and generally, although the term is unfortunately imprecise, witchcraft, might be identified by the title "sage." These are people whose religiomagical training makes them specialists in divining information from the gods. They have a personal connection and the professional skills that enable them to know information otherwise unavailable to mere mortals. These people have to know how to read and write. They must consult manuals that describe how to perform correctly the specific religiomagical activities to effect a desired result. Thus, in a largely illiterate world, their reading ability gives them a high degree of respect and even awe, especially when it can be put to use in the service of persuading the gods to act on behalf of the petitioner. Of course, the texts that mention the high regard in which sages were held were written by the sages themselves. It may be, therefore, that some of these ancient accounts of the sages' social value overestimate their importance, shamelessly so in some cases. It remains obvious, nonetheless, that wisdom has never been limited to only a certain class or profession. Qohelet (Ecclesiastes) 9:13–16 mentions the quiet, neglected poor man who, although he saved the city by his wisdom, was soon after forgotten.

This, too, I have observed under the sun about wisdom, and it has affected me profoundly. There was a small town with just a few people in it. A great king came, surrounded it, and laid siege to it. There was a poor wise man in the city and he delivered the city by his wisdom, yet no one remembered that poor man at all. Now this I declare: Wisdom is better than valor, but the wisdom of a poor man is despised, and his words are not heeded.

The sages, being the ones who wrote most of the ancient documents that have come down to us, controlled in many ways their own press. Nonetheless, knowing the value of learning and writing to urban life, their value to society was enormous.

The Hebrew Bible itself attests to the various roles of sages (חכמים) in royal courts. The Egyptian pharaoh had sages, sorcerers, and magicians to advise him (see Exodus 7:10–11 and Isaiah 19:11–13). The Persian king likewise consulted his sages (חכמים) for advice on customs and official protocol (Esth 1:13). Another example is Daniel. The narratives in Daniel 1–6 present Daniel as a learned young man in the service of the Babylonian and Persian courts. The story suggests that the Babylonians selected Daniel for service in their royal court because he was a handsome and intelligent young man. They taught him "the writings and language of the Chaldeans" (Dan 1:4). The term "Chaldeans" (כשדים, kasdim) refers here to a group of learned professionals, and Daniel was taught all the skills of their trade. "Chaldeans" is related to the Assyrian term kaldû and the Babylonian term kašdû and designates a group of learned professionals who were experts in various forms of divination.[3] Daniel, as well as his three Jewish compatriots, was trained to be one of these experts, and in fact he excelled at the job, especially in interpreting dreams (Dan 1–2). But Daniel's wisdom comprised not just what he learned from his Babylonian teachers: Daniel claimed that his wisdom came from God who alone knows the unknowable and reveals it to those who are faithful to him (Dan 2:20–23, 27–30; cf. Isa 44:24–25). Daniel bested the Babylonian sages at their own game thanks not only to his wisdom and training, but to his piety. Daniel is thus a model for how one can excel in exile—by observing the divine commandments and their accompanying traditions.[4] The book of Genesis mentions that the Egyptian pharaoh had technicians whose job was to interpret dreams (Gen 41:8), but the young Hebrew Joseph was superior to all the official dream interpreters of Egypt. In fact, there was a well-developed tradition of oneiromancy (i.e., their dream interpretation) in ancient Mesopotamia, and to perform this task well one had to master a vast body of material.[5] The following are just a few excerpts from this dream-interpreter's instruction literature. Note that the texts describe an image that one might see in a dream, and then they explain what this image means for the dreamer.

> If a man in his dream ascends to heaven and the gods bless him,
>> this man will die.
> If a man in his dream ascends to heaven and the gods curse him,
>> this man will live long.
> If a man kisses a dead person,
>> he will stand up in court against his adversary.
> If a dead person kisses a man,
>> one near to him will die.
> If a man in his dream enters the gate of a city,
>> wherever he turns he will not attain his desire.
> If he ascends to heaven,
>> his days will be short.
> If he descends to the netherworld,
>> his days will be long.
> If he goes to set a wood-pile afire,
>> he will see days of sadness.
> If he goes to plant a field,
>> he will be set free of hardship.
> If he goes to hunt in the desert,
>> he will become sad.
> If he goes to a fold for sheep,
>> he will become a chieftain.[6]

Other religiomagical professions were likewise demanding and respected. The witch was someone who could consult the gods, persuade the gods to act, perform rituals that would benefit the petitioner by warding off harmful spells cast by others or, obviously, cast spells to harm an enemy or opponent.[7] Because they had spent considerable time learning the vast religiomagical tradition and could theoretically influence the demonic forces, witches were highly valued in their cultures.

One needed these experts' skills to ward off evil and promote welfare. For these reasons they became guardians of a society's cultural values. Their literary training gave them knowledge of the past, and their professional skills gave them power to use this knowledge for the benefit of the present.

The sages of the "Wisdom" tradition provided one of the likely backgrounds for Israelite scribes and scribalism.[8] Within this tradition learning—in both its practical and its philosophical dimensions—was promoted. Crenshaw has eloquently described the loci, work, and ethos of sages and their part in the educational "system" of ancient Israel.[9] Sages were the deposit of the community's values and cherished traditions as well as what might be called scientific learning. While it is only with Ben Sira that we learn of a schoolhouse for learning (51:23), most of a child's education occurred within the confines of the home. Sages were available in the community and often in conjunction with official institutions. Beyond the leaders in Jerusalem and the regional centers of power, the Hebrew Bible is replete with references to the community leaders known as "the elders." These would have been the local leaders who guided the community and administered justice at certain levels. They met in the city gates and there conducted their business and passed on the community's history, traditions, and values.

Book of Baruch

The Book of Baruch is found in a collection of texts traditionally designated "the Apocrypha."[10] The word *apocrypha* is the plural form of the Latin word *apocryphus* that is itself based on a Greek word (ἀπόκρυφος) meaning "hidden" or "secret." The term designates books that were somehow regarded as "hidden away" because they were thought to contain secret or perhaps even heretical teachings (although nothing could be further from the truth). The gripping narratives, lovely poems, ecstatic visions, and didactic wisdom found in these "apocryphal" texts demonstrate the intellectual and religious vitality of the various early Jewish communities that produced and cherished this literature. These Jewish texts were relegated to the dubious category of apocrypha by leaders of the church and synagogue who lived much later and who arrogated for themselves the right to decide what was and was not acceptable religious literature. In their day, circa 200 B.C.E.–50 C.E., these texts formed part of a vast popular literature that was well known across all segments of Jewish society. In Roman Catholic Christian circles these books are known as the "Deutero-canonical Books" of the Bible. This term, along with the designation "apocrypha," indicates that these books were thought to be somehow secondary (the prefix *deutero* means "second") or inferior in status. Still, for many Orthodox Christian communities, at least some of these books belong to their canonical Scriptures. They accord these texts as much honor and value as they do the other books of the Bible. Jews have, however, traditionally designated these books the "the external books" (הספרים החיצונים), or perhaps even "the heretical books." The designations "apocrypha," "deuterocanonical," and "external," all un-fortunately suggest that the origins and religious value of these books are questionable. These somewhat derogatory designations all refer to the same collection of fourteen or fifteen separate books that are treated as a supplement to the Hebrew Bible. These texts actually form just a small part of an enormous and amorphous body of early Jewish literature known as the "apocrypha and pseudepigrapha."[11] These early Jewish apocrypha and pseudepigrapha, together with the Dead Sea Scrolls, the works of Josephus, Philo, and some early rabbinic texts, as well as the archaeology of Greco-Roman Palestine, are our primary sources for information on early Jewish history and culture.

Christians have designated the many apocryphal and pseudepi-graphic texts the "intertestamental literature," and the period from which they stem—roughly 200 B.C.E. to 100 C.E.—the "intertestamen-tal period." The Christian bias in the term *inter*testamental is obvious. Until the mid-1960s, and even today in some circles, Christians were interested in this literature simply because they thought it might shed some light on the origins and early history of Christianity.[12] Jews had no *"inter"* period, and for the most part either ignored this material or mined it for what light it might shed on the origins of rabbinic Judaism. Both the Christian and the Jewish communities, therefore, held biased views on the history and literature of this period. Since the mid-1960s, however, a major shift has taken place in the study of these texts. This material has overcome its subservience to the agendas of the traditionalists in both the Jewish and Christian communities and has come to form the basis of an independent field of research. No longer the handmaiden of biblical, Jewish, or Christian studies, the field is now itself so vast that there are subspecialties in Dead Sea Scrolls, Philo, Josephus, early Jewish apocalyptic literature, and other fields.

The actual role of the Apocrypha in Jewish and Christian religious history is not as marginal as the rabbis and some church leaders might have preferred. The history of the Apocrypha is in part closely tied to the Greek translation of the Hebrew Bible. This translation is commonly designated the "Septuagint." The Greek Bible was not a Christian, but a Jewish one. Jewish communities were widely spread across the Mediterranean basin where the primary language was Greek, and many of these Jews neither read nor understood Hebrew. Such Greek-speaking Jewish communities required a Greek Bible to serve the religious needs of the community and the individual. The Septuagint and other translations of the Bible into Greek by Jews served in many respects as "the Bible" in these communities.[13] Nevertheless, for religious and liturgical purposes the Hebrew text remained the principal version of the Bible for Jewish communities worldwide. The books of the Apocrypha were written largely in Greek, and even a cursory reading of these texts indicates how interesting they are. As a result, the Jewish communities came to value these books. It is not at all certain that they ever gained true canonical status in the Jewish communities, but they certainly did enjoy widespread popularity. We cannot say at this point whether or not these texts were part of the Bible for Jews because the great codices of biblical manuscripts in Greek that include the Apocrypha alongside the standard biblical texts—codices that date from the fourth and fifth centuries C.E.—are Christian codices, produced for and by Christians.

The Book of Baruch, one of the books of the Apocrypha, consists of four anonymous units that originally circulated independently:

1:1–14	Narrative Introduction
1:15–3:8	Prayer of Confession
3:9–4:4	Poem in Praise of Wisdom
4:5–5:9	Message of Consolation

These four components were eventually combined into a new text. This new text was closely associated with the book of Jeremiah and was not known separately as the Book of Baruch until as late as the eighth century C.E. in the Latin Church.[14] Some Greek fathers of the church quote from the Book of Baruch, but identify their source as "Jeremiah," while other Greek fathers cite this text as "Baruch." Still other Greek fathers are inconsistent: they will quote from what we call the Book of Baruch but cite the source as "Jeremiah" in some places and then later cite it as "Baruch" in others.[15] This inconsistency in identifying the Book of Baruch demonstrates that the early Christian (and perhaps also the Jewish) communities were uncertain about the authorship of this small book. The authorship of the book is anonymous apart from its narrative introduction, the only place in the book where Baruch's name appears (1:1,3). The book as a whole, therefore, could not have been associated with Baruch until the introduction was added.[16] This evidence indicates that there was considerable fluidity in defining the exact limits of the Greek version of Jeremiah. Eventually, however, these "additions" were collated as an independent work and ascribed, based on the introduction, to Baruch. Moreover, it must also be remembered that these "additions" appear attached to the Greek version of the biblical book of Jeremiah—precisely that book which hinted that Baruch would be Jeremiah's prophetic successor.

Determining this text's original language and date of composition has been difficult. The book has been preserved in several translations—Armenian, Coptic, Ethiopic, Greek, Latin, and Syriac, with the Greek of the Septuagint being, obviously, the most important witness. Most scholars have concluded that at least 1:1–3:8 was composed in Hebrew, yet others maintain that the entire book was composed in Hebrew.[17] Given that one section, as we shall see shortly, quotes the book of Daniel, that part of the Book of Baruch can have originated no earlier than the book of Daniel, which was composed circa 165 B.C.E. And as there are no clear historical references or allusions in the text, save for the ones to the Babylonian era in which Baruch lived, no precise dates of composition can be offered. Instead, we can only say that the various parts of this text were composed and combined sometime between the late second century B.C.E. and the mid–first century C.E.[18] This is admittedly a rather broad time frame; nonetheless, the Book of Baruch represents almost certainly the next postbiblical text to be associated with Baruch. The textual and thematic evidence vis-à-vis Baruch's persona suggest that the components of this book most likely originated earlier in this time frame than later, say late second or first century B.C.E. The Book of Baruch attests, in any case, to the religious values of that era and provides a glimpse into how Baruch was imagined at that time.

Baruch 1:1–14—Narrative Introduction

The Book of Baruch opens with Baruch living among the Judaean exiles in Babylon (1:1–2). Baruch's name is given here as Baruch the son of Neriah, the son of Mahseiah, son of Zedekiah, son of Hasadiah, son of Hilkiah (1:1). This form of his name adds apocryphal details of his lineage that were lacking in the book of Jeremiah, for Jeremiah never mentions ancestors beyond Baruch's father and grandfather (Neriah and Mahseiah). The names Zedekiah and Hilkiah are names of important biblical figures, but it does not seem that this text is trying to connect Baruch to those figures. The name Hasadiah appears in a list of descendants of David in 1 Chr 3:20, but again, this Hasadiah is certainly not the person mentioned in Baruch 1:1, since the Chronicler identifies Hasadiah's father as Zerubbabel. The Book of Baruch either preserves additional details about Baruch's lineage that were not recorded in the Bible, or, and this is much more likely, the text simply tries to fill out his ancestry.

This narrative introduction to the Book of Baruch serves as an introduction to the entire work and gives it the appearance of a book that Baruch wrote and read to a gathering of all the exiles in Babylon (1:3–5). The opening words, "these are the words of the book which Baruch wrote," (1:1) recall Jeremiah 29:1 and link Baruch's activity and book with that of Jeremiah:

> These are the words of the letter (literally "book") which Jeremiah the prophet sent from Jerusalem to the rest of the elders of the exilic community, the priests, the prophets, and to all the people whom Nebuchadnezzar exiled from Jerusalem to Babylon.[19]

Thus, Baruch, like Jeremiah before him, wrote words to comfort and instruct the exilic community. The wording in Baruch 1:3 is, moreover, reminiscent of 2 Kgs 23:2 and Josiah's reading of the recently "discovered" Book of Deuteronomy "to their ears" of all the people, "from the least to the great" (2 Kgs 23:2; 2 Chr 34:30; cf. Ex 24:7; Deut 31:11). It also parallels what the book of Jeremiah says about Baruch's work in Jerusalem prior to being exiled—he read from Jeremiah's scroll "to the ears" of the people (Jer 36:6, 10, 13–15; cf. Jer 2:2, 36:20–21). As H. M. Orlinsky once suggested, the phrase "to read to the ears of" appears to be a technical phrase indicating that the text being publicly read is somehow important or authoritative.[20] The phrase is used of Moses when he read the book of the Covenant to the people on Sinai (Ex 24:7) and of Ezra when he read the book of the Torah to the post-exilic community in Jerusalem (Neh 8:3). Perhaps even more significant is the fact that this "reading to the ears of" is precisely what Baruch did when he read Jeremiah's "scroll of disaster" publicly on behalf of Jeremiah (Jer 36:6,10). The Book of Baruch opens, therefore, with a statement connecting the contents of this book both to Baruch's earlier work and to a longer tradition of authoritative texts. The use of this biblical phrase is clearly tendentious: the author wishes the readers to receive this book as an inspired, prophetic message. Thus the opening section of the book portrays Baruch as a leader of the exiles by having the exiled Judaean king Jehoiachin and all the people gather to hear the words of his book. In this activity Baruch functions like Moses, Jeremiah, Ezekiel, and Ezra, who also had people gather around them to hear "the word of the Lord" (Ex 24:7; Jer 25:1–2, 26:7; Ezek 8:1, 33:30–32; Neh 8:3).

The author who added this narrative introduction intends the phrase "the words of this book" (1:3) in the introduction to refer to the entire Book of Baruch as we now have it. After the exiles allegedly had heard the contents of this entire book, they responded in a penitential manner: they wept, fasted, prayed, and prepared sacrifices, activity that is part of a biblical model for repentance (Bar 1:5–7; cf. Judg 20:26; 2 Sam 1:2; 2 Kgs 19:15; Neh 1:4; and Esther 4:3). The exiles took up a collection, "each as much as was able," to send to Jerusalem. They intended the priests and people in Jerusalem to use these resources for sacrifices to be made on behalf of the exiles and their oppressors (Bar 1:10–12). This introduction thus rehabilitates the Babylonians and portrays them as friends of Jerusalem and the Jews. Moreover, Baruch's request that the people pray for the welfare of the Babylonian king is

part of an exilic ideology whereby Jews living under foreign domination or in foreign lands should work for the well-being of their over-
lords. The other nations are no longer the focus of divine wrath, as was
common in much of the Hebrew Bible, rather, thanks to Jeremiah's
viewing them as potential instruments of Yahweh's justice, these
nations are now also the potential recipients of divine favor. Daniel is
presented as a model of how Jews are to behave in exile so that they
might enjoy the favor of both their heavenly and their earthly mas-
ters.[21] He maintains his Jewish identity and practices, and even works
for the Babylonian and Persian kings. This theme is echoed in the
book of Ezra as well—another book with an exilic setting. Ezra 6
reports how the Persian King, Darius, ordered his officials to support
the restoration of the Jerusalem temple and its cultic practices so that
the people there "may offer pleasing sacrifices to the God of Heaven
and pray for the life of the King and his sons" (Ezra 6:10).[22] These
favorable words about the Babylonians portray Baruch as a promoter
of the pro-Babylonian ideology that had been favored by Jeremiah.
After the initial transfer of exiles to Babylon, Jeremiah wrote to them
telling them to make the best of the situation:

> Thus says Yahweh of Hosts, the God of Israel, to the entire community
> that I exiled from Jerusalem to Babylon: build houses and live in them!
> Plant gardens and eat their produce! Take wives and have sons and
> daughters! Let your sons and daughters marry so that they, too, might
> have children. Multiply there and do not decrease! Seek the well-being of
> the city to which I exile you and pray to Yahweh on its behalf, for when
> it prospers, you shall prosper (Jer 29:4–7).

Baruch also repatriated the holy vessels used in the Temple (Bar 1:8–9).
These were not the Temple's original holy vessels fashioned in
Solomon's day, for those were looted by Nebuchadnezzar when he
conquered Jerusalem (2 Kgs 24:13). These, the text claims, were the
vessels that king Zedekiah made to replace the ones Nebuchadnezzar
stole (Bar 1:8). The text is perhaps trying here to solve an interpretive
problem. It is mentioned in 2 Kgs 24:13 that Nebuchadnezzar "carried
away from there (i.e., Jerusalem) *all* the treasures of Yahweh's Temple
and the treasures of the king's palace. He smashed *all the golden vessels* which Solomon, king of Israel, made for the Temple of Yahweh"

(italics mine). The phrase translated here as "golden vessels," ‏כלי הזהב‎, could also be translated "golden decorations" or "golden items." Since Nebuchadnezzar is said to have "smashed," or perhaps "torn down" (‏קצץ‎) these items, it seems unlikely that these are the golden vessels that were used in the cultic practices. These vessels likely would have been transported intact. It is reported in 2 Kgs 25:13–16 that on a later campaign against Jerusalem in the days of Zedekiah the Babylonians committed additional acts of ruthless pillaging.

> The Chaldeans broke up the bronze pillars of the Temple of Yahweh as well as the stands and the bronze basin that was in the Temple of Yahweh, and they carried away the bronze to Babylon. They took the pots, the ladles, the snuffers, the dishes for incense, and all the bronze vessels as well as the pans and the bowls that served in the cult. Whatever was made of gold the captain of the guard took away for the gold, and whatever was made of silver, for the silver. The two pillars, the one basin, and the stands, which Solomon made for the Temple of Yahweh, the bronze of all these vessels was beyond weighing.

Baruch 1:8–9 is not alone in providing somewhat confusing information about which cultic vessels went to Babylon and when. The Chronicler was likewise confused somewhat by his source, the Book of Kings. The Chronicler's history recounts that, in Jehoiakim's day, Nebuchadnezzar "brought to Babylon some of the vessels of the Temple of Yahweh and put them into his palace in Babylon" (2 Chron 36:7). This expands the story as recounted in Kings, for nowhere did the Kings' version of the story mention where these holy vessels were deposited. Moreover, the Chronicler notes that in Zedekiah's day Nebuchadnezzar took "all the vessels of the Temple of God, the big ones and the small ones, and the treasures of the Temple of Yahweh and of the king and his officers, all these he brought to Babylon" (2 Chron 36:18). The authors of Baruch 1 have conflated the story somewhat and turned the bronze vessels of Zedekiah's day into silver ones. Moreover, in trying to explain the origin of these items, Baruch 1 claims that Zedekiah actually fashioned new vessels for use in the temple cult. The Chronicler's resolution of the discrepancy is rather more elegant. The Chronicler notes that in Jehoiachin's day the Babylonians took "some" of the holy vessels and then in Zedekiah's day the

Babylonians took "all" of the remaining vessels. This is precisely how Jeremiah described the fate of the temple vessels: the Babylonians took some of these when they first conquered Jerusalem in 587 B.C.E. and then took the rest in 586 B.C.E. when they reconquered the rebellious city (Jer 27:16–28:6). In any event, Baruch 1:1–14 places Baruch squarely in the events surrounding the exile to Babylon and the creation of Jewish life there. Moreover, these Jews are portrayed as not having lost their concern for the well-being of Jerusalem and the Jews living there. Baruch's concern with repatriating the temple vessels portrays him as one who sought to realize Jeremiah's hopes, expressed in Jer 27–28, for the eventual restoration of these cultic vessels. In a sense, Baruch's restoration of the temple vessels and the people's support of the cult symbolize both the immanent end of the exile and the beginning of the renewal of the cult in the Temple of Yahweh in Jerusalem. Thus, the introduction to the Book of Baruch portrays Baruch as a person concerned for the well-being of the Jewish community and for the restoration of the Yahweh cult in Jerusalem.

Baruch 1:15–3:8—Prayer of Confession

The second unit of the Book of Baruch is a lovely penitential prayer. This anonymous prayer became associated with Baruch only after it was connected to the introduction, since Baruch's name appears nowhere in the text; actually, the prayer comes from the people of Jerusalem and Judah (1:15). By associating this otherwise anonymous prayer with Baruch, the editor of the Book of Baruch is portraying Baruch as a penitent who prays like Daniel.[23] The editor's desire to associate Baruch's piety with Daniel's is unmistakable: this prayer consists of a patchwork of excerpts from Daniel 9.[24] This prayer depicts Baruch (literally, the people of Jerusalem) as one who has accepted the Deuteronomistic explanation of the fall of Jerusalem and the exile of the people—namely, that all this came about because of the religious failures of the people who did not worship Yahweh alone.[25] This connection with the Deuteronomistic ideology is made explicit through quotations from and allusions to the book of Deuteronomy in general and to the prophets Daniel and Jeremiah in particular.[26] This prayer, then, once it became part of the Book of Baruch, portrays Baruch in the tradition of pious people like Daniel who were concerned for the exiles and the state of the holy city.[27] Like Daniel, Baruch accepted the exile as God's punishment for religious infidelity and asked for divine forgiveness for Israel's sins. Baruch (i.e., the people) pleaded with God to remember the promise he made to Moses, that if they repented of their iniquities, he would restore them to their land (Deut 28–30). Although the prayer is actually a communal prayer of confession, its placement in the Book of Baruch transforms it into Baruch's prayer— he becomes part of the people of Jerusalem and Judah. That Baruch anguished over the destruction of Jerusalem was evident already in Jeremiah 45:2: "Woe is me because Yahweh has added grief to my pain. I am weary with my groaning, and I can find no rest." The decision of the book's editor to associate this prayer with Baruch, then, is perfectly understandable: Baruch, as a leader in the Jerusalem community, was the kind of pious person who would have prayed a prayer like this. Thus, by adding this component to Baruch's popular persona, the editor is further developing Baruch's legacy as a person of great piety.

Baruch 3:9–4:4—Poem in Praise of Wisdom

The third unit in the Book of Baruch (3:9–4:4) is a poem in praise of Wisdom.[28] This poem calls people to pursue "Wisdom" in a manner that draws on imagery from Job 28 and Proverbs 1–9. Job 38–39 recounts a speech by God in which the Almighty asks a long series of rhetorical questions that point out human limitations. This material is part of a wider Wisdom tradition in the ancient Near East and intends to show that humans, no matter how learned they may be, cannot fathom the deep mysteries of life and the cosmos. Job 28:12–28 likewise relates that Wisdom is indeed a rare commodity, but with Job we encounter a distinctly Israelite perspective on Wisdom.

> Where can wisdom be found,
>> and where is the location of understanding?
> No one knows the way to it;
>> it cannot be found in the land of the living.
> The deep says, "it is not in me;"
>> the sea says, "it is not with me."

Pure gold cannot buy it;
>   its price cannot be weighed out in silver.
It cannot be weighed against the gold of Ophir,
>   nor against precious onyx or lapis lazuli.
Gold or glass cannot match its value;
>   nor can vessels of fine gold be exchanged for it.
Coral and crystal cannot be mentioned alongside it;
>   a collection of wisdom is better than coral.
Topaz cannot match its value;
>   it cannot be weighed against pure gold.
But where does wisdom come from?
>   Where is the location of understanding?
It is concealed from the eyes of the living;
>   hidden from the birds of the sky.
Abaddon and Death say,
>   "we have only heard a report about it."
God understands the way to it;
>   he knows its location.
For he sees to the ends of the earth;
>   he observes all that is under the heavens.
When he made weight for the wind,
>   he apportioned the waters.
When he set a limit for the rain,
>   he made a path for the thunderbolts.
He saw it [i.e., Wisdom] and he evaluated it;
>   he considered it and also investigated it.
And he said to humanity:
The fear of the Lord is wisdom,
>   and turning from evil is understanding.

The Psalmists would agree with the final verses of this passage: "The beginning of Wisdom is the fear of Yahweh; it grants sound judgment to those who live by it" (Ps 111:10). Moreover, the "fear of Yahweh" as the foundation for Israelite Wisdom is the central theme in another book of Israelite Wisdom—the book of Proverbs.

> The fear of Yahweh is the beginning of knowledge;
>   fools despise wisdom and discipline (Prov 1:7).

The fear of Yahweh is the beginning of wisdom,
>and the knowledge of the Holy One is understanding (Prov 9:10).

Moreover, the book of Proverbs teaches its readers that there is a pay-off for "fearing Yahweh," the goal of Yahwistic wisdom:

The fear of Yahweh prolongs life,
>but the years of the wicked will be cut short (Prov 10:27).
The fear of Yahweh is a fountain of life,
>turning away from the snares of death (Prov 14:27).
The fear of Yahweh is life;
>sated with it one endures and suffers no evil (Prov 19:23).
The result of humility and the fear of Yahweh is riches, honor, and life (Prov 22:4).

Prov 2:1–22 makes the issues at stake clear:

My child, if you accept my words
>and store my commandments within you,
making your ear attentive to wisdom
>and inclining your heart to understanding;
if you cry out for insight,
>and raise your voice for understanding;
if you seek it like silver,
>and search for it as for treasures,
then you will understand the fear of Yahweh
>and find the knowledge of God.
For Yahweh gives wisdom;
>from his mouth come knowledge and understanding.
He stores up prudence for the upright;
>a shield to those who walk blamelessly,
protecting the paths of justice,
>he guards the way of his faithful ones.
Then you will understand righteousness and justice—every good path.
For wisdom will come into your heart,
>and knowledge will delight your soul;
Foresight will guard you,
>and understanding will protect you.
It will save you from the way of evil,

from the people who speak deceitfully,
who forsake the paths of uprightness
    to walk in the ways of darkness,
who rejoice in doing evil,
    delighting in the perverseness of evil;
whose paths are crooked,
    and who are devious in their ways.
It will save you from the corrupt woman,
    from the adulteress with her smooth talk,
who forsakes the companion of her youth,
    and forgets the covenant of her God.
For her house leads down to death,
    and her paths to the shades.
All who go to her never return,
    nor can they return to the paths of life.
So, walk in the way of the good,
    and keep to the paths of the just.
For the upright will dwell in the land,
    and the blameless will remain in it.
But the wicked will be cut off from the land,
    and the treacherous will be rooted out of it.

In Proverbs 1–9, Wisdom, personified as a woman, stands in the streets calling for people to come and learn from her. Thus, Wisdom is like a Greek teacher who must market himself to attract students to come and acquire the Jewish equivalent of Greek *paideia,* training in the traditions, morals, and intellectual values that define and characterize a culture.[29] In this section of the Book of Baruch, however, Wisdom is equated with obedience to the divine commandments, the Torah.[30] This is a crucial step, for now Wisdom is the property of everyone who knows or has access to Mosaic religion. Wisdom now resides with the people and is readily accessible in the book, the Torah (cf. Deut 30:11–14). Although Wisdom in the Hebrew Bible is multifaceted, its essential character is reduced to Torah-obedience in the Book of Baruch and Ben Sira (Ben Sira 24). While biblical Wisdom literature affirms that Yahweh is the source of every conceivable aspect of wisdom, the Book of Baruch affirms that access to Yahweh's wisdom is now gained only through obedience to Mosaic religion. In other words, the author of this text is stressing the importance of both orthodoxy and orthopraxy as prerequisites for becoming wise. Obedience to Mosaic religion will enable one to become wise, and that wisdom will promote further devotion to that very religious system, the one given to Moses by God. Wisdom now is not simply knowledge-based, but founded on both knowledge (which itself is gained only by divine grace/revelation) and proper behavior. For this text James Crenshaw has epitomized the issue clearly: ". . . true wisdom is attained only through embodiment of virtue, for which divine assistance is required. In short, a sage needed a gift from the deity to grasp the full meaning of information processed by arduous intellectual effort and to put knowledge to effective use." In his survey of Israelite and ancient Near Eastern wisdom circles and traditions, Crenshaw has identified four qualities that distinguish the wise from the foolish: "silence, eloquence, timeliness, and modesty."[31] Beginning if not in the late monarchic or exilic periods then certainly with the Persian and Hellenistic periods, we must also add "Torah-obedience." That is to say, upon the completion of the Deuteronomistic History with its fiercely monotheistic and aniconic ideology, the cultural foundation of the community revolved in many ways around the religious program that the text and subsequent tradition claim was given by God to Moses. A truly wise person must by definition follow and encourage others to follow Mosaic religion, for that is the God-given pattern for humans to follow in order to avoid calamity and to warrant divine approval.

Baruch appears here as just such a sage. Interestingly enough, during a period of history when, in the Mediterranean basin, Greek civilization was reaching its zenith in terms of science and philosophy, many of the sages of Israel, at least as far as the preserved texts indicate, were concentrating their speculations on practical ethics and passing on the ancient traditions and practices as they understood them.[32] Actually there must have been a vibrant interest in science in Israel throughout its ancient history, at least as far as astronomy/astrology is concerned—an interest obviously paralleled in Greece.[33] The denunciations of astronomy in the Hebrew Bible attest to the prevalence of the practice of observing and worshiping stars, the "hosts of heaven" in the biblical period (e.g., Deut 4:19, 17:3; 2 Kgs 17:16, 21:3,5, 23:4–5; Isaiah 47:13–14; Jer 8:3, 19:13; Amos 5:26; Zeph 1:5; 2 Chron 33:3,5). Moreover, astronomy must have been important in some Wisdom circles because one of the earliest non-biblical Jewish texts, the "Astronomical Book of Enoch" (1 Enoch 72–82), which dates at least to the early third century B.C.E., attests an intense interest in observational astronomy.[34] This interest in astronomy and astrology appears also among the texts of the Dead Sea Scrolls (e.g., 4Q317–319). The fact that astronomical speculations were attributed to Enoch is not surprising given that Enoch lived 365 years—a solar year—before being "taken" by God (Gen 5:21–24).[35] Jews undoubtedly conducted scientific speculation much like the Greeks, but this work is not what characterized the traditional Jewish depictions of their sages.

This third unit of the Book of Baruch, therefore, adds to the developing persona of Baruch an element of Wisdom.[36] Baruch is becoming a paradigm of a Second Temple period sage who is devoted to a Wisdom that is not simply familiarity with ancient lore (Ecc 1–2, 12:9–12) or scribal skill, but is focused on behavior and characterized by obedience to the commandments of the Torah as given to Moses by God.[37] To be sure, this is not entirely new, for already Jeremiah equated "the word of Yahweh" with "the Torah of Yahweh," and claimed that to reject one is to reject the other (Jer 8:8–9). Baruch is portrayed in this section of the Book of Baruch, then, as the type of leader who models fidelity to the traditional religious and cultural teachings honored by the community. If one wishes to know how to live a pious Jewish life, Baruch provides a perfect example to follow; here the community's socioreligious interests are reflected in how they depict their ideal leaders. With respect to educating its people, especially the young, to cherish and follow its traditions, morals, and intellectual values, the early Jewish sages closely resembled their Greek counterparts: they sought to civilize their compatriots according to their community's customs so that people's lives would be better and that their culture would endure.

Baruch 4:5–5:9—Message of Consolation

The final unit of the Book of Baruch (4:5–5:9) is a discourse meant to console the exiles and inspire them to remain faithful to God in spite

of their sufferings.[38] This unit encourages the exiles to take heart, obey
the commandments of God, and prepare to return to Jerusalem. Their
reason for hope is that the God who sent them into exile because of
their religious infidelity will also bring them back to their land once
they return in obedience to him. The imagery and sentiment of
Baruch 4–5 is inspired by Isaiah 40–41, passages that offer comfort to
the exiles.

> Comfort, comfort my people,
>> says your God.
> Speak tenderly to Jerusalem,
>> and declare to her
> that her service is over,
>> her iniquity is expiated.
> For she has received from the hand of Yahweh
>> double for all her sins (Isa 40:1–2).

> They draw near and come.
> Each one helps the other,
>> saying to his companion, "take courage!" (Isa 41:5b–6).

> But you, O Israel, my servant,
>> Jacob, whom I have chosen,
>> the offspring of Abraham, my beloved,
> you whom I took from the ends of the earth,
>> and from its remotest regions I called,
> saying to you,"you are my servant,
>> I have chosen you and have not cast you off.
> Do not fear, for I am with you;
>> do not be afraid, for I am your God.
> I will strengthen you, I will help you;
>> I will support you with my victorious right hand" (Isa 41:8–10).

The first major movement of this section is an address by the personified city of Jerusalem to the exiles (4:5–29). The author of this material
remains anonymous, but the editor who assembled the anonymous
materials to create the Book of Baruch has now associated this anonymous address with Baruch. This movement, like the second, begins with
the verb "take courage" (θαρσέω; 4:5, 30), and is also punctuated with

two other occurrences of this verb (4:21,27). The section begins with Baruch addressing his people and then quoting to them Jerusalem's lament—a lament in which Jerusalem speaks to her now-exiled inhabitants and tenderly encourages them amidst their sufferings. The exiles' pain is superceded only by Jerusalem's torment at their loss, as indicated by how touchingly Jerusalem refers to her inhabitants: they are her "sons and daughters," her "children." The lament turns to optimism at 4:21 as Jerusalem assures her exiled children that God will deliver them from their exile as soon as they turn to him in repentance: "Take courage, little children, and cry out to God, for you will be remembered by him who brought this upon you. For just as you resolved to turn away from God, return and seek him with tenfold zeal. For the one who brought evils upon you will bring upon you eternal joy when he delivers you"(4:27–29). Thus these comforting words now associated with Baruch portray him as one who cares for the sufferings of the exiles and for Jerusalem's torment: he looks forward to the exiles' repentance and their restoration, as well as Jerusalem's comfort.

Associating this section of the Book of Baruch with Baruch is at least in part inspired by the first of two letters that Jeremiah sent to the exiles (Jer 29:1–23).[39] Jeremiah encouraged them to settle down and make a life for themselves in Babylon, quoting a divine oracle:

> Build houses and live in them; plant gardens and eat their produce. Marry and have sons and daughters. Let your sons take wives and your daughters husbands so that they may have children of their own. Multiply there and do not decrease. Seek the welfare of the city to which I exile you and pray to Yahweh on its behalf, for when it has peace, you will have peace (Jer 29:5–7).

Baruch 4:5–29 focuses on the end of the process: repentance and restoration. In fact, the final paragraph (Bar 4:27–29) appears to draw on vocabulary from the Greek version of this chapter in Jeremiah. Because of the different chapter sequences in the Hebrew and Greek versions of Jeremiah, Hebrew (and English) Jeremiah chapter 29 appears in Greek Jeremiah as chapter 36. A form of the term used to describe how the exiles must turn and seek ($\zeta\eta\tau\acute{\epsilon}\omega$) Yahweh prior to their restoration in the Book of Baruch 4:28 appears in Greek Jeremiah

36:13 (ἐκζητέω) with the same sense. Moreover, the very next verse in the Book of Baruch, 4:29, mentions the evils (κακά) that God brought on the people for their disobedience, and this seems to draw on Greek Jeremiah 36:11 which uses this same term "evil" (κακά) in referring to how Yahweh will one day bring not "evil" but peace to the exiles. These are admittedly somewhat tenuous links, but the select vocabulary and the overall ideology suggest that the editor is trying to have Baruch do and say the kinds of things Jeremiah did and said in leading the community.

The second movement in this "Message of Consolation" addresses Jerusalem who languishes as the mother bereft of her children (4:30–5:9). This section draws on many biblical images of restoration. Baruch 4:30 draws on images and vocabulary from Zephaniah 3:16 and Zechariah 8:13,15: God will turn to do good to Jerusalem in the midst of her sufferings.[40] The message of hope in this section draws on restoration themes that appear in a variety of texts such as Isa 51–52, 60, Jer 30–31, and Ps 137. The message is that the bad times are now over and the good times are on the horizon. Compare Isa 60:4 with Bar 4:36–37.

> Lift your eyes and look around.
> They have all gathered together and are coming to you.
> Your sons shall be brought from afar,
>> your daughters carried like babies (Isa 60:4).

> Look around to the east, O Jerusalem,
>> and see the joy that is coming to you from God.
> Behold, your children are coming,
>> whom you saw being sent away.
> They are coming, gathered from the east and west,
>> at the command of the Holy One,
>> rejoicing in the glory of God (Bar 4:36–37; cf. 5:5–6).

Baruch thus heralds the return from exile. The one who had once heralded the exile now announces its end. Jerusalem had earlier lamented that "I have taken off the garment (στολή) of peace and put on the sackcloth of supplication" (Bar 4:20). Here, however, she is told: "take off your garment (στολή) of sorrow and affliction, O Jerusalem, and put on the robe (διπλοΐδα) of divine justice" (Bar 5:1). The Book of Baruch thus closes on a positive note. The point that the editor of this text seems to be making is that the tragedy that Baruch witnessed in 586—when the Babylonians devastated Judah, destroyed the Temple, and exiled the people—will soon be resolved. The exile will end, the exiles will return, and Jerusalem will be comforted. This message of hope for national restoration and preservation formed part of the foundation of the ancient Jewish identity. The hope was for the opportunity to live their lives in the land of Israel without foreign domination.

By associating this final unit of the book (Bar 4:5–5:9) with Baruch, the editor has portrayed Baruch as a leader who, like Jeremiah (cf. Jer 29–31), encouraged the exiles to remain faithful to their God while awaiting their eventual repatriation.[41] Baruch is once again gaining prominence, for just as Jeremiah wrote to instruct and encourage the exiles, so Baruch is here depicted as offering comfort and guidance to the exiles outside of Judah and tenderly lamenting the sufferings of Jerusalem.[42] By adding this originally anonymous material to a book being ascribed to Baruch, the editor is portraying Baruch as a leader who is concerned for the well being of exiled Jews and for the state of the holy city of Jerusalem.

The images associated with Baruch in the Book of Baruch bring to life the biblical character, depicting him as a great spiritual leader of the people. This reflects the community's interest in a leadership that promotes Torah obedience as the way to achieve Wisdom and that tenderly attends to the aspirations of Jews living outside of the land for a connection to Jerusalem as the focal point of their piety. But this is just one of the initial stages in the transformation of Baruch from a scribe to a great sage and apocalyptic seer.[43] As is becoming clear, the popular perception of Baruch was changing with time: the professional scribe was becoming a character of central religious importance to the community.

Paraleipomena of Jeremiah

The Paraleipomena of Jeremiah, "the things omitted from (the book of) Jeremiah," completes Jeremiah's story by supplying information about the prophet's final days and death. Here Baruch is depicted as the loyal colleague of Jeremiah who took a leadership role in Jerusalem during the time that Jeremiah was exiled to Babylon. Jeremiah 43–44 recounts how Jeremiah and Baruch were taken forcibly to Egypt by their compatriots. The Paraleipomena of Jeremiah, however, preserves another tradition regarding the fate of these two people.[44] When the Babylonians conquered Jerusalem, they took Jeremiah away to Babylon, but Baruch remained in Jerusalem. Overwhelmed by the tragedy, Baruch went into a tomb to grieve.[45] While he was sitting in the tomb, angels came and "explained everything" to him (4:11). We learn no details of these angelic revelations, but this does indicate that the authors of this text believed that Baruch was worthy to receive divine revelations. This tradition builds on the story of the private oracle delivered to Baruch in Jer 45 and the theme that Baruch is worthy of divine revelations. The brief mention of these angelic revelations is immediately followed by the story of Abimelech's sixty-six year nap in the fields outside Jerusalem. Abimelech (also known as Ebed-Melech) was another member of the pro-Jeremiah faction in Jerusalem and the only person besides Baruch to whom a private oracle was delivered by Jeremiah (Jer 38:4–13). The Paraleipomena of Jeremiah relates that Abimelech, thanks to his righteousness and his care for Jeremiah when the prophet was thrown into a pit (Jer 38:1–13), was spared the pain of seeing Jerusalem destroyed and its people deported by being put to sleep for 66 years in the "field of Agrippa" outside of the city.[46] The Baruch narrative resumes with Abimelech finding Baruch still grieving in the tomb (6:1). The juxtaposition of the stories leads the reader to conclude that while Abimelech was sleeping for sixty-six years, Baruch was learning from the angels. Baruch welcomed his friend and immediately began praying for wisdom regarding what to do next. The answer came mid-prayer, clearly an indication of Baruch's influence with the Almighty (6:11). An angel revealed to Baruch God's plans for the exiles' repatriation to Jerusalem, plans that included the commandment that the exiles abandon their foreign wives. An eagle then miraculously carried a letter detailing these plans to Jeremiah in Babylon. Baruch and Jeremiah put these plans with their religious overtones into action, thus showing how they meticulously obeyed God's commands. The book closes with Baruch and Abimelech burying and memorializing Jeremiah.

The Paraleipomena of Jeremiah follows Hebrew (Masoretic) Jeremiah's portrayal of Baruch as Jeremiah's assistant. It also, however, follows Greek Jeremiah in suggesting that Baruch became Jeremiah's successor. Baruch prayed and wept for Jerusalem and its citizens just as Jeremiah did, and along with Jeremiah he effected the exiles' return. Baruch's prayers were immediately answered, and he received angelic revelations. While the text provides no details of these revelations, the authors have introduced a new element into Baruch's persona—he has become an apocalypticist who receives divine revelations.

The Paraleipomena of Jeremiah is an originally Jewish text that was transmitted in Christian circles and underwent some Christian editorializing; this is especially evident in the Christian components that have been incorporated into chapter 9.[47] Dating this text has proven difficult, a problem faced with most early Jewish and Christian apocrypha and pseudepigrapha. This text refers to the destruction of Jerusalem, but the destruction at the hands of the Babylonians in 586 B.C.E. is used here, as is the custom in many pseudepigraphic texts, as a veiled reference to the destruction of Jerusalem by the Romans in 70 C.E. That this is the case is made certain by the mention of the "field of Agrippa" (3:14), which indicates that this text was composed after the reign of Agrippa I.[48] The reference to the destruction of Jerusalem fits, therefore, with the Roman destruction of Jerusalem. Adding Abimelech's sixty-six-year sleep after "the destruction" to the 70 C.E. date suggests that this text was composed circa 136 C.E. Since, however, the text describes, and bitterly laments, the destruction of the temple and the cessation of the temple cultus, it seems unlikely that it was composed in the wake of the second or Bar Kochba revolt against Rome in 133–135 C.E., because at that time the temple and its cult had ceased to exist for over a generation. Many scholars have also argued that this text postdates *2 Baruch (Syriac Apocalypse)* and is dependent on it.[49] It may be, however, that the material that is common to both the Paraleipomena of Jeremiah and *2 Baruch (Syriac Apocalypse)* is due to their authors' independent use of earlier sources or traditions.[50] It is even possible that the Paraleipomena of Jeremiah antedates both *2 Baruch (Syriac Apocalypse)* and *3 Baruch (Greek Apocalypse)*, or at the very least contains a different tradition about the location where Baruch lamented the destruction of the city and the deportation of Jeremiah and his compatriots. The apocalypses open with Baruch lamenting while sitting amid the ruins of the temple.[51]

Had the Paraleipomena of Jeremiah known this tradition, it would have been unnecessary to introduce the image of Baruch receiving revelations while sitting in a tomb. The Paraleipomena of Jeremiah thus either antedates these two texts or simply depends on a different tradition about the locus of Baruch's laments and revelations.

The Paraleipomena of Jeremiah and *2 Baruch (Syriac Apocalypse)* begin with parallel accounts of the fall of Jerusalem to the Babylonians.[52] These accounts, however, depict the relationship of Jeremiah to Baruch differently. The differences between the depictions in these two books reflect the two different views of Baruch in the two versions of the book of Jeremiah: according to Hebrew (Masoretic) Jeremiah, Baruch was simply Jeremiah's amanuensis, while in Greek (LXX) Jeremiah Baruch was Jeremiah's successor. The passages where these differences appear are Par. Jer. 1:1–2:1 and *2 Bar.* 1:1–2:1. These two texts have the following elements in common: 1) both texts state that God spoke directly to the person (Par. Jer. 1:1 and *2 Bar.* 1:1); 2) both texts state that the sins of the people brought about God's judgment (Par. Jer. 1:1 and *2 Bar.* 1:2–4); and 3) both texts mention the effectiveness of the prayers or works of Jeremiah, Baruch, and their associates (Par. Jer. 1:2 and *2 Bar.* 2:1).[53]

These parallels indicate either that one of these texts depends on the other or, more likely, that both depend on a common source for their introductory narratives.[54] These two texts differ, however, over whether God spoke to Jeremiah and told him to instruct Baruch or whether God spoke to Baruch and told him to instruct Jeremiah. In the Paraleipomena of Jeremiah, whenever Jeremiah is in the picture, he eclipses Baruch. On the other hand, while Jeremiah is in Babylon, Baruch dominates the scene. In the Paraleipomena of Jeremiah God addressed Jeremiah directly ("God spoke to Jeremiah") and instructed him to go and tell Baruch what to do. This follows the pattern in Jeremiah 36:5 where Jeremiah "commanded" Baruch to go to the Temple and read from a scroll that contained warnings to the people. In *2 Bar.*, however, just the opposite happened: God spoke directly to Baruch ("the word of the Lord came to Baruch") and commanded him to go and tell Jeremiah what to do. Moreover, these two accounts differ over how Jeremiah learned that he should accompany the exiles to Babylon. The Paraleipomena of Jeremiah (3:14–16; 4:6–12) says that God himself spoke directly with Jeremiah and instructed him to go to Babylon with the exiles. In *2 Bar.* 10:1–5, however, God spoke directly to Baruch and told him to instruct Jeremiah to accompany the exiles to Babylon.

It is clear that these two texts have different perspectives on the relationship between Jeremiah and Baruch. In the Paraleipomena of Jeremiah, Jeremiah remains the central figure, a role clearly dependent on his biblical background as a great prophetic leader.[55] The account in *2 Baruch (Syriac Apocalypse)* of these events surrounding the fall of Jerusalem identifies Baruch as the leader of the people. In *2 Bar.* 5:5–7 Baruch led several leaders of the city (including Jeremiah) to the Kidron valley in order to tell them what God had revealed to him about the imminent fall of the city. According to *2 Bar.* 6–9, Baruch alone saw angels enter the city, break down the city walls, and hide the sacred vessels, while in Par. Jer. both Baruch and Jeremiah witnessed these events. The account in *2 Baruch (Syriac Apocalypse)* parallels the depiction of Baruch in Greek (LXX) Jeremiah and seeks to emphasize the emergence of Baruch as Jeremiah's successor.

The narratives about the fall of Jerusalem in the Paraleipomena of Jeremiah and in *2 Baruch (Syriac Apocalypse)* have markedly different perspectives on the nature of the relationship between Jeremiah and Baruch. Given the overall prominence of Jeremiah in Jewish and Christian tradition, we may assume that the work that has Baruch appearing equal to or superior to Jeremiah is trying either to promote Baruch over Jeremiah, or, more probably, to show how Baruch suc- ceeded Jeremiah as a leader of the people and a qualified recipient of divine oracles.[56] These texts, therefore, reflect the transition reflected already in Greek Jeremiah—Baruch became Jeremiah's successor; he was the one who would lead the people in Jeremiah's absence.[57] It is also noteworthy that the Paraleipomena of Jeremiah is known by two titles: The Greek manuscripts entitle it "The Paraleipomena of Jere- miah" ("the things omitted from Jeremiah"), while the Ethiopic manuscript entitles it "The Rest of the Words of Baruch." The two titles, therefore, further indicate that there were two opinions on who was the central figure of this text. If Jeremiah eclipses Baruch in a text, then that text is simply following the portrayal of these two characters in the Hebrew Bible; however, whenever Baruch eclipses Jeremiah in a text, then that text is following a clear tendency in Greek Jeremiah to promote Baruch. The two were not really in competition. Nor are the editors who created and passed on these texts intending to suggest that there was a rivalry between the two. Rather there seems to have been a movement that imagined Baruch as Jeremiah's successor. This group therefore portrayed Baruch as a sagacious leader who took up a communal leadership role in Jeremiah's absence or after the great prophet's death.

The sage was an important figure in Second Temple Period Judaism. These people could perform mundane scribal functions as well as the more communally significant roles of professional philosopher, biblical interpreter, and source of wisdom. For early Jewish communities the role of community leader was particularly important to survival. The Jewish sages were esteemed in their communities not simply for the knowledge they acquired, although that was indeed important, but also for their wisdom. This wisdom entailed not just familiarity with ancient lore, but with knowledge of Torah—Jewish law, tradition, and culture. For many Jews of the Second Temple Period, Wisdom is Torah, as Ben Sira put it many times.

> All wisdom is from the Lord,
>> and with him it remains forever (1:1).
> To fear the Lord is the root of wisdom,
>> and her branches are long life (1:20).
> If you desire wisdom, keep the commandments,
>> and the Lord will lavish it upon you (1:26).
> The whole of wisdom is the fear of the Lord,
>> and in all wisdom is the fulfillment of the law (19:20).
> Whoever keeps the law controls his thoughts,
>> and the fulfillment of the fear of the Lord is wisdom (21:11).

Baruch ben Neriah came to be imagined as a great sage. He was a skilled scribe who not only knew his profession and a wealth of ancient lore; he was also popularly imagined as a great man who knew what pleased God and taught his people how to do this. He became, at least in the memory of many people, one of those community leaders who were prophetic-like in their inspired leadership. The people imagined that God spoke to Baruch and that Baruch in turn communicated those revelations to his community. He passed on traditions, beliefs, and practices that came to define the community. Many people appear to have thought of Baruch as Jeremiah's successor. The editors or pseudepigraphers who created new Baruch texts and who ascribed anonymous texts to him fashioned Baruch in their image of the perfect communal leader. The texts discussed in this chapter indicate, therefore, that many people viewed Baruch as a sage. As Jewish communities developed other ideas about what constituted an ideal religious leader, the editors/pseudepigraphers set out to refashion Baruch. As the next chapter will illustrate, Baruch eventually became an apocalypticist who received revelations from God and who traveled through the heavens. Baruch's legacy grew with time, and Ben Sira's words in praise of sages certainly fit Baruch ben Neriah:

> He who is devoted to the study of the Law of the Most High
>> will seek out the wisdom of all the ancients,
>> and be concerned with prophecies.
> He will preserve the sayings of renowned people,
>> and delve into the subtleties of parables.
> He will seek out the secrets of proverbs,
>> and be conversant with the obscurities of parables.
> He will serve among the great,
>> and appear before rulers.
> He will travel in foreign lands,
>> and learn what is good and evil among humanity.
> He will set his heart to rise early to seek the Lord who made him,
>> and will make supplication before the Most High.
> He opens his mouth in prayer,
>> and makes supplication for his sins.
> If the great Lord is willing,
>> he will be filled with the spirit of understanding.
> He will pour forth words of wisdom of his own,
>> and in prayer will give thanks to the Lord.
> He [God] will direct his counsel and knowledge,
>> as he meditates on his [God's] mysteries.
> He will reveal instruction in his teaching,
>> and will glory in the law of the Lord's covenant.

Many will praise his understanding;
>it will never be blotted out.

His memory will not disappear,
>and his name will live through all generations.

Nations will speak of his wisdom,
>and the congregation will proclaim his praise.

If he lives long, he will leave a name greater than a thousand,
>and if he goes to rest, it is enough for him (Ben Sira 39:1–11).

The many texts and traditions that speak of or are attributed to Baruch ben Neriah confirm Ben Sira's insight. Baruch's legacy has reached through the ages; his memory lives on.

Chapter Three

THE APOCALYPTIC SEER

The angel of hosts said to me, "Come and I will reveal to you the mysteries of God"

3 Baruch 1:8

During the Greco-Roman period a new outlook on life emerged in the Mediterranean world—apocalypticism. For Jews, this new way of viewing their world developed as part of the changes wrought by the interaction of ancient Jewish traditions and beliefs with the newer Hellenistic civilizations. Societal changes seemed to be undermining traditional Jewish culture: the old largely Near Eastern ways of life were being supplanted by Hellenistic approaches. For many people this led to an alienation from traditional ways of imagining themselves, their gods, their history, and their image of the cosmos. "Apocalypticism" is a social movement or ideology that unites people who have rejected the standards and ideology of the dominant culture and are attempting to create a radically different worldview or counter-culture.[1] This social movement is characterized by an utter dissatisfaction with the world as it is, a fascination with the cataclysmic intervention of God on their behalf, and a longing to be ushered into a messianic era or into the heavenly realm. The texts discussed in this chapter are part of this ancient apocalyptic world, and the images they create of Baruch are of one who is part of this esoteric culture. These texts, as well as the ideology that undergirds them, create alternative worldviews that attempt to make sense of a changing and, in many ways, inhospitable world. These texts are the products of people who have become disenchanted with the traditional ideologies and approaches to life, feel alienated from the power structures of their society, and have a sense of deprivation, although it is only relative deprivation. No matter what their station in life may be, these people sense that they are somehow deprived or oppressed, and it is this sense of deprivation that convinces them that they are in fact deprived or oppressed. In most cases they are honest people who are just trying to make sense of their world, but in some cases these people are fomenting social unrest and intending to overthrow the powers that be. In general, however, they are on a quest to transcend both the pain of their mundane circumstances and, on a more existential level, their personal mortality.[2] The world they imagine is one where, after they have successfully endured their present sufferings, God eventually intervenes to save them and lead them to a life of peace, harmony, and personal fulfillment—a true utopia. But this is more than just a future expectation for most of these people. They believe that the way they live their individual and group lives here on earth is a reflection of life in heaven.

One can think of any number of modern apocalyptic groups, but probably one of the most famous, or infamous, was the Branch Davidians in Waco, Texas. This group withdrew into its compound to protect itself from the allegedly corrupting influences of society and especially of the federal government. Their "inspired" leader, David Koresh, taught them about their duties in this life and how to prepare for the future. In the end they were at least partially responsible for bringing on their own apocalyptic end. The most familiar apocalyptic group from the ancient world is probably the apocalyptic sectarians of the Dead Sea Scrolls who lived at the site of Qumran on the northwest shores of the Dead Sea. These people imagined themselves as the only true Jews, and they thought that all other Jews were corrupt. They claimed that they withdrew to their desert refuge in protest against the corruption of the priesthood in Jerusalem, but the reason was more likely because their ideology made them barely tolerable outcasts from mainstream society and because they adopted an entirely different calendar, thus putting their holy days on different days then those of the traditional Jewish calendar used in Jerusalem and elsewhere. In their isolation they developed an apocalyptic theology and demanding way of life.[3] These people imagined themselves a community of angels whose rigidly pious life was thought to imitate that of the angels in heaven.[4] They also believed themselves to have access to divine mysteries just like the angels via their group's inspired leaders. Thus they had transcended death and lived the life of the heavenly angels here and now. Their most famous leader, the "Teacher of Righteousness," was, much like David Koresh, a bold and dynamic interpreter of the Bible whose teachings drew people into the group.

Apart from the social aspects of apocalypticism, there are literary texts that are designated "apocalypses." The most well known ancient Jewish and Christian apocalypses are those of Daniel in the Hebrew Bible/Old Testament and of John in the New Testament. It would be a mistake, however, to assume that all apocalypses and all apocalyptic communities were the same. Throughout the course of the modern study of both this literature and this social phenomenon the images created by the biblical books of Daniel and Revelation have remained the primary focus. That is to say, the kind of apocalypse represented in these two biblical texts has been thought to adequately characterize apocalypses and apocalypticism. In fact, there are a variety of apocalypses and apocalyptic movements. The literary form "apocalypse" has been defined as follows:

> Apocalypse is a genre of revelatory literature with a narrative framework, in which a revelation is mediated by an otherworldly being to a human recipient, disclosing a transcendent reality which is both temporal insofar as it envisages eschatological salvation, and spatial insofar as it involves another, supernatural world intended to interpret present, earthly circumstances in light of the supernatural world and of the future, and to influence both the understanding and the behavior of the audience by means of divine authority.[5]

This technical definition of apocalypses requires further explanation. First, an apocalypse is a text wherein "a revelation is mediated by an otherworldly being to a human recipient." That is to say, an apocalypse contains the information revealed by an otherworldly being, typically an angel, to a human being. The angel is thus God's messenger. Second, this revelation discloses "a transcendent reality," or information that could not be known by any ordinary human. Apart from this divinely granted revelation, then, humans could not have known this information, for knowledge of the future, of the secret workings of the cosmos, and of the secrets of the human soul are far beyond human ken. Third, this information "is both temporal insofar as it envisages eschatological salvation, and spatial insofar as it involves another, supernatural world." Furthermore, this revelation of otherwise unknowable secrets is "intended to interpret present, earthly circumstances in light of the supernatural world and of the future." All this means that this revelation has two foci: the future salvation of the righteous and/or the existence and nature of the supernal or infernal worlds—heaven and hell. Because the recipient of this allegedly divine revelation has God-given knowledge about what the future holds and can now confirm the existence of the places for future, post mortem punishment and reward, the reader is well advised to heed the apocalypse's warnings. Fourth, the overall purpose of an apocalypse is "to influence both the understanding and the behavior of the audience." That is to say, this kind of literature intends to persuade people to adopt certain religious beliefs and to follow a prescribed lifestyle in order to warrant divine blessing both now and in the hereafter. The authors of this material did not imagine themselves to be involved in trivial matters: they were dealing with matters of life and death— eternal life and death. Finally, this revelation comes directly from God and therefore has divine authority. One neglects it at one's own peril. The author is not just spouting his or her own novel ideas, but is communicating what God in fact told him or her in a vision or during an ascent into the divine presence.

Thus, apocalypses are not solely interested in personal or corporate eschatology—what an individual's or group's ultimate fate will be— although that is of course a main theme and is the central theme in the biblical apocalypses of Daniel and Revelation. Interestingly, the earliest Jewish apocalypse, the "Astronomical Book of Enoch," focuses on astronomy and the secret workings of the cosmos. Its authors were highly educated people who were fascinated with "scientific" speculation.[6] Thus, although the biblical apocalypses focus exclusively on the temporal axis, on what the future holds, most other early Jewish and Christian apocalypses are not so myopic, and a good many concern themselves with the secrets of the cosmos and of heaven and hell.

Apocalypses have commonly been attributed to socially disenfranchised segments of society whose overall goals were socially subversive. And while the biblical apocalypses of Daniel and Revelation do have this element and were born of the sufferings of people at the hands of foreign domination, this is not the case for every apocalypse. Some are born out of deep emotional crisis (e.g., Fourth Ezra), some are purely scientific (e.g., Astronomical Book of Enoch), and some focus on providing an *ex eventu* prophecy of historical events (e.g., Ascension of Isaiah). If there is any true disenfranchisement, or crisis situation, it is only a perceived one. This is to say, one's individual experience determines what is and is not a crisis. These perceived crises occur for an individual (4 Ezra) or a group (Dead Sea Scrolls, Branch Davidians).

Ancient and modern apocalypticists and apocalyptic groups are very diverse. Those with militant approaches to the governing authorities tend to attract more attention because they force showdowns with the ruling powers. Apocalyptic pacifists, on the other hand, gain little attention because they rarely enter into the spotlight. If they perceive themselves as unsuccessful in transforming society, then they either disband, become aggressive towards outsiders, or take out their frustrations on themselves by committing suicide in the hope of hastening the apocalyptic end and sending themselves to their heavenly reward.

2 Baruch (Syriac Apocalypse)

Baruch, owing perhaps to his image as a man of wisdom, a sage, became a popular figure among early Jewish and Christian apocalypticists, and they attributed several texts to him pseudepigraphically. The term "pseudepigrapha" refers to an amorphous collection of texts bearing the names of biblical figures. These texts, however, were not written by that person whose name they bear, but by someone who lived much later. The term literally means "falsely written," the point being that these books were written by people who falsely attributed their own writings to great figures from the past.[7] Although we may think it odd (if not downright unethical) to attribute a work falsely to another individual, the ancients had no such ethical dilemma. The reasons for attributing these texts to ancient figures were likely quite varied. The authors could have been trying to gain a wider audience for their text by attributing it to notable ancients. They might have been trying to hide behind the veil provided by pseudepigraphy to escape detection for writing things that might have upset their communal or national leaders. They might also have been trying to infiltrate the broader market, which was in those days becoming dominated by "Scripture" and by the rabbinical or ecclesiastical writings. In any case, pseudepigraphy helped these authors gain the attention they sought.

The apocalypticists were attempting in their writings to answer some of the most difficult questions about life. One of these questions centered on a perennial source of human turmoil: the question of theodicy, or "why do the righteous suffer?" Or, to paraphrase from a popular modern book, "why do bad things happen to good people."[8] As remains the case for us today, the book of Job in the Hebrew Bible/Old Testament was the primary source for the apocalypticists on this issue. The protagonist, Job, experienced tremendous personal pain. The tragedies he and his family suffered were seemingly without cause. Throughout the course of the book, both Job and the reader learn that God's ways are inscrutable. As Job himself says: "I came forth from my mother's womb naked, and naked shall I return. Yahweh has given; Yahweh has taken. Blessed be the name of Yahweh" (Job 1:21). *2 Baruch* is thoroughly consumed with the issue of theodicy and resolves it with an apocalyptic answer: although the righteous suffer and the wicked prosper, God is still just and this will be made fully manifest only at the end of history when the wicked will be punished and the righteous rewarded. Baruch learned this not through any earthly wisdom or dialogue with his contemporaries, but through a series of divine revelations.

Although the literary setting of *2 Baruch* is the Babylonian destruction of the Jerusalem temple in 586 B.C.E., the text was likely written sometime after the destruction of the temple in Jerusalem by the Romans in 70 C.E. Like most early Jewish and Christian apocryphal and pseudepigraphic texts, *2 Baruch* has been preserved only in later manuscripts—no originals or very early copies exist. Many Jewish texts that were composed in either Hebrew, Aramaic, or Greek were not preserved in these languages. Fortunately, Christian communities came to value these texts and so translated them into their languages—Greek,

Latin, Syriac, Coptic, Armenian, Slavonic, and others. As a result, to study what was originally a Jewish text scholars of this material must now know the several languages used by the churches that preserved these texts. Thus, to study the principle manuscripts of the text now called *2 Baruch* one must know Syriac, an Aramaic dialect, the language of the Syrian Orthodox Church.

As stated above, *2 Baruch (Syriac Apocalypse)* was written some time after the destruction of Jerusalem in 70 c.e., but exactly when after this date is not certain.[9] On first glance *2 Baruch* appears to be a disjunctive collection of prayers, fasts, dialogues between Baruch and God, apocalyptic visions, and bitter laments. Nonetheless, the greater portion of the book is segmented by a series of fasts followed by dialogues between Baruch and God or his angel. The overall structure of the book has seven movements, or sections: chapters 1–9, 10–20, 21–34, 35–47, 48–52, 53–76, 77–87. Structurally, then, it is similar to 4 Ezra, which has an unmistakable seven-vision structure. The formal similarity between *2 Baruch* and 4 Ezra has naturally led to a debate over whether 4 Ezra is modeled after *2 Baruch,* or vice versa: in other words, which came first, 4 Ezra or *2 Baruch?*[10] *2 Baruch* lacks the passion of 4 Ezra, and the sevenfold structure is less clear-cut than in 4 Ezra. I would agree, therefore, with those who maintain that *2 Baruch* was written after 4 Ezra and in part used 4 Ezra as its model. This would mean that *2 Baruch* was written after 100 c.e., as that appears to be when 4 Ezra was written.

Theodicy in *2 Baruch*

For the author of *2 Baruch,* the suffering that Jews experience at the hands of their conquerors—Babylonians then, Romans now—is only temporary. The embodiment of this suffering occurs in the destruction of the temple in Jerusalem. The question arises of how the Jewish community can survive without the temple? Can it, in fact, survive? The author solves the problem in two ways, by addressing both the place of the temple in post-destruction Judaism and the role of the Torah in this community. As we shall see, the author holds out the hope that the earthly temple will be replaced by a heavenly temple in the eschaton. Moreover, in the meantime Jews must follow the long-cherished and still evolving religious teachings and practices of their community: the prescriptions of the Torah.[11] The proper response to the disasters they face, therefore, is to wait patiently for God's means of resolving this terrible problem and to remain loyal to standard religious beliefs and practices. Such an acceptance of the destruction of the temple and the role of Torah obedience does not occur in 4 Ezra. There, God is taken to task for the sufferings of the people, and the author unhesitatingly questions God's justice. Ezra's questioning of God in 4 Ezra remains unrelenting until Ezra undergoes a conversion of sorts and thereafter drops his objections and adopts God's viewpoint.[12] Each of the dialogues between Baruch and God in *2 Baruch,* however, ends with Baruch acquiescing and accepting God's explanations. These dialogues between Baruch and God lack, therefore, the sustained tension found in the dialogues between Ezra and God.

2 Baruch begins with vocabulary that harkens back to the book of Jeremiah. In the first chapter God asks Baruch, "have you seen all the things that this nation has done to me? The *evils* that the two tribes that remain have done" (1:2)?[13] God then informs Baruch of how he intends to deal with the evil perpetrated by the people: "Therefore, behold, I will bring *evil* on this city and its citizens" (1:4). The idea of God "bringing evil" upon an individual or a city has deep roots in biblical tradition. This very phrase, in fact, is used for what God does to wicked kings like Jereboam I (1 Kgs 14:10), Ahab (1 Kgs 21:21), or Manasseh (2 Kgs 21:12). In exchange for all the *evil* they did, God brought upon them another *evil:* a disastrous end.[14] As we see, these passages all appear in the books of Kings. These books were composed by editors commonly called "Deuteronomists." These people were the leaders of the strict "Yahweh-alone" component of the Israelite and Judaean religious milieu: they believed that "Yahweh alone" was the true God and that the only place where he was properly worshiped was the Yahweh temple in Jerusalem.[15] The leaders among this religious movement were responsible for composing, editing and promulgating the books from Deuteronomy through 2 Kings—the "Deuteronomistic History." One of the leading figures of this group was the prophet Jeremiah, and in Jeremiah's book we learn that because of all the *evil* that the people were doing, God repaid them with another kind of *evil*, destruction at the hand of a foreign power.[16]

Jeremiah, as would his deuteronomistic compatriots, defined this *evil* as refusal to obey the dictates of strict deuteronomistic Yahwism, especially as it relates to the ban on worshipping other gods.[17] Moreover, these deuteronomistic historians created a book recounting the history of the pre-state period: the book of Judges. In that book they show that by "doing evil" the Israelites set in motion a cycle that led to divine punishment (e.g., Judges 2:11–14, 3:7–15).[18] In a similar manner, although God had sent prophets to warn Israel, they did not listen and continued to sin, and this led to God sending *evil* their way (Jer 35:13–17). In *2 Baruch* the principle of God repaying *evil* in kind is applied again to Jerusalem and the rest of the nation, just as it was in Jeremiah. *2 Baruch* opens, then, with the idea initiated in the Deuteronomistic History and the book of Jeremiah that God is just in bringing calamity upon Jerusalem and its environs because of the people's sin.

Immediately following the introduction Baruch's lament and dispute with God begins. Here Baruch is attempting to reconcile God's justice with human suffering—specifically asking how God can use nations that are, at least in Baruch's mind, much more depraved to punish Israel? This, too, was the concern of the prophet Habakkuk (Hab 1). How can God allow his temple and city, the temple and city that bear his name, to be destroyed by people who revile his people and who do not follow him anyway? If Jerusalem, its environs, and its people are destroyed, who will ever hear of Yahweh's great deeds or listen to the interpretations of his Torah? In fact, without Yahweh's city, temple, and people, the world might even revert to primordial chaos (*2 Bar.* 3:4–9).[19] God told Baruch that what matters are not the earthly institutions, but the heavenly ones, the ones that have existed since, and even before, creation. Earthly institutions will come and go. The eternal city and temple remain secure in heaven with God (*2 Bar.* 4:1–5:4). Thus, God's initial answer to Baruch, that his focus should not be on the earthly institutions but on the heavenly realities, solves the problem of why God's people suffer at the hands of those more wicked than they. Baruch, however, was not convinced.[20]

Before God allowed the invaders to destroy Jerusalem, angels came and removed the sacred vessels from the Holy of Holies and deposited them in an opening in the earth (*2 Bar.* 6). After the angels had torn down the walls of the holy city, the Babylonians entered and plundered the place (*2 Bar.* 8). Baruch witnessed these events and later wept over the destruction of the city (*2 Bar.* 9). Although the book of Jeremiah does not indicate where Baruch or Jeremiah were when the city actually fell, an account almost identical to this one in *2 Baruch* appears in the Paraleipomena of Jeremiah (Par. Jer. 1–4). Jeremiah 39 and 52 and 2 Kgs 24–25 contain narratives that recount the fall of the city to Nebuchadnezzar and his commander Nebuzaradan. None of these texts mentions, naturally, the involvement of angels. In fact, all of the destruction is wrought by the Babylonians themselves. Although he was writing about the destruction of the city and temple by the Romans, Josephus, the first century Jewish historian, curiously mentions several ominous events that attended the fall of the city in 70 c.e. (*War* 6.288–300). Perhaps the narratives in the Paraleipomena of Jeremiah and *2 Baruch* were drawing in part on traditions concerning the miraculous events surrounding the fall of Jerusalem in 70 c.e. known also to Josephus. In fact, one passage leaves open the question of how the city walls were initially breached: 2 Kgs 25:4 states simply, "the city was breached." The city had been besieged by the Babylonians and then suddenly "the city was breached." This passage says nothing about who breached the walls or how.[21] Later the Babylonians "demolished the walls of Jerusalem on every side" (2 Kgs 25:10). Still, the question remains, who breached the walls initially? This text does not in any way intimate that angels were involved. Nonetheless, it appears that the tradition concerning angelic involvement attested in *2 Baruch* 6–8 may stem from a creative interpretation of the ambiguous statement in 2 Kgs 25:10. Later authors simply read the angels into this story since that was how these people imagined that God accomplished his will on earth.

Baruch's protracted debate with God begins in earnest in chapter 10, and after this debate (*2 Bar.* 10–77) Baruch writes a letter to the exiled Jews (78–87). Baruch's lament focuses on the issue of theodicy:

> Now I, Baruch, say this against you, O Babylon:
> Had you been prosperous and Zion remained in its glory,
>> our pain would have been great that you were equal to Zion.
> But now, behold, the pain is limitless,

> and the lamentation is measureless.
> But you, behold, you are prosperous,
> and Zion is destroyed (*2 Bar.* 11:1–2).

Baruch ended his first complaint with a seven-day fast after which he heard a voice. This voice was God answering Baruch's complaint (*2 Bar.* 13:1–12). God sought to console Baruch by informing him that he would indeed survive this tragedy and would therefore be present to tell the people that although God had chastised his people, he would eventually restore them. Moreover, Baruch should tell the people that God will also hold all other nations accountable as well. This seems to play off of the enigmatic words of Jeremiah 45:2–5:

> Thus says Yahweh the God of Israel to you Baruch: You said, "Woe is me because Yahweh has added grief to my pain. I am weary with my groaning, and I can find no rest." Thus you shall say to him, "thus says Yahweh: Behold, I am going to tear down what I have built, and uproot what I have planted—even the whole land. And you, do you seek great things for yourself? Do not seek them, for I am going to bring evil upon all flesh, says Yahweh. But I will give you your life as a prize of war in every place wherever you may go."

2 Baruch 13:1–3 interprets this to mean that Baruch will survive the calamity to tell others about the events and their historical and theological significance. Moreover, these words now relate to the apocalypse that bears Baruch's name. That is to say, Baruch's testimony to the events and causes of Jerusalem's fall—both to the Babylonians and now to the Romans—is contained in this apocalypse. God's promise to Baruch in Jeremiah 45, therefore, is being kept.

The prelude to the contentious debates between Baruch and God is a lament by Baruch over the terrible fate of his people at the hands of the Babylonians (10–12). God had told Baruch to remain in the ruins of Zion for a vision of "the end of days" (10:3). Baruch responded to this promise with a lament and a seven-day fast. The first round of the debate (chapters 13–20) is circular: Baruch claims that God is unjust in punishing the righteous Zion by means of the wicked Babylonians. Moreover—and this is really the heart of Baruch's complaint—God is unjust in holding humans eternally accountable for the sins they commit during their brief and painful lives. God defends himself by saying that he gave them a guide, the Torah, and had they obeyed it, they would have been rewarded and not punished. There is no climax or resolution to the debate. Both sides remain resolute in their positions. God had promised Baruch that he would reveal what would happen at "the end of days," but this comes at the end of the debate and only vaguely indicates that the times are progressing quickly to the end (20:1–2). God finally tells Baruch to go and fast seven more days—he had already fasted fifteen days (5:7; 9:2; 12:5)—and afterward he would receive further true revelations about the course of history.

These fasts are not only important structural devices, they also hint at actual visionary practices. Fasts can serve as part of an induction technique or ritual intended to promote the visionary/dream experience. This same structural and psychological feature appears also in 4 Ezra.[22] The ancient visionaries ruminated over their personal and theological turmoil incessantly, and eventually their theological beliefs influenced how they resolved their deep personal and national struggles. In other words, these people saw in their dreams and visions exactly what they had trained themselves to see. In Baruch's case he fasted for a day before the Babylonians destroyed the city (5:7) and for seven days after that cataclysmic event (9:2). Immediately following the seven-day fast in *2 Baruch* 9:2, Baruch reports that "the word of God came to me" (10:1). Then after concluding his lament over the disaster that befell Zion and another seven-day fast (12:5), Baruch was again standing on Mt. Zion when "a voice came to me from on high" (13:1), initiating the first round in Baruch's contentious debate with God (13–20). Again, a seven-day fast produced a visionary, or in this case auditory, experience. Baruch and God contest point and counterpoint, making little progress in convincing one another of either the justice (God's position) or the injustice (Baruch's position) of God's destroying Jerusalem and exiling the people.

The second round of the debates (21–34) also follows a fast, but this time the result is that Baruch's soul was flush with "many thoughts" and he "began to speak before the Mighty One" (21:3). This time the seven-day fast induced a state wherein Baruch imagined himself standing in God's presence and addressing the Almighty. During this dialogue with God, Baruch learns about the future in more detail. Though not a day-by-day chronicle of the eschaton, this information does indicate what the future holds: terrible times will precede the end and this will affect all living things. In the end, however, the righteous will be rewarded while the wicked endure the torment and punishment they deserve. Armed with this information, Baruch turns to his people to encourage them amidst their sufferings (chapters 31–34). Baruch's encouragement follows the tone of God's words to him: the current disaster is terrible, but there will be even greater disaster in the future. The only way to survive all these turmoils is to obey the precepts of the Torah. Baruch thus becomes the mouthpiece for traditional answers to the issue of the suffering of the righteous. He does not receive revelations from God that contain information with simply a personal eschatological focus; his revelations concern the entire nation. When he turns to leave the people to prepare to receive further revelations, the people he was addressing implore him not to leave. He responds by saying that he was not abandoning them permanently or even for an extended time. Rather, he was going to return to the ruins of the temple so he could receive further information from God.

> God forbid that I should forsake you or leave you. I am going alone to the Holy of Holies so that I may ask from the Mighty One on your and Zion's behalf if I may be enlightened some more, and afterward I will return to you (*2 Bar.* 34).

Baruch is showing himself, or better the editor/author of *2 Baruch* is showing Baruch as a person committed to the well-being of the community. He teaches them that the way to survive is by following the Torah, the divinely-instituted, community defining and sustaining religious, moral, and social precepts. Baruch also understands his continuing responsibility to seek more light from God for the people. He would never abandon them, no matter how terribly he might despair about the current situation. Baruch appears as a model leader. The second debate between Baruch and God does not end with a seven-day fast. Instead, Baruch goes to the temple ruins, sits down, and weeps.

The third dialogue between Baruch and God, chapters 35–47, begins with Baruch weeping, quite literally, over the ruin of the temple. He weeps to the point of exhaustion and then has a night vision, or dream (36:1). In this instance a kind of ritual weeping, and not a fast, induces Baruch's encounter with God. Baruch has a symbolic vision in which a forest is washed away by water. God interprets this dream for Baruch and tells him that the forest represents the wicked kingdoms of the earth and that the waters represent the Anointed One who will come to assert God's authority and to rule the entire earth in the eschaton (*2 Bar.* 36–40). Although this is an important sketch of the future, it is not enough for Baruch. He responds to God's interpretation of the vision with even more questions about how to determine exactly who the righteous and the wicked are (41–43). Again, Baruch concerns himself with the people and not with his own personal fate. He learns, not surprisingly, that the righteous are those who believe and obey God's commandments and the wicked are those who do not believe and obey (42:2). Baruch is himself an example of a righteous person and his confession of this indicates how one ought to believe and observe the commandments to warrant divine reward.

> O Lord, my Lord, you always enlighten those who conduct themselves with understanding. Your Torah is life and your wisdom is righteousness. Make known to me, therefore, the meaning of this vision. For you yourself know that my soul has always been concerned with your Torah, and [all] my days I have not departed from your wisdom (*2 Bar.* 38:2–4).

Baruch's petition indicates that he models the kind of piety that God expects of his people. It is this lifelong commitment to following God's commandments that gives God confidence in assuring Baruch throughout the book that he will receive divine blessing. This second in the series of dialogues with God ends with Baruch addressing a few of the other leaders of the community. Here, as will be discussed in more detail below, Baruch appears as one who is training his successors. He told them that he was eventually going to "go the way of the whole earth" (i.e., that he was going to die). In the meantime conditions would worsen and their task was to keep Baruch's work on behalf of the people going:

> Behold, I am going to my ancestors, according to the way of all the earth. You, however, must not depart from the way of the Torah but must protect and illumine the people who remain so that they do not depart the commandments of the Mighty One. . . . For if you continue and persevere

in fearing him and do not forget his Torah, the times will change for the better for you and you will see the consolation of Zion. . . . For those are the future ones who will inherit this time that was spoken about, and to them belongs the inheritance of the promised time. They are the ones that prepared for themselves treasuries of wisdom, and treasures of insight are found in them. From mercy they have not departed, and the truth of the Torah they have guarded. So, to such as these will be given the world-to-come, but the dwelling place of many others is in the fire. Thus you, as much as you are able, must admonish the people because this is our duty. For when you teach them you make them live (*2 Bar.* 44:2–3, 7, 13–45:1–2).

By adjuring them to do these things, Baruch ensures that his personal mission will be carried on after his death. Understandably, the leaders were dismayed at the prospect of losing Baruch, the one who brought God's messages to them and thereby served as the mediator between the community and the Divine. Baruch assured them, as we be discussed below, that God would continue to provide inspired leaders to guide them (*2 Bar.* 46:3–6).

Baruch fasted another seven days, prayed, grew weak, and then received another revelation, beginning the fourth round in his series of debates with God (*2 Bar.* 48–52). This time, however, the debate is more of a lecture by the Almighty on what will happen to the final generation. The biting tenor of the disputes between Baruch and God has become muted. Still, God insists on his right to condemn the wicked and reward the righteous, while at the same time Baruch concerns himself more with the fate of the wicked, especially since God knew beforehand that there would be many more sinners than saints. This phase of the book ends with Baruch falling asleep.

The next section in *2 Baruch* is the so-called "apocalypse of the clouds" (*2 Bar.* 53–76), a symbolic vision. This vision is actually a historical apocalypse that reveals—or more correctly, reviews—history from the creation of the world until the eschaton when the Messiah will rule over the world in righteousness, abundance, and peace. Baruch did not understand his vision initially, and an interpreting angel, Ramael, came and interpreted the symbols and their meanings for him. That God should send an angel to help Baruch is another indication of his favor with the Almighty. Baruch is worthy enough both to have God reveal the future to him and to have an angel come to make sure he has the meaning right. This is important because Baruch is learning things that are otherwise unknowable and because he is communicating them for the edification of his people. The angel came in response to Baruch's prayer, clearly indicating that Baruch has God's ear, as the angel indicated: "This is the vision that you have seen, and this is its interpretation. For I have come to say these things to you for your prayer has been heard by the Most High" (*2 Bar.* 71:2). We thus learn again that Baruch, as his name suggests, is "blessed." In Baruch's vision the movements of history are depicted in the form of alternating black and white clouds. The black clouds represent, naturally, the dark days in Israelite and Jewish history when the people sinned against God, were led by wicked rulers, or were oppressed by foreign powers. The white clouds, by contrast, represent those bright days when the people obeyed God or were led by righteous leaders.

2 Baruch ends with two letters that Baruch wrote to the Jewish exiles (chapters 78–87). He wrote these letters in response to a request by the people in Jerusalem that he send "a letter of instruction and a roll of hope so that you might strengthen them" (*2 Bar.* 77:12). Baruch told them that he was not the only source of light remaining in the world. Moreover, the important thing is to know and to observe the instructions in the Torah (77:15–16). Like the letter mentioned in the Paraleipomena of Jeremiah (Par. Jer. 7:1–12), Baruch sent one of his letters via an eagle to the nine and a half tribes in the diaspora (*2 Bar.* 77:17, 19–26; 87:1).[23] Clearly these two texts are drawing on the same tradition of Baruch sending a communiqué to the exiles via a carrier-bird. This, too, points to Baruch's favored status—even the birds willingly work on his behalf. He also sent a letter in the hands of three men to the exiles in Babylon. Again, this shows Baruch's concern for his people, wherever they may be, to remain faithful to Torah, for this is the only way the Jewish community can survive, as history and God's explicit words in both the Bible and this apocalypse unambiguously indicate. These communiqués indicate a belief that Baruch had an impact even among the exiles in Babylon. As will be discussed in chapter four, several later traditions locate Baruch in Babylon.

The letters that conclude *2 Baruch* emphasize three important issues. First, the righteous will one day see God's punishment meted out on those who oppress God's people or who despise the Almighty and his commandments (82–83). This thought, as selfish as it may be, is an example of the sinister thoughts that people harbor toward their enemies and certainly toward their oppressors. The psychological reason why many of the early Jewish and Christian apocalyptic visionaries see their enemies being punished in the afterlife is to assuage their real anger at their current sufferings. Seeing their oppressors suffering indescribable torment at God's hands, as uncomfortable as this theme may be for modern readers, gives them some comfort and is also an expression of their confidence in divine justice. This further empowers Baruch's audience to remain steadfast in their religious beliefs and practices. In fact, what these authors are doing by describing in graphic detail the pleasures that await the righteous and the torments that await the wicked is simply to promote certain kinds of religious belief or praxis.[24] Second, the theological tenant that troubled Baruch so much in the beginning sections of this book has become the foundation of his exhortation: those who obey God will be rewarded and those who do not will be accordingly punished (84:1–2, 6–9; 85:3–4). This belief is one of the hallmarks of the Deuteronomistic History, the books from Deuteronomy through 2 Kgs in the Hebrew Bible. Thus, even though he can engage God in critical debate over the issue of his, the Almighty's, justice, in the end Baruch heartily endorses the long-standing, community-defining belief in God's justice and in Israel's responsibility to obey the Torah. The need for God's people to be righteous is pressing because the end is near:

> The youth of this world is past, the power of creation is already exhausted, and the coming of the times is short and even has passed. The pitcher is near the well, the ship to the harbor, the journey to the city, and life to the end. Therefore, prepare your souls so that when you sail and ascend from the ship, you will have rest and not be condemned when you have departed (*2 Bar.* 85:10–11).[25]

Baruch's revelations are, therefore, both timely and absolutely essential. Now is the time to act in order to warrant divine blessing in the afterlife. Baruch appears as one of the last prophets. He receives revelations from God, but not in the same manner as his biblical prototypes.

His debates with God are much like Job's, and his visions, like Daniel's, are apocalyptic visions of the future and of the world-to-come that are made intelligible by an interpreting angel.

2 Baruch and Inspired Revelation

2 Baruch also provides evidence of an important shift that was taking place in Judaism: the shift from scribes writing down divine revelations, as Baruch did for Jeremiah, to interpreters providing inspired interpretations of previously revealed material. This shift and how it appears in *2 Baruch* marks an important chapter in the history of Judaism, for it was part of the complex processes that led to the emergence of both Jewish sectarianism and the rabbis' ability to shape Jewish belief and practice.

The author of *2 Baruch* clearly portrays Baruch as the prophetic successor to Jeremiah. To connect Baruch explicitly with the biblical prophets, the author uses the standard biblical formula to introduce the divine speeches addressed to Baruch: "the word of the Lord came to Baruch ben Neriah" (hw' ptgmh dmry' 'l brwk bn nry', cf. *2 Bar.* 1:1, 10:1, etc.).[26] Just as the divine word "came to Jeremiah" (היה דבר יהוה אל ירמיהו, cf. Jer. 1:2, 4, 11, 13; 2:1, etc.) or other prophets in ancient Israel, so did Baruch receive "the word of the Lord." The author's use of this stereotypical formula is part of a typological technique to link Baruch to the line of the classical prophets.[27] By associating this ancient biblical formula with Baruch, the author intends to show that Baruch is a legitimate successor to the prophets of the Bible—he received divine messages just as they did. In the author's view Baruch was Jeremiah's successor, a prophet who functioned as the intermediary between God and his people.

The author of *2 Baruch* attempts to further legitimate Baruch as a prophetic successor by linking him with the greatest prophet, Moses.[28] Baruch's fidelity to the Torah is irreproachable (38:2–4), and God revealed secrets about the end of time and the measurements of the future temple to him just as He did to Moses (59:4).[29] Just as Moses ascended Mt. Nebo before his death and there learned divine mysteries (Deut. 32:48–52; 34:1–8), so Baruch ascended a mountain to learn divine mysteries before he departed from the earth (76).[30] God also told Baruch that although he would depart this world, he would not die (76:2). This theme directly parallels a tradition that Moses did not die but ascended into heaven.[31]

Baruch also reconfirmed the Mosaic Covenant. Whatever commandments Moses gave to the people, Baruch reiterated (84).[32] Moreover, he reiterates the promise that if the people diligently obey the Torah, God will bless them (84:6–8). Baruch instructs them in how to live in order to merit divine favor just as Moses had done (cf. Deut 30).[33] Baruch resembles a tradent of what had become cherished or community-defining traditions. Baruch's visions and revelations reconfirm and are based on ancient traditions. By linking the ideas in *2 Baruch* with long-standing traditions, the author hopes to make this new text part of a continuing tradition of Jewish thought; what is new in this text is not revolutionary. What Baruch is declaring to the people is both old and new. The new is legitimated by its continuity with the old. Baruch is the prophetic successor to Jeremiah, but he is also a prophet like the greatest of all prophets after whom all other legitimate prophets are patterned: Moses (Deut 18:15–22).

As mentioned earlier in this chapter, the author of *2 Baruch* puts speeches into the mouths of Baruch's followers that indicate how those people esteemed Baruch. These speeches come in response to Baruch's addresses. In these addresses Baruch related or interpreted for the people what God has taught him or showed him about their present conditions or about the future. The people's responses indicate that they consider Baruch their divinely sent and inspired leader. After one address Baruch turned to leave when the people begin lamenting that he is leaving them as a "father who leaves his children as orphans and goes away from them" (32:9). They believed that they would be better off dead than for him to leave them (33:3). Baruch calmed the people's fear by telling them that he would be away only temporarily in order to go to the Holy of Holies to receive further communications from God (34:1). The community's expressed need for Baruch's immediate presence indicates that they regarded him as their source of life and their connection to God. Behind the pseudepigraphic veil of this text, however, it seems that this account reflects the attitudes of a community toward their leaders. Their leaders are those people without whose immediate presence the community senses that its existence and its view of reality is at risk. In this way the text reinforces the authority of the author of this text who, I suspect, wants to present himself as the tradent of Baruch's teachings. The author intended that the readers put themselves in the position of the people addressed by Baruch and that they view him, the author of *2 Baruch*, as a divinely inspired seer and this text as the product of divine revelation.

When Baruch told the people that he was about to leave them once again (44–45), their response clearly indicates that they regarded him as their inspired interpreter of the Torah. Baruch is depicted here as the heart of the community, and without him their existence is threatened.

> And my son and the elders of the people said to me: "Would the Mighty One humiliate us to such an extent that he would take you away from us quickly? Then we shall truly be in darkness! There will be no light for the people who remain! Where shall we again investigate the Torah, or who will distinguish between death and life for us?" So I said to them, "I cannot resist the throne of the Mighty One. Nonetheless, Israel shall not lack a wise man, nor the tribe of Jacob lack a son of the Torah. But prepare your hearts so that you heed the Torah, and submit yourselves in fear to those who are wise and understanding. Prepare your souls so that you do not depart from them. If, therefore, you do this, those good tidings about which I spoke to you earlier will come to you, and you will not fall into the torment of which I spoke to you earlier" (*2 Bar.* 46:1–6).

This passage depicts Baruch as the inspired or the divinely authorized interpreter of Torah. Without him the people are lost, for he alone has the ability to "distinguish between life and death," that is to say, between the things that please God and bring his blessing and the things that displease God and bring his curse.[34] Baruch is the inspired interpreter to whom people turn for correct instruction in Torah. Baruch further declares that God will provide inspired interpreters for each generation: "Israel shall not lack a wise man, nor the tribe of Jacob lack a son of the Torah. But prepare your hearts so that you heed the Torah, and submit yourselves in fear to those who are wise and understanding" (46:4–5). As Baruch followed Moses and others, so there would always be someone to follow Baruch as the inspired interpreter whose teachings would preserve the life of the community. This recalls the promise in Deut 18:15–22 that Israel would always have a prophetic presence like Moses. Thus, the biblical promises are still being fulfilled in the community. Moreover, this claim demonstrates the author's interest in showing the continuity between Baruch's teachings and the community's long-standing traditions. In fact, the actual author of this text would have the readers regard him, the author of *2 Baruch*, as a legitimate successor to Baruch. He continues Baruch's work of instructing the community in the correct interpretations of Torah, a tradition of inspired instruction with links all the way back to Moses himself.

This theme indicates a different concept of ideal leadership. The charisma of the biblical prophet who recorded divine revelations is supplanted by the charisma of the divinely inspired interpreter who could find meanings long hidden in the ancient, authoritative texts.[35] These new, inspired interpretations make the dated words of the Hebrew Bible/Old Testament pertinent and applicable to a new generation living in a new world; the words, commandments and prophecies thus live again. In essence, prophecy—or perhaps better, intermediation—did not cease, but took on different expressions, and one of these was the inspired interpretation of authoritative texts.[36] The ancient prophetic texts achieved religiously authoritative status, and consequently devout people needed to know what these texts meant and how they were to be actualized in their day. The inspired interpreter thus continued the mission of communicating God's word to the community. However, the Word of God now consisted not so much of immediate revelations, though that certainly took place in some groups (i.e., the apocalypticists and their followers), but of the meticulous interpretation of religiously authoritative texts that the community believed had been divinely revealed to previous generations. These interpretations are in no sense secondary or compromised forms of revelation, for the revelatory nature of the interpretations stems from the interpreter's divine inspiration. God is still ultimately in control of the results so that later generations could be confident about God's will and their responsibilities. This is actually an ingenious way to ensure that what had become community-defining traditions and beliefs continued to guide the community. Although inspired interpretation largely supplanted immediate revelation, the tradition did not ossify because the interpretative process was able to accommodate change. Whatever was new in the interpretations of ancient documents was not entirely new since it was based on the inspired interpretation of texts that had been long cherished by the community. The inspired interpreter was thus the crucial element in keeping the community-defining texts and traditions alive and relevant. According to Nahum Sarna, the ongoing interpretation of authoritative documents, including the interpretation of the Hebrew Bible "was informed by the ever-abiding consciousness that it was the major source for the national language, the well-spring of the peculiar life-style of the Jew, the font of Jewish values, ideals, and hopes. These were matters of transcendent seriousness that demanded not surface reading but deep study and interpretation, and interpretation itself became a propaedeutic discipline indispensable to the training of the cultivated Jew."[37]

Baruch not only taught his generation as their inspired interpreter, but he also appointed others to pass his teachings accurately to succeeding generations.

> I, Baruch, went from there and came to my people. I called my firstborn son and the Gedaliahs, my friends, and seven of the elders of the people, and I said to them, "Behold, I am going to my ancestors according to the way of all the earth. You, however, must not depart from the way of the Torah but must protect and illumine the people who remain so that they do not depart the commandments of the Mighty One" (*2 Bar.* 44:1–3; cf. 84:9).

Here, like Moses (Deut 27–33) and Joshua (Josh 23–24) before they "departed," Baruch is giving a farewell address in which he urges the people to remain faithful to the divine commandments. This passage more importantly draws clearly on the biblical tradition in Numbers 11:16–17, according to which God distributed some of the divine power given to Moses to seventy elders of Israel so that they might assist him in leading Israel.

> Yahweh said to Moses, "Assemble for me seventy men from the elders of Israel whom you know to be elders and officers of the people. Take them to the Tent of Meeting, and they shall take their place there with you. Then I will come down and speak with you there. I will remove some of the spirit that is on you and put it on them. They will carry with you the burden of the people, and you will not have to carry it alone."

Thus Baruch is again portrayed like Moses in that he had seven (an obvious multiple of Moses' seventy) elders of Israel to help him carry out the divine mission. This passage provides public certification of those who would claim to be latter-day tradents of Baruch's revelations, be they traditions with longstanding associations with Baruch or ones more recently "discovered," or more accurately, invented. This is how the author of *2 Baruch* created a fiction regarding the fidelity with which Baruch's teachings were transmitted through the generations. Mishnah Avot 1:1 recounts how Moses' teachings were passed on through the generations to the rabbis: "Moses received the Torah from Sinai and passed it on to Joshua, and Joshua to the elders, the elders to the prophets, and the prophets to the men of the Great Synagogue." In similar fashion, Ben Sira 8:8–9 instructs the young on how to benefit from their predecessors:

> Do not ignore the discussion of the sages, but engage yourself with their proverbs because from them you will learn instruction and how to serve great people. Do not miss the discussion of the elders, for they learned also from their ancestors. From them you will learn understanding and how to give a timely answer.

This is part of the education process and relates to how community values in ancient Israel were transmitted from one generation to the next.[38] The author of *2 Baruch* understands the need for passing on teachings and he creates this fiction both to justify what he is doing and to persuade others to pass on the traditions he has included in this new Baruch book. Moreover, this author included another means whereby Baruch tried to assure the continuance of his mission: he wrote letters to the Judaeans living in exile instructing them to pass on the teachings he gave to them.

> Behold, I have given you knowledge while I am alive. I said that above all you should learn the commandments of the Mighty One which I instructed you. I shall set before you some of the commandments of his judgment before I die. . . . Therefore, let this letter be a witness between me and you so that you will remember the commandments of the Mighty One. . . . Now transmit this letter and the traditions of the Torah to your children after you just as your ancestors transmitted [them] to you (*2 Bar.* 84:1, 7, 9).

In these passages the author creates two stories to show how Baruch attempted to pass on his teachings. In the first passage, Baruch selected certain individuals to become his successors, continuing his work of teaching the people the correct interpretations of Torah. Their teaching of the Torah is the source of life for their followers: "Thus you, as much as you are able, must admonish the people because this is our duty. For when you teach them you make them live." (*2 Bar.* 45:1–2).[39] In the second passage (*2 Bar.* 84:1, 7, 9), Baruch instructed the older generation to pass on his teachings to the younger generation just as they had the teachings of the Torah and the biblical prophets (cf. Deut 6:4–9). The author is attempting to make Baruch's interpretations of the Torah as important as the words of the Torah and the biblical prophets. They are words that guide people in the right way to live. The people's fear at being left without an inspired interpreter stems from their belief that the ancient prophets are no longer among them. What they expect is not immediate, prophetic revelations, but inspired interpretation of existing authoritative documents and traditions.

> "Do this for us your people. Write also to our people in Babylon a letter of doctrine and a scroll of hope so that you might strengthen also them before you depart from us. For the shepherds of Israel have perished, the lamps that gave light are extinguished, and the fountains from which we used to drink have withheld their streams.[40] Thus we have been left in the darkness, in the thick forest, and in the thirst of the desert." I answered and said to them, "shepherds and lamps and fountains came from the Torah. Still, when we go away, the Torah will remain. So if you look earnestly into the Torah and are intent upon wisdom, then the lamp will not be wanting, the shepherd will not fail, and the fountain will not dry up" (*2 Bar.* 77:12–16).

What the people seek is not new prophetic messages, but inspired interpretation based on the Torah. This view represents a shift from direct revelation to inspired exegesis of revealed texts and traditions. The author's community now values a different kind of leadership (cf. *2 Bar* 85:1–4).[41] Baruch is presented in *2 Baruch* as this type of divinely inspired interpreter of Torah.[42] His position of authority in the community is based, as was the case for the Teacher of Righteousness, Jesus, and Paul, on his inspired interpretations. The people who follow the interpretations and other teachings pseudepigraphically attributed to Baruch do so because they believe these are the only teachings which correctly interpret the Torah and which alone lead to salvation.[43] The author of *2 Baruch* desires that his audience regard this apocalypse as part of a collection of inspired Baruch documents; the teachings the author provides here are inspired because God gave them to Baruch, an inspired authority, and Baruch passed them on to people like the author.[44]

The emergence of the role of the inspired interpreter is part of a larger cultural transformation that was taking place in Judaism at this time. This transition "involves making the movement from a culture based on direct divine revelations to one based on their study and reinterpretation."[45] We can observe this transformation in later prophets, like Joel, who became interpreters of tradition rather than recipients of immediate revelation.[46] Evidence of this transition can be found also at Qumran. The "Teacher of Righteousness" was the sect's inspired interpreter of Torah whose interpretations of Scripture the people of Qumran accepted as the only true interpretations by which they ordered their lives (1QpHab. 2:1–10; 7:3–5, 17–8:3).[47] He held, therefore, a position of supreme authority in the community. After his death they awaited another inspired teacher (CD 19:35–20:1, 14). It is possible that the Teacher wrote at least some of the Pesharim (biblical commentaries) from Qumran.[48] The Teacher believed that he was inspired by God both to interpret the Torah and to reveal only to his followers the mysteries God had revealed to him:

> But God considered their deeds for they sought him wholeheartedly. He raised up for them a Teacher of Righteousness to guide them in the way of his heart. He made known to the last generations what God did to the last generation, a congregation of traitors (Damascus Document 1.10–12).[49]

> You have set me as a banner to the Elect of Righteousness,
> a discerning interpreter of wonderful mysteries, . . .
> To try [the people of the] truth,
> and to test those who love learning.
> I am a man of contention to the interpreters of error,
> [but a man of pea]ce to all those who see truth (Hodayot 10.13–15).[50]

These are the regulations for the Teacher by which he is to conduct himself with all the living according to the precept for each era and the value of each and every person. He is to do the will of God according to all that has been revealed for each period and is to study all the learning discovered in earlier times, as well as the regulation of the era. He is to separate out and weigh the Children of Zadok [Righteousness] . . . according to their spirituality. He is to preserve the Chosen Ones of the era according to his [God's] will which he commanded. He is to judge a person according to his spirituality. He is to include a person according to the purity of his hands and let him advance according to his understanding. So shall be his love and his hate. . . . He shall not reprove or dispute with the men of the Pit, but should conceal the counsel of the Torah from perverse people. He is to reprove by true knowledge and righteous judgment those who have chosen the Way, each according to his spirituality, according to the regulation of the time. He is to guide them in knowledge, and thus instruct them in marvelous mysteries and truth. Everyone among the people of the Yahad is to walk blamelessly with one another by all that has been revealed to them.[51] This is the time for "preparing the way in the desert."[52] He is to instruct them to do everything that is expected in that time and to separate from everyone who has not turned away from all perversity. . . .

These are the precepts of the Way for the Teacher in these times regarding his loving and hating—eternal hatred for the People of the Pit in a spirit of secrecy! He is to leave them wealth and material goods as a slave does his master and a poor person his oppressor. He is to be a zealot for the regulation whose time will be the Day of Vengeance. He shall do the will [of God] in all deeds and in all his realm as he [God] commanded him (Community Rule 9:12–23).

They are the violat[ers of the Covena]nt who will not believe when they hear everything that will co[me up]on the last generation from the mouth of the Priest in [whom] God put [understand]ing to interpret all the words of his servants the prophets by [whose] hand God declared all that will come upon his people (1QpHab 2:6–10).

It was only by faith in the Teacher of Righteousness as the divinely inspired interpreter of Torah that a person could gain salvation, as the interpretation of Hab 2:4 in 1QpHab 8:1–3 indicates:

But the righteous shall live by his faith

> Interpreted this concerns all those who keep the Torah in the House of Judah whom God will deliver from the house of judgment because of their suffering and their faith in the Teacher of Righteousness.

The Teacher's interpretations helped forge the identity of the Qumran community. His interpretations structured their lives and their view of the world. The many texts shot through with biblical allusions and quotations as well as the atomistic biblical interpretation found in the Qumran Pesharim all indicate that the Bible was an authoritative document for the people of Qumran. This authoritative text was viewed as only part of the divinely inspired authoritative documents: together with the Hebrew Bible/Old Testament went the interpretations of it by the Teacher of Righteousness. Both were equally authoritative and divinely inspired because the Teacher was the one "to whom God made known all the mysteries of the words of His servants the prophets" (1QpHab 7:4–5).[53] The interpretative principles utilized by the Teacher of Righteousness and his contemporaries had a long history in ancient Israel and were used also by later rabbinic interpreters.[54] Through the use of these interpretive techniques the Teacher of Righteousness and his contemporaries developed new interpretations of the classical, authoritative texts. While the hermeneutical techniques were the same, it was the differences in the interpretations of the authoritative documents that led to the development of the many sects within early Judaism.

That the various sects within Judaism developed on the basis of differences in the interpretation of Torah is clear. The early Christian community began, at least in part, because of a conflict over the correct interpretation of Scripture. The gospel writers depict Jesus as an inspired interpreter who gives new interpretations to the ancient, authoritative Scriptures. Several times in the Sermon on the Mount Jesus declares, "you have heard it said," before citing a commandment from the Torah. He then says, "but I say to you," before offering his new interpretation of the particular passage (cf. Mt 5:21–48). Jesus' interpretations of the Torah led to disputes with other Jewish leaders, as the debate with some Pharisees over the ritual cleansing of hands indicates (Mt 15:1–3 and parallels). The apostle Paul also created a following based on his claims to authority and his unique interpretations of Scripture. He considered himself a divinely inspired interpreter, and he often warned his followers to obey his teachings and to avoid those of his opponents (cf. 1 Cor 11:2; Col 2:8; 2 Thess. 2:15, 3:6; and 1 Tim 6:3–4). In both these cases, each leader had his own interpretation of what the scriptural passages meant. As a result, separate communities formed around the different interpreters based on their charisma, their rhetoric, and their claim to authority.

2 Baruch, then, presents Baruch as a legitimate successor to Jeremiah. He received revelations from God and even debated with the Almighty over the suffering of the righteous. *2 Baruch* is an example of an historical apocalypse with no otherworldly journey: Baruch encountered God in visions without having to journey into the heavenly realms.[55] Baruch's revelations come from encounters with the Divine, and he appears as a leader whom God inspires to provide the correct interpretation of Scripture. By his visions and inspired interpretations Baruch guides the community in obeying God's commandments and living holy lives. His teachings provide the answers to life's problems and mysteries. Thus Baruch the sage has become Baruch the apocalyptic seer, one who debates with God and who receives revelations of mysteries otherwise unknowable to human beings. This is a new feature for the Jewish sage.[56] The people who created and cherished *2 Baruch* valued apocalyptic seers whose visions and teachings guided the community, and so they re-imagined Baruch in that role.

3 Baruch (Greek Apocalypse)

The *Greek Apocalypse of Baruch (3 Baruch)* is an entirely different kind of apocalypse than *2 Baruch:* it is an ascent apocalypse that presents Baruch as an apocalyptic seer who ascended into the heavenly realms and returned to tell about it. Such ascent apocalypses are not unique to Jewish or Christian circles. Borrowed from the Greco-Roman world, this motif was a powerful tool in the hands of people who wished to promote a particular ideology or religious teaching.

The Hebrew Bible/Old Testament, with the exception of the Book of Daniel, does not promote ascent to heaven as an hallmark of piety. In fact, two verses from the book of Psalms succinctly summarize the

Hebrew Bible's general view of the possibility of humans ascending to the heavenly realm: "Heaven is Yahweh's heaven, but the earth he has given to humans. The dead do not praise Yahweh, nor all those who go down to silence" (Ps 115:16–17). Humans, according to the biblical editors, have no place in the heavenly realm. Ever since the expulsion of Adam and Eve from the Garden of Eden, God and humans have been separated: the Divine retreated forever into the heavens, while humans scattered across the face of the earth. Humans belong on earth both while alive and after death. The clearest suggestions of an ancient Jewish belief in a beatific afterlife in heaven appear only vaguely in the later biblical materials (e.g., Psalms 16, 49, 73; Ecc 3:21).[57] The earliest Jewish idea of the dead joining God in the heavenly realm emerges only in the Hellenistic period (Dan 12:1–3; 2 Macc 7:9, 11, 14, 23; 1 En 51:1, 61:5; 4 Ezra 7:32). Other than Enoch (Gen 6:21–24) and perhaps the prophet Elijah (2 Kgs 2:1–2), ascent to heaven does not figure into ancient Israelite piety (cf. Deut 30:12; Prov 30:4), no matter how desirable or laudable it might seem (Amos 9:2; Ps 139:8). In fact, to intend to ascend to heaven is evidence of wickedness, not piety. Isaiah derided the hubris of the king of Babylon, portraying him as one who imagined himself worthy of admission into heaven.

> Sheol below was excited to greet your arrival;
>> rousing the shades of all leaders of the earth;
>> raising from their thrones all kings of the nations.
> All of them speak and say to you:
>> "Even you are affected like us!
>> You have become like us!"
> Your pride has been brought down to Sheol,
>> and the sound of your harps.
> Worms are the bed beneath you,
>> and maggots are your blanket.
> How you are fallen from heaven,
>> O Day Star, son of Dawn!
> How you are cut down to the ground,
>> O destroyer of nations!
> You said in your heart,

> "I will ascend to heaven;
> I will raise my throne
>   above the stars of God;
> I will sit on the mount of assembly
>   on the heights of Zaphon;
> I will ascend to the tops of the clouds,
>   I will make myself like the Most High."
> But you are brought down to Sheol,
>   to the depths of the Pit (Isa 14:9–15; cf. Ezek 28:2,6).

And as the rhetoric of Proverbs further indicates, to go into the heavenly realm and know heavenly secrets is far beyond human ken.

> Who has ascended to heaven and come back down? Who has gathered the wind in the palm of his hand? Who has wrapped up the waters in a garment? Who has established all the ends of the earth? What is his name? And what is his child's name? Surely you know! (Prov 30:4).

Deuteronomy 30:11–13 also inveighs against the idea that a human could ascend to heaven or cross to the mythical regions beyond the ocean.

> This commandment that I am commanding you today is not too difficult for you, nor is it far from you. It is not in heaven that you should say "who will ascend to heaven for us and get it for us and declare it to us so that we can do it?" Neither is it beyond the ocean that you should say "who will cross over to the far side of the ocean and get it for us and declare it to us so that we can do it?"

This passage states that God's commandments are near at hand, and that mortals need not expend extraordinary efforts to learn or follow them. God's commandments, the commandments that guide one in proper living, are sequestered neither in heaven above in the realm of the gods nor at the ends of the earth. The general ideology of the Hebrew Bible, then, is that God's rightful place is in heaven while humanity's is on earth (Ps 115:16; Ecc 5:1). The prophets Micaiah ben Imlah, Isaiah, and Ezekiel had visions of the divine presence, but their feet remained firmly on earth; they did not "ascend" into heaven.

The Hebrew Bible begins with narratives about humanity's frustrated quest for eternal life (Adam and Eve) and frustrated attempt to enter heaven (Tower of Babel).[58] In Mesopotamia the quest for eternal life was undertaken by Gilgamesh, while the ascent to heaven motif figures in the myths of Enmeduranki, Etana, and Adapa. The Bible also contains two people who, like Adapa and Etana, may have ascended into heaven (Enoch and Elijah). Regarding what happens to a person at death, the biblical view is best summarized by the following:

> Remember that my life is a breath; my eye will never again see good. The eye that beholds me will see me no more; while your eyes are upon me, I shall be gone. As the cloud fades and vanishes, so those who go down to Sheol do not come up; they return no more to their houses, nor do their places know them any more (Job 7:7–10).[59]

Thus, except for a few suggestive but unfortunately ambiguous passages, the Hebrew Bible does not evince a belief that humans during life or even in the afterlife can ascend to heaven; heaven is the realm of God and earth is the realm of humans. The only biblical texts to suggest a belief in the heavenly ascent of the righteous are Ecclesiastes and Daniel.

> For in the matter of fate, human and animal have one and the same fate: as the one dies so does the other. Both draw the same breath. The human is in no way superior to the animal since both come to nothing. Both go to the same place—both came from the dust and both return to the dust. Who knows if a man's breath/spirit rises upward and if a beast's descends downward to the earth. I saw that there is nothing better for humans than to enjoy their possessions since that is their lot, for who can enable a human to see what will happen afterward? (Ecc 3:19–21)

> At that time the great prince Michael, who stands beside your compatriots, will appear. There will be anguish such as has never been since they became a nation and until that time. But at that time your people will be delivered, everyone whose name is written in the book. Many of those who sleep in the dust of the earth will awake, some to eternal life, others to reproaches and eternal abhorrence. The knowledgeable will shine like the splendor of the firmament, and those who led many to righteousness will be like the stars forever and ever (Dan 12:1–3).

Ecclesiastes' reference to the afterlife is much more ambiguous than Daniel's, but it does seem to at least hint at an awareness of the idea of the post mortem ascent of the soul. If this interpretation is correct, then Ecclesiastes (in some sense) and Daniel (quite clearly) break with the strong biblical tradition against heavenly ascent. This deviation is completely understandable, however, since Ecclesiastes may have been composed in the Persian period, and Daniel was certainly composed in the Hellenistic era (ca. 165 B.C.E.).[60] By this time many Jews had adopted Persian and Greek ideas of heavenly ascent and astral immortality. Ecclesiastes seems aware of the idea of heavenly ascent; Daniel unashamedly adopts it.

The early Greeks, much like the editors of the Hebrew Bible, were hesitant to imagine that any earthling could enter the heavenly realm. Book 11 of Homer's *Odyssey* recounts a tale of the giants Otus and Ephialtes who intended to stack mountain upon mountain in order to climb into heaven (11.305–20), but their plans were thwarted when they were killed in their youth by one of Zeus' sons. This story appears to be a polemic about ascending into heaven, much like the tale of the Tower of Babel in the Hebrew Bible (Gen 11:1–9). For the early Greeks, Mt. Olympus and the heavenly realm were home to the gods alone. By the fourth century B.C.E., however, most Greeks located the post mortem residence of the human soul in the heavenly realms. This belief stems from Pythagorean and Platonic ideas that the human soul originated in the ethereal realm, became imprisoned in the earthly body, and longs to return to the spiritual realm.[61] An example of this belief found in the writings of Plato is the "Myth of Er," recounted at the end of the *Republic*.[62] The hero, Er, dies, but before his funeral his soul leaves his body to visit the underworld and the heavens where it witnessed people being rewarded or punished according to their behavior while on earth. Er's soul returns to his body on earth after this heavenly tour; he then revives and tells his contemporaries what the other world was like. Likewise, Cicero's "Dream of Scipio" describes how Romans in the first century B.C.E. imagined that people would find an "eternal home" in the heavenly realm in reward for having lived nobly.

> But, [Scipio] Africanus, be assured of this, so that you may be even more eager to defend this commonwealth: all those who have preserved, aided, or enlarged their fatherland have a special place prepared for them in the heavens, where they may enjoy an eternal life of happiness.

Consequently, if you [Scipio] despair of ever returning to this place [i.e., the heavenly realm], where eminent and excellent men find their true reward, of how little value, indeed, is your fame among men, which can hardly endure for the small part of a year? Therefore, if you will only look on high and contemplate this eternal home and resting place, you will no longer attend to the gossip of the vulgar herd or put your trust in human rewards for your exploits. Virtue herself, by her own charms, should lead you on to true glory.

Strive on indeed, and be sure that it is not you that is mortal, but only your body. For that man whom your outward form reveals is not yourself; the spirit is the true self, not that physical figure which can be pointed out by the finger.

And as a spirit is the only force that moves itself, it surely has no beginning and is immortal. Use it, therefore, in the best pursuits! And the best tasks are those undertaken in defense of your native land; a spirit occupied and trained in such activities will have a swifter flight to this, its proper home and permanent abode [i.e., in heaven]. And this flight will be still more rapid if, while still confined in the body, it looks abroad, and, by contemplating what lies outside itself, detaches itself as much as may be from the body. For the spirits of those who are given over to sensual pleasures and have become their slaves, as it were, and who violate the laws of gods and men at the instigation of those desires which are subservient to pleasure—their spirits, after leaving their bodies, fly about close to the earth, and do not return to this place except after many ages of torture (*Republic* 6.13, 23, 24, 29).[63]

According to Cicero, therefore, the human spirit, or soul, desires to return to its true home in the highest reaches of the cosmos, but to do so it must have first prepared itself through living a life devoted to "the best pursuits" while also avoiding all manner of sensual pleasures. Otherwise the soul will undergo punishment to purge it of the earthly vices that prevent its ascent into the higher, purer realms. These disqualifying vices indicate the belief that there are qualifications one must meet in order to obtain the heavenly realm. While later Jewish and Christian ascent texts such as *3 Baruch* develop this theme of prerequisites for admission into heaven as a tool to encourage fidelity to behavioral and theological codes, here the goal is to encourage valiant patriotism and moral conduct.[64]

Since heavenly tourists like Baruch claimed to have actually learned their material while in the realm of the divine, their ideas were beyond challenge: they learned these things directly from God or his heavenly assistants, the angels. It is precisely because the teachings of such people could not be controlled that the rabbis attempted to marginalize this activity. The rabbis were not completely successful in this, so they reframed the discussion of the idea of ascents to, or visions of, the heavenly realm in their own terms. In fact, there was a wide variety of esoteric rabbinic speculation on the heavenly realms and the divine presence. A famous example of one kind of this literature is the *Hekhalot* ("palaces") literature. *Sepher Hekhalot* (ספר היכלות), the "book of palaces," also known as *3 Enoch,* claims to be an account of Rabbi Ishmael's journey through the seven heavenly palaces or heavens.[65] This famous second century rabbi was escorted on this heavenly tour by the archangel Metatron, who eventually reveals to Rabbi Ishmael that he is none other than Enoch (hence the title *3 Enoch*) who, according to the traditional interpretation of Genesis 5:21–24, was taken by God into heaven. During the course of his heavenly tour, Rabbi Ishmael saw God seated on his heavenly throne and learned about the secret workings of the cosmos, the organization of the heavenly hosts, and the ultimate fate of the just and the wicked. All this is part of the standard itinerary for people who are granted a tour of the heavenly realms with an angelic escort. So we see that the rabbis did occupy themselves somewhat with speculating on the appearance and contents of the heavenly realms. Their problem with most other accounts of ascents to the heavenly realm is that the figure involved was not a recognized rabbinical authority. These non-rabbinic ascents posed potential religious dangers: since these people claimed to have visited the heavenly realm, to have seen God face-to-face, and to have learned secrets unknowable to humans, they could concoct almost any theological program and claim that it has divine warrant. It all boiled down to a matter of religious authority: either these apocalypticists and their claims would guide people, or the rabbis and their ways would determine the faith, practice, and future of Judaism. While the apocalypticists based their authority on visions and other ecstatic experiences, the rabbis based their religious authority on expert knowledge and reasoned interpretation of religiously authoritative biblical and rabbinic texts, and this is the heart of traditional Judaism.[66] While the rabbis based their authority on "thus it is written" or "thus rabbi so-and-so said," the apocalypticists' claim was based on "thus I have seen in heaven" or "thus a heavenly being revealed to me." In a sense the heavenly tourists are like Moses himself who got his revelation directly from God, and his glowing face (Ex 34:29–35) was visible proof of his having been in the divine presence and served as the sign of his divine authority.[67] While Moses went up on a mountain to encounter the Divine (or into the Tent of Meeting as in Ex 33:7–11, cf. Ex 34:33–35, Numb 11–12, Deut 31:14–15, 23), the apocalypticists went up to God's heavenly abode itself and there received revelations of otherwise unknowable secrets. Moreover, as Moses' authority was linked to his intimate interactions with God—"Behold, I am coming to you in a thick cloud so that the people will hear as I speak with you and so will trust you forever"—so the apocalypticists' claims to having been in the divine presence above the clouds substantiated their authority.

The ascent theme appears in Jewish literature during the Greco-Roman period. Its growing prominence suggests a shift in perspective among some Jews regarding the nature and means of authority. The ascent as a means of claiming religious authority was promoted neither in the anteceding biblical materials nor in the subsequent rabbinic materials. According to Genesis 5:21–24, Enoch was the first to ascend into heaven, and this owing to his great piety. Likewise, at the end of his life Elijah allegedly ascended to heaven (2 Kgs 2). The rest of the biblical materials demonstrate at points that some did not view the idea of heavenly ascent quite as favorably. Deuteronomy 30:11–14 indicates that the divine teachings are not secreted away in heaven where one need ascend to learn them, rather they are immediately at hand in the Torah (cf. Deut 29:29). In addition, Isaiah 14:12–20 indicates that the Babylonian king's claim to ascend to heaven and be like God demonstrates the height of his pride and hubris. For a human to want to ascend to heaven is evidence of wickedness, not piety. For the tradents of these biblical materials, therefore, the claim to ascend to heaven was not welcome. Outside of the Enoch and Elijah narratives it was a claim born of human pride, not piety. The prevailing view assumes that man's place is on earth, not in heaven. Nonetheless, God did allow some humans to peer into the divine realm. While the tribes of Israel were encamped at Mt. Sinai it is reported that "Moses, Aaron,

Nadab, Abihu, and seventy of the elders of Israel went up [to the mountain] and saw the God of Israel" (Exodus 24:1–2, 9–11).[68] Other than a brief description of the pavement under God's feet, the text lacks the elaborate description of the divine presence characteristic of later texts. Although these people "went up" (עָלָה) and "saw" (רָאָה) God, they ascended only to the top of Mt. Sinai; they did not ascend into heaven itself. Another person to see the divine presence was Micaiah ben Imlah (1 Kgs 22). He "saw Yahweh sitting on his throne with all the host of heaven standing to his right and left" (1 Kgs 22:19). This passage, however, lacks a description of the divine presence. Amos reports that he saw Yahweh but describes only what the Almighty was holding in his hand (Amos 7:7–8). Isaiah, too, saw Yahweh sitting on a throne (Isaiah 6:1–5). Isaiah, somewhat less restrained than the Micaiah passage, adds a brief description of the beings around the throne. By the Exilic or the post-Exilic period there is even less restraint about describing the presence of the divine. Ezekiel saw "the appearance of the image of the glory of Yahweh" (Ezekiel 1:28) and described the chariot of God in detail. Although Ezekiel's descriptions are not as elaborate as later Jewish mystical texts (e.g., *Ma'aseh Merkabah, Hekalot,* and *Shi'ur Qomah*), his descriptions still evidence an advance from the earlier materials. The Bible, therefore, does not completely restrict speculation on the divine presence. What is does completely restrict is the idea of a human actually entering into the divine realm. All of these people may catch glimpses of the divine presence, but their feet never leave the earth. These are visions of the divine presence, not journeys into the divine presence. For the biblical tradents earth is the human realm and heaven is the divine realm. Humans other than Enoch and Elijah do not enter into the realm of God. Ascent to heaven, therefore, plays no part in revelatory experiences recounted in the Bible.

The authority of the prophet in the Bible rests in the claim of having received "the Word of the Lord." The phrases "the Word of the Lord was upon me," and "thus says the Lord" are the basis of prophetic authority.[69] The revelation is immediate and bears divine authority. The written, authoritative, prophetic word was subsequently reinterpreted. For example, Daniel 9 is part of an exegetical tradition of reinterpreting the oracle of Jeremiah 25.[70] The authority of select prophetic oracles was accepted early, and the subsequent reinterpretation of these oracles can be found within the Bible itself. This starts a process of the interpretation of authoritative documents as a basis for authority.

The authority of the prophetic speech was based in the first-hand reception of the divine word. The authority of the exegetical interpretation rests both on the authority of the interpreted document and on the claim to divine inspiration by the interpreter. Eventually the claim to having the inspired interpretation of an authoritative document was augmented by the appeal to the authoritative interpreters or teachers themselves.[71] As discussed above, this feature of the authority of an inspired interpreter is apparent in the attitude of the people towards Baruch in *2 Baruch*, in the attitude of the people of Qumran towards the Teacher of Righteousness, and in the attitude of several early Christian churches towards Paul. The citation of prominent teachers characterizes also the rabbinic literature. Not only did the rabbis support their teachings on the basis of an appeal to authoritative documents (i.e., "thus it is written"), but they also appealed to authoritative teachers ("thus rabbi so and so said"). This is all part of the exegetical tradition. By claiming a connection to a religiously authoritative document or person, an author can contextualize his ideas within the bounds of the accepted traditions.

With regard to the ascent texts like *3 Baruch*, however, the appeal to authority is much different. Those who have ascended to heaven have an altogether different basis for authority: they can claim that they ascended into heaven and saw all this. This could be termed the "experiential" claim to authority. This basis for authority cannot be challenged, for it is based on personal experience, a claim to have had a first-person encounter with God and/or his heavenly servants. This reveals the central function of the ascent narrative: the ascent qualifies or authorizes the seer and his message. *3 Baruch* as an apocalyptic ascent text uses the "experiential" approach to validating an author's claims. It narrates a heavenly ascent whose purpose is to convince Baruch that God hears and attends to human prayers. The community that created and initially transmitted this text valued the idea of heavenly ascent as a means of gaining or demonstrating divine authority.

3 Baruch, therefore, attests that the popular image of Baruch took on an additional feature.[72] Baruch became one of those apocalyptic seers who had taken a guided tour of the heavenly realms. The heavenly tour in *3 Baruch* comes in response to Baruch's turmoil over the destruction of Jerusalem.[73] The text opens with Baruch sitting on the ruins of the Holy of Holies and weeping over the Babylonian (read: Roman) destruction of the city. This setting, with Baruch weeping over the fate his people must endure, was surely inspired by the image in Jeremiah 45:3 that describes Baruch's grief: "Oh woe is me! Yahweh has added grief to my suffering. I have exhausted myself with groaning and have found no rest." While in the book of Jeremiah Baruch received comfort in the form of a divine oracle delivered via Jeremiah (Jer 45:4–5), in *3 Baruch* the divine response and comfort came in the form of a tour of the heavenly realms. God sent the angel Phamael to lead Baruch through five heavens: "the Lord God Almighty . . . has sent me to you to proclaim and show you all the things of God. For your prayer has been heard by him and has entered into the ears of the Lord God (*3 Bar.* 1:3–5). Baruch immediately became calm (1:6) and then began his ascent into the heavens where he learned "the mysteries of God" (1:8). The ascent, then, is the most obvious indication of Baruch's worthiness in God's eyes, but the angel's address to Baruch also indicates something of Baruch's character. At 1:3 the angel addresses Baruch as ἄνερ ἐπιθυμιῶν, "a greatly beloved man." This is precisely the phrase used of Daniel in a Greek version (Theodotion) of Daniel 9:23 and 10:11.[74]

In the first heaven (2:1–7) Baruch saw a vast plain where there lived people "with ox faces, deer horns, goat feet, and sheep torso" (2:3). The angel told Baruch that these were the people who built the "tower of the war against God" (2:7) (i.e., the Tower of Babel) and were sent here for punishment. At the first stop on his tour, therefore, Baruch learned that those who oppose God will eventually be held accountable and punished for their deeds. This is important because this very idea of the wicked people oppressing the righteous concerns Baruch at the outset of this apocalypse. Baruch's heavenly tour was already addressing his concerns. Interestingly, in the second heaven (3:1–4:1) Baruch saw another group of grotesque people who looked like dogs yet had deer feet (3:3). The angel explained to Baruch that these people were the ones who plotted to build the tower and forced others to do the work on this sacrilegious project (3:8). Genesis 11:7–9 recounts that God responded to the building of the Tower of Babel by confusing the languages of the builders and spreading them out over the face of the entire earth. *3 Baruch,* then, adds a new perspective to the story: not only were there immediate temporal consequences for these people's acts, there were extratemporal, or postmortem, consequences. That is to say, their sin earned them punishment in the afterlife. Baruch learned that sin never goes unpunished, and while this comforts those who await the punishment of their tormentors, it also challenges individuals to live rightly now lest they, too, suffer punishment in the afterlife. Baruch thus appears as a preacher promoting obedience to God and righteous living as the only way to avoid postmortem, and, presumably, eternal punishment in the afterlife.

In the third heaven Baruch learned about secret workings of the cosmos: he learned how the sea, although it is continuously fed by a multitude of rivers, never overflows; he learned how evil reappeared in the world following the Flood; and he learned about the movements of the celestial bodies. The Bible explains how evil first became manifest in the world, but not how it reappeared after the cataclysmic Flood. Here in the third heaven Baruch learned that a twig of the Tree of the Knowledge of Good and Evil, the very tree that led Adam and Eve astray, floated on the waters of the Flood and escaped the Garden of Eden. When Noah went out to replant the earth after the Flood, he happened upon this innocuous twig. The angel Phamael, the same angel who was serving as Baruch's guiding angel during his tour through the heavens, appeared to Noah and told him about the twig. This led Noah to question whether he should plant the twig or not. After Noah had prayed fervently for forty days about the matter, God sent the angel Sarasael who persuaded Noah to replant the twig. In spite of the obvious danger, God intended to use this plant, which formerly had been the cause of so many of humanity's ills, to display his glory even more magnificently. In what is an obvious Christian interpolation into the text, we learn that the twig came from a grapevine and that its fruit was wine. This formerly devastating fruit would become the symbol of the rejuvenating blood of Christ (4:15–17).

Baruch also learned about another mystery: how is it that the rivers flow incessantly into the sea, yet the sea never overflows. Our author eschews any scientific answer in favor of a mythical one: the sea never overflows because there is a primordial serpent who swallows "one cubit" of water daily from the sea (5:1–3). Thus, the waters that flow into the sea from the rivers replenish the water extracted by this monster with an enormous stomach.

Apart from these fanciful tales, the focus of Baruch's attention in the third heaven is astronomy. The archangel Phamael revealed to Baruch otherwise unknowable secrets that explain the mysterious workings of the celestial bodies. Cosmic speculation is a central aspect in early Jewish apocalyptic thought, and this intellectual pursuit is commonly associated with the figure of Enoch in both Jewish and Christian traditions.[75] According to the traditions included in the several texts that constitute *1 Enoch*, Enoch learned all manner of cosmological secrets including the secrets regarding the heavenly abodes of the righteous, the lightning and thunder, the storehouses of the winds, dew, hail, mist, and clouds, and the regular courses of the sun and moon (*1 Enoch* 41, 43–44, 72–82). It is certainly understandable that such secrets should be revealed to the antediluvian hero who was the first and perhaps only person in the Hebrew Bible to have gone into the heavenly realm. Moreover, these features are fairly standard items a visionary encounters when viewing the secrets of the cosmos.[76] According to *3 Baruch* the archangel Phamael enabled Baruch to trace the movements of the sun. Rather than making careful mathematical calculations of the sun's movements as Enoch did in the Astronomical Book (*1 Enoch* 72–82), Baruch offers mythological explanations. The sun moves as it does because it rides in a chariot drawn by a multitude of angels (*3 Bar.* 6:1–2). After the sun rises from one of the 365 gates it uses on the eastern horizon, the mythological Phoenix bird interposes itself between the earth and the sun to protect humans from the sun's burning rays (*3 Bar.* 6:3–7:6). Once the sun sets in the west, angels come to remove its crown—presumably the symbol for its rays and brightness—and take it to heaven to be renewed because it becomes defiled as it looks down on the evils being perpetrated on earth during the day (8:1–7). Baruch then observed the moon during the course of its nighttime travels (9:1–8). He learned that the moon, like the sun, travels in a chariot drawn by angels. He also learned that the phases of the moon are a result of its participation in the sin of Adam in the

Garden of Eden. That is, the moon, the lesser of the two great lights (Gen 1:14–19), changes size and shape because of a curse put on it by God for allowing its light to shine while Adam was eating the forbidden fruit (9:5–8). Again, rather than attempting some kind of scientific explanation as Enoch did (e.g., *1 Enoch* 73–74, 78:5–17), Baruch proffers a mythological/theological explanation for the workings of the cosmos. This is entirely in keeping with the author's goal, for he or she intends to show that sin does not go unpunished: since the heavenly bodies who did wrong do not go unpunished, so too will those who are oppressing the righteous eventually suffer divine punishment, and that eternally.

In the fourth heaven Baruch saw another vast plain and living there were the righteous who appeared in the form of birds living along the banks of a lake in the middle of the plain (10:1–9). Baruch and his angel then ascended to the fifth heaven. Oddly, they did not pass through the gates to enter this heaven as they had in the first four heavens: they stood outside the locked gates of heaven and waited. Angels eventually arrived to deliver human prayers to God at the appointed hour. The archangel Michael then came from the presence of God and opened the gates. Michael greeted Baruch and his angelic guide warmly and then received the prayers from the angels. He then went back through the gates, locking them behind him, and presented the prayers to God. He returned shortly thereafter and meted out God's responses. To the righteous and exceptionally virtuous God granted reward, and even to those who were only somewhat virtuous, God granted a limited measure of reward (14–15). To the wicked, however, God said to send pain, suffering, and demonic torment (16:1–4). This is the climax of Baruch's heavenly tour. True, he did not see God face to face, and this may in part be a statement warning against seeking such an encounter.[77] Nonetheless, Baruch did learn that God was acutely aware of what people were doing on earth and that he held everyone responsible, good or bad.

In *3 Baruch,* Baruch learned during the course of his ascent that God was still in control. This knowledge comforted Baruch in his turmoil over the destruction of Jerusalem. Baruch learned that although this world may be characterized by chaos, and the righteous appear to suffer unjustly, nonetheless God is still in control and listens daily to the prayers of his people. Like Enoch in the many texts and traditions about him, according to *3 Baruch,* Baruch, too, learned otherwise unknowable secrets about the workings of the cosmos. Baruch was now viewed as a person whose unimpeachable righteousness afforded him a guided tour of the heavens. He had ascended to heaven and returned to reveal some of its secrets. Baruch was imagined as a truly exceptional person, and his teachings carried heavenly authority.

The authors of *2 Baruch (Syriac Apocalypse)* and *3 Baruch (Greek Apocalypse)* built on the traditions they had inherited and then re-invented Baruch as an apocalyptic seer. They portrayed him as one who had revelatory visions in which he argued with God and as one who had taken a guided tour of the heavens in the company of an angel. These narratives about Baruch's debates with God and his heavenly journeys, while certainly very entertaining in their own right, addressed people's self-perceived socioreligious needs. These apocalyptic texts make it clear that the communities that created and cherished these texts longed for an explanation of the political, religious, and existential turmoil they suffered. They wanted to know why: "Why are we tormented and suffering as we do? If we are the righteous ones whom God promised to reward for our religious fidelity, then why do we suffer at the hands of infidels?" The authors of these texts, and the communities they served, found solace in these stories of Baruch's visions and heavenly journeys. On one level they could identify with Baruch. Baruch lamented his suffering just as they did: "Woe is me because Yahweh has added grief to my pain. I am weary with my groaning, and I can find no rest" (Jer 45:3). Moreover God revealed to Baruch that he would escape the present troubles and escape with his life: "Yet I will give you your life as a prize of war in every place wherever you may go" (Jer 45:5). These people also knew from existing traditions that God favored Baruch. He was a righteous sage who served God faithfully. He also was a prophet—or at least many thought he was—and was so righteous that God granted him revelatory visions. These people lived in the Roman era, and in this era esoteric knowledge and mystical encounters with God were widely valued as signs of piety. This was a time when many people esteemed apocalyptic seers. The pseudepigraphers behind *2 Baruch* and *3 Baruch* reinvented

Baruch so that he might address the needs of their communities in modes that they valued. The pseudepigraphers' goal was not to deceive, but to inspire and give hope. They gave their communities a Baruch who perfectly matched their image of an ideal, inspired leader. Apocalyptic Baruch gave them hope that through all the vicissitudes of life, God still cared for them, knew of their suffering, and would one day in future, either in this world or the next, reward them. All they had to do was to remain faithful to the community's cherished traditions, values, and morals. Apocalyptic Baruch, therefore, served to define and transmit these community-defining traditions, values, and morals to present and future generations. Baruch's legacy as a spiritual leader thus continued to endure.

Chapter Four

BARUCH IN LATER JEWISH, CHRISTIAN, AND ISLAMIC TRADITION

By the second century C.E. Baruch's persona had evolved quite significantly from that of the loyal scribal assistant to the prophet Jeremiah. The historical Baruch had become much greater in death than he had been in life. These evolutions in the depictions of Baruch ben Neriah were not haphazard. New facets in Baruch's postbiblical persona were purposefully designed to meet specific needs based on various communities' images of their ideal leader. The postbiblical pseudepigraphers thus reinvented Baruch to fit new communal realities. This process of reinventing Baruch continued well into the Middle Ages. This chapter surveys several later traditions about Baruch in an attempt to show how Christians, Jews, and Moslems continued to recreate the historical Baruch. As has become clear with the texts and traditions discussed in the preceding chapters, each community or new generation reinvented Baruch to accord with their particular socioreligious needs. Likewise, later pseudepigraphers and tradents of Jewish and Christian traditions continued to remake Baruch. In his various reincarnations Baruch thus continued to serve the religious needs of people long after his death.

Baruch the Angel

In his brief discussion of apocryphal texts attributed to biblical figures, M. R. James mentions a book ascribed to Baruch in which Baruch appears as an angel.[1] The book was written by Justin the Gnostic, whose teachings eventually drew the criticism of the third century

Roman heresiologist, Hippolytus. At the end of the fifth book of *Refuta-tio omnium haeresium* (Refutation of all Heresies), Hippolytus describes Justin's teachings.[2] Although Justin's book is entitled "Baruch," it is named not after the scribe/sage/seer of Jewish and Christian tradition, but after the most prominent of the twelve good angels in Justin's Gnostic cosmology.[3] The angel Baruch in this book is a spokesperson for God, revealing mysteries to Justin, but this figure is not Baruch ben Neriah. The angel is named Baruch not because of any connection with Baruch ben Neriah, but because the name means "blessed," a fitting name for an angel. Nonetheless, as Harlow has noted, it is indeed tempting to speculate that perhaps in some circles Baruch was imagined to have attained angelic status.[4] The evolution of the portrayals of Baruch has been complex indeed, and the possibility that some may have tried to imagine him as an angel is intriguing. Perhaps this would have been a fitting final transformation for a figure whose biblical afterlife in Jewish and Christian tradition was so multifaceted.

Baruch the Prophet

As the Baruch materials surveyed in the previous chapters indicated, there was an ongoing debate as to whether or not Baruch was a prophet. This ambivalence about Baruch's prophetic status appeared already in the biblical materials that mention Baruch. The final editors of the Hebrew (Masoretic) version of the book of Jeremiah did not imagine Baruch as a prophet. This is most clearly evident by the titles given to Jeremiah and Baruch: Jeremiah is "the prophet," while Baruch is "the scribe." The Greek (Septuagint) version of the book of Jeremiah is somewhat more ambiguous about Baruch's status and at least appears to suggest that Baruch succeeded the prophet Jeremiah as the spiritual leader of the people.

This debate over Baruch's role in the community continued in early Jewish and Christian literature. Some texts indicate that certain rabbis regarded Baruch as a prophet.[5] Moreover, several Christian texts appear to follow the Jewish tradition that Baruch was a prophet.[6] Although Baruch does not appear in the Greek *Vitae Prophetarum*, a Byzantine collection of various biblical and postbiblical traditions about the lives and deaths of the prophets, there is a brief vita of

Baruch in an Armenian work entitled "The Names, Works, and Deaths of the Holy Prophets."[7] Baruch's name also appears in an early Christian list of seventy-two prophets and prophetesses.[8] Clearly some ancient Jewish and Christian communities revered Baruch as one of the ancient prophets.

The *Mekhilta d'Rabbi Ishmael,* an early rabbinic commentary on a large part of the book of Exodus, however, continued the perspective of Masoretic Jeremiah in denying that Baruch was a prophet.[9] In this text Baruch actually complains of not having received the prophetic spirit from his teacher Jeremiah, as Elisha received it from Elijah and Joshua from Moses. The alleged reason for Baruch's being denied the prophetic spirit was because he wanted it for his own benefit and not for Israel's.[10] According to Jer 45:5, Baruch sought "great things" (גדלות) for himself. Exactly what this term ultimately refers to is unclear. Nonetheless, as was suggested in chapter one, the term appears to have something to do with seeking the prophetic office or a prophetic revelation, and at the very least had something to do with improving Baruch's status or wealth. This quest was misdirected in God's opinion, so the Almighty denied Baruch these "great things." As also noted in chapter one, the Psalmist points out that seeking "great things" (גדלות) is inappropriate for the devout people. Psalm 131:1–2 states:

> O Yahweh, my heart is not lifted up,
> > and my eyes are not elevated too high.
> I do not concern myself with *great things,*
> > and marvels that are beyond me.
> Rather, I have calmed and quieted my soul,
> > like a weaned child with its mother;
> > like the weaned child is my soul with me.

In fact, this understanding of the quest for "great things" as something evil may be what the Damascus Document is alluding to when it refers to the words Jeremiah spoke to Baruch. The Damascus Document was an important document among the sectarians at Qumran, the people of the Dead Sea Scrolls. In describing God's attitude to the people who do not follow their sectarian lifestyle, the authors of the Damascus Document state that:

because of his [God's] hatred for the builders of the wall, his anger
rages. . . . And like this judgment so will it be for all those who reject the
commandments of God, forsake them, and turn instead towards the
stubbornness of their heart. . . . This is the word that Jeremiah spoke to
Baruch son of Neriah . . . and Elisha to Gehazi his servant (CD 8:18–20).

The import of this final sentence is unclear. That God told Baruch via
Jeremiah not to seek "great things" (Jer 45:5) is clear. Although it is a
stereotypical biblical designation for God's wonders, especially those
related to delivering Israel (cf. Josh 24:17; Neh 9:18; Ps 71:19, 106:21,
136:4; 1 Chr 17:21), the term 'great things' (גדלות) appears in Jer 33:3
in connection with divine revelations: "Call on me, and I will answer
you. And I will declare to you 'great things' (גדלות), secrets you have
not known." Baruch appears to have wanted to become a prophet
himself—he sought these "great things." On the other hand, Gehazi,
the prophet Elisha's servant (2 Kgs 4:12–36; 5:20–27; 8:4–5), never
asked that he inherit the prophetic mantle from Elisha, although this
may not be out of the question for Gehazi since he certainly knew that
Elisha had inherited it from Elijah (2 Kgs 19:16, 19; 2:15). Gehazi did
recount the "great things" (גדלות) of Elisha to the king (2 Kgs 8:4–5),
but these "great things" are the miracles Elisha performed. Interestingly, however, Elisha later criticized Gehazi for going out to the people Elisha had helped and taking money from them by deceit (2 Kgs
5:20–27). This using of Elisha's miracles as an opportunity to enrich
himself appears to have been Gehazi's mistake. It may be that this is
what the Damascus Document is referring to—a tradition that Gehazi
and Baruch both sought to use the prophetic office for personal
enrichment. It was for this reason, then, that both were denied the
prophetic mantle. In a similar way some Christians also denied that
Baruch was a prophet. Ishodad of Merv, the ninth-century Nestorian
bishop of Hedatta, states that Baruch, upset because he had not
received the gift of prophecy, left Jerusalem, became the founder of
Zoroastrianism, and wrote the *Avesta,* the sacred books of the Zoroastrians.[11] There seems to have been a tradition, therefore, that Baruch
was not appointed a prophet because of avarice. This suspicion of Baruch's avarice seems to stem from the divine criticism that Baruch not
seek "great things." This may be in part why *2 Baruch (Syriac Apocalypse)*

continually stresses Baruch's concern for the well being of the community and not his own fate. The author of *2 Baruch* may have been attempting to counter the tradition that Baruch was driven simply by self-interest.

Baruch in the *Ethiopic Apocalypse of Baruch*

Another pseudepigraphon attributed to Baruch, the *Ethiopic Apocalypse of Baruch,* circulated among the Falashas, a group of non-rabbinic, Ethiopian Jews. This work has two parts: the first recounts Baruch's ascent to heaven where he sees places of reward and punishment, while the second records a series of apocalyptic predictions by Baruch. Although the *Ethiopic Apocalypse of Baruch* was composed by Ethiopian Christians some time after the mid sixth century C.E., the Falashas subsequently removed the Christian elements and transmitted it as one of their holy books.[12]

Baruch's relationship to Jeremiah is never mentioned in this apocalypse. In fact, instead of being Jeremiah's scribe, Baruch is a gate-keeper for the temple. This anomaly suggests that the original Christian author(s) and the later Falasha tradents thought that Baruch was a priest.[13] The ascent and its question-and-answer format indicate that the communities who created and transmitted this text regarded Baruch as a holy man worthy to be ushered into the divine realm to receive answers to his questions about the structure of the cosmos, the eschaton, and the ultimate fate of sinners and saints. Given the late date of this text, it is likely that its original Christian authors and readers were already familiar with the idea of Baruch as an apocalyptic seer (*2 Baruch*) and heavenly tourist (*3 Baruch*). This text simply develops both of these themes further.

Baruch and Zoroaster

Oddly enough, several medieval Christian commentators identify Baruch with Zoroaster.[14] This curious connection appears in a tradition describing how Baruch/Zoroaster prophesied the birth, life, death, and resurrection of Jesus. As Jacob Neusner has shown, however, this identification of Baruch with Zoroaster is a medieval Christian tradition that has no parallel in Jewish sources and stems from medieval debates between Christians and Zoroastrians.[15] The tradition further demonstrates, however, that some Christians regarded Baruch as a prophet who predicted the coming of Jesus as Messiah. That Christians believed, or wished to prove, that Baruch prophesied events in Jesus' life is apparent also in several Christian interpolations of messianic import in the Baruch pseudepigrapha.[16]

Baruch and Ebed-Melech

In rabbinic tradition Baruch is identified occasionally with Ebed-Melech, the Ethiopian eunuch who rescued Jeremiah from the pit into which King Zedekiah's officials had placed him (Jer 38:1–13).[17] As a reward for saving the prophet's life, God promised to spare Ebed-Melech from suffering during the fall of Jerusalem (Jer 39:15–18). Rabbinic tradition takes Ebed-melech's designation as a "Cushite" to mean that just as a Cushite is distinguished by black skin, so Ebed-Melech is distinguished by his good works.[18] Although Ebed-Melech's deeds show him to be a righteous person, why do *Sifre Num* 99 and *Pirqe R. El.* 53 identify him with Baruch? The answer lies in the exegetical techniques of the rabbis. In the book of Jeremiah both Baruch and Ebed-Melech received oracles of personal deliverance containing virtually identical vocabulary.[19]

וְהָיְתָה לְךָ נַפְשְׁךָ לְשָׁלָל "you shall have your life for booty" (Jer 39:18 for Ebed-Melech).

וְנָתַתִּי לְךָ אֶת־נַפְשְׁךָ לְשָׁלָל "I shall give to you your life for booty" (Jer 45:5 for Baruch).

This verbal parallel prompted the rabbis to equate the two figures. Moreover, Ebed-Melech and Baruch have equal status as disciples of Jeremiah in the *Paraleipomena of Jeremiah*.[20] Thus, the equating of Baruch with Ebed-Melech occurs late and stems from the rabbinical practice of reading two verbally similar biblical passages as if they were referring to the same person. Since both Baruch and Ebed-Melech were given virtually the exact same promise in Scripture, and since one is prominent while the other is otherwise unknown, the rabbis understand the two to be the same person. This is how *Sifre Num* 99 and *Pirqe R. El.* 53 come to identify Baruch with Ebed-Melech.[21] Moreover, just as some interpreters thought that Baruch escaped death (cf. *2 Bar.* 13:3, 25:1, 46:7 and 76:2), so some believed that Ebed-Melech "entered the Garden of Eden alive" (*b Der. Er. Zut.* 1).

The Fate of Baruch

What ever became of Baruch? Where did he live after the fall of Jerusalem to the Babylonians? There were more answers to this question than one might expect, given the book of Jeremiah's account of Baruch and Jeremiah's fate—both were taken against their will to Egypt.

> So Johanan son of Qareach, all the commanders of the forces, and all the people did not obey the voice of Yahweh and remain in the land of Judah. Instead, Johanan son of Qareach and all the commanders of the forces took all the remnant of Judah who had returned from all the nations to which they had been driven to settle in the land of Judah— the men, the women, the little children, the princesses, and everyone whom Nebuzaradan the captain of the guard had left with Gedaliah son of Ahiqam son of Shaphan—and the prophet Jeremiah and Baruch son of Neriah. They came into the land of Egypt because they did not obey the voice of Yahweh. And they came to Tahpanhes (Jer 43:4–7).

Such an unambiguous biblical statement should have left no doubt as to Baruch's fate. Although not mentioning Baruch specifically, the fragmentary Qumran texts 4Q385b (=*4QApocryphon of Jeremiah^c* fragment 16, 2:6) and 4Q389a (=*4QApocryphon of Jeremiah^e* fragment 3, 5) follow the biblical tradition that Jeremiah went to Tahpanhes in Egypt.[22] Several ancient texts and traditions, however, locate Baruch and/or Jeremiah in other places. The first-century C.E. Jewish historian, Josephus, preserves a tradition according to which Baruch remained in Jerusalem (*Antiq.* 10:158). Likewise, *2 Baruch (Syriac Apocalypse)* 10:1–3, *Paraleipomena of Jeremiah* (1:1; 4:6–7; 5:17–18; 7:36; 8:6–7), and the famous medieval Jewish scholar Rashi (commenting on Jer 44:14) report that Baruch remained in Jerusalem.

The preface to the Book of Baruch (1:1–2) and some other Jewish texts, nonetheless, report that Baruch lived in Babylon.[23] In addition, Rabbi Petachia, a late-twelfth-century rabbi famous for his travels, reported that he saw Baruch's tomb outside of Baghdad.[24] One text,

Pesikta Rabbati (26:6; 33:1–2) mentions that although Baruch did at one time go to Babylon, he eventually returned to Jerusalem. *Shir HaShirim Rabba* notes that Baruch lived in Babylon, but it also includes a curious tradition about Baruch's appearance, describing Baruch as an old and overweight man who was physically incapable of returning to Jerusalem, even were he to be carried the entire way. There was another tradition according to which Baruch and Jeremiah did enter Egypt but did not remain there very long. According to this tradition Baruch and Jeremiah were taken by force to Egypt—exactly the tradition recounted in Jeremiah 43:4–7. But when king Nebuchadnezzar of Babylon conquered Egypt he took all the Jews who were living there captive to Babylon. Thus Baruch ended up living in Babylon.[25] All these differing traditions indicate that it is not certain where Baruch spent his last days, but there is one tradition about his alleged tomb.

Baruch's Tomb

Rabbi Petachia of Ratisbon traveled through the Near East and Asia in the late twelfth century.[26] While in the region of Baghdad the locals told him about the nearby tomb of Baruch ben Neriah. Baruch's tomb was located just outside of Baghdad and was once adjacent to the tomb of the prophet Ezekiel, who the locals believed was Baruch's teacher. Once, on orders from the Islamic king, Muslims tried to open Baruch's tomb but were struck dead. Realizing the greatness and miraculous power of Baruch, the king ordered some local Jews to move Baruch's coffin away from the tomb of Ezekiel so that Baruch might have his own shrine and not share one with Ezekiel. When the Jewish workers had carried Baruch's coffin approximately one mile from the tomb of Ezekiel, neither they nor their pack animals could move the coffin any farther. The king took this as a miraculous sign and ordered that Baruch be reinterred immediately at the spot and that a lavish shrine be built over his grave. Petachia also states that a portion of Baruch's prayer shawl protruded from the coffin, leading the locals to believe that Baruch's body miraculously had not decayed.

Petachia's account of the legends concerning Baruch's tomb reflects the kinds of miraculous events that are often attributed to the graves of saints. Beliefs about the miraculous powers available at these sites serve to promote both the reputation of the person commemorated and the financial success of the place as a pilgrimage site.[27] Obviously, these legends about Baruch's tomb depend on the tradition that after the fall of Jerusalem in 586 B.C.E. Baruch resided in Babylon.

Although the Masoretic version of the book of Jeremiah and many later traditions would deny that Baruch was a prophet, in the minds of many people he was indeed a prophet and spiritual leader of his community. Not only did he record Jeremiah's visions and sermons, he also recorded the revelations God gave to him. Baruch could have passed from the pages of history without notice, but his memory was kept alive by individuals and communities who continued to speculate about his actions and whereabouts. They saw in Baruch someone with whom they could identify, someone whose portrayal in the Bible suggested that he would have been concerned for them and their needs. He became depicted as a saint, a holy man, a person who could help them. Even in death he could help, for at his tomb powers were available to work miracles. Baruch's legacy was indeed larger than life.

THE EVOLUTION OF BARUCH FROM SCRIBE TO SAGE AND SEER

Baruch ben Neriah, the prophet Jeremiah's scribal assistant and close colleague, lived during tumultuous times when the kingdom of Judah fell to the mighty Babylonian empire. Baruch himself appears only in the book of Jeremiah in the Hebrew Bible/Old Testament, and that in only a few scenes. The final editors of the book of Jeremiah depict Baruch as a notable figure in Jerusalem. Nonetheless, Baruch has not drawn a great deal of scholarly attention, especially among biblical scholars. Indeed, the major commentaries on the book of Jeremiah give Baruch only limited attention. I have been fascinated for years by Baruch ben Neriah and how he is depicted in biblical and postbiblical literature. I hope that this slender volume has provided some insight into the evolution of Baruch's persona. This evolution evidences the creativity of the multifaceted pseudepigraphic imagination.[1] Although the different postbiblical images of Baruch tell us precious little about the Baruch of history, they do reveal a great deal about the religious interests of the communities who continued to honor him. Moreover, these images teach us more about the creativity of the pseudepigraphic imagination and how it works. The postbiblical creators of new traditions about Baruch were reinventing him to address the pressing socioreligious needs of their day. They were reinventing Baruch in their image and for their needs. These pseudepigraphers were not trying to deceive people with their new Baruch texts and traditions. They were trying to inspire people to follow what they understood to be longstanding, cherished, community-defining beliefs and practices.

Baruch ben Neriah was presented in the Masoretic textual tradition of the book of Jeremiah as Jeremiah's scribal assistant. Although his was a highly respected profession, this portrayal clearly shows that Jeremiah played the leading role in the Jerusalem community while Baruch occupied a secondary position. This study followed a leading trend in Jeremiah studies by maintaining that the text of Hebrew/Masoretic Jeremiah is in many ways secondary to that preserved in the Greek Jeremiah. That being the case, the clear subordination of Baruch to Jeremiah in Hebrew/Masoretic Jeremiah is a revision of what must have been the portrayal of Baruch in the Hebrew text that served as the basis for the version of Jeremiah preserved in the Greek Septuagint and in some of the fragments of the book of Jeremiah among the Dead Sea Scrolls.

The Greek version of the book of Jeremiah presented Baruch as Jeremiah's successor. The editors of this version of the book of Jeremiah configured the chapters to emphasize Baruch's role as the great prophet's successor. Baruch became much more than a scribe; he became a leader of the people. The Book of Baruch, an addition or supplement to Greek Jeremiah, added more detail to the evolving image of Baruch. With the Book of Baruch we move from the realm of history to the realm of the pseudepigraphic imagination. The people who composed this text from existing materials portrayed Baruch as a penitent and man of wisdom who addressed the Jewish people as one of their sages. Baruch came to be viewed as a man who knew, obeyed, and transmitted the beliefs and traditions of the past to the current generation. Baruch was seen as the Jewish people's link to the past. Moreover, according to the *Paraleipomena of Jeremiah,* Baruch was revered as a pious man of great learning. When the early Jewish and Christian communities imagined Baruch, they thought of him as a person like Daniel, Ezra, or even Moses, who taught his people what God expected of them and modeled for them how to follow these divine expectations.

2 Baruch (Syriac Apocalypse) added other elements to the persona of Baruch: he became an apocalyptic seer and inspired interpreter of Torah upon whose divinely inspired teachings people depended for eternal life. In this text we find Baruch arguing with God about issues of theodicy—why do bad things happen to good people, God's people?

Baruch appears like the biblical image of Job or like the postbiblical image of Ezra (i.e., Fourth Ezra). Because of his piety and his mastery of Torah, Baruch could debate with God on his own terms. *2 Baruch* also portrays Baruch as a learned Torah-sage who taught Torah to a small group of disciples and who revealed to this special group divine and cosmic secrets that God had revealed to him. He thus appears as a Torah-sage who ensured that there would be people to follow in his footsteps when he left this world. This classic example of a community leader teaches his generation and prepares disciples to carry on that mission to succeeding generations.

3 Baruch (Greek Apocalypse) took the somewhat radical step of portraying Baruch as one who had ascended into heaven and returned with a report of what he had experienced. Because of the heavenly ascent attributed to him in *3 Baruch,* Baruch can teach divine mysteries that otherwise cannot be known. The mysteries are not meant just to titillate. They import knowledge to Baruch's earthly audience that can enable them, too, to be fit one day for admission into God's presence in heaven. Baruch's teachings, therefore, enable his followers to endure the difficulties of life on earth, and also prepare them for a better life in heaven.

This evolution of the persona of Baruch as it can be traced in the texts pseudepigraphically attributed to him parallels a cultural shift in early Judaism: there was an evolution from the priority of the sage/scribe who inscribed and transmitted the divine words to that of the sage/scholar who interpreted and extended the divine words for the benefit of the community. The Baruch of history was clearly a member of the former group: as a scribe he wrote down the words of God and Jeremiah. By way of contrast, the Baruch of the pseudepigraphic imagination took those ancient texts and traditions and reinterpreted them, breathing new life into them and making them applicable in new ways for later generations. The apocalyptic seer feature of Baruch's later persona likely served a limited Jewish audience, and this restricted readership is why these Baruch texts were not preserved in their original languages; the rabbis who dominated the Jewish religious institutions were not much interested in this apocalyptic element. The early Christian community thrived on this literature, however, and so various Christian communities preserved these texts in their vernacular languages. The images and words of the apocalyptic Baruch addressed their needs through the apocalyptic visions and heavenly ascents that captivated their religious imaginations.

According to Ben Sira 38–39, the sage was respected for wisdom, piety, and knowledge of Torah. The depictions of Baruch ben Neriah in the early Jewish and Christian texts and traditions associated with him included all these elements. Baruch's persona developed from his actual historical role as Jeremiah's scribal assistant to that of an ideal sage and apocalyptic seer. The stages in this metamorphosis reflect the many spiritual and cultural aspirations of the communities that created, cherished, and transmitted the many Baruch texts and traditions: some groups valued sages while others valued apocalyptic seers. These images tell us more about these people than about the historical Baruch ben Neriah himself. The pseudepigraphic imagination, thus, is part of a larger exegetical imagination whose goal was to make the biblical traditions relevant to each new generation. By reinventing Baruch ben Neriah, the ancient tradents of Baruch texts and traditions made Baruch address issues relevant to later generations. Although some would deny Baruch the prophetic mantle, others viewed him as an ideal prophet, sage, and seer. Baruch's legacy was greater than even he could have imagined. According to Jer 45:5, God told Baruch that he should not seek "great things": "But you, do you seek great things for yourself? Do not seek them" (Jer 45:5). What these "great things" that Baruch sought are is not entirely clear; but, as we have seen, they appear to be either the position of prophet, the reception of divine revelation, or some leading role in the community. God's response to Baruch's quest for these "great things" was unambiguous: "Do not seek them!" Nonetheless, according to the Jewish and Christian texts and traditions discussed here, later generations imagined Baruch as a sage, a prophet, a recipient of divine revelations, and a leader of the community. Thus, Baruch's legacy was quite remarkable. He ultimately obtained, albeit only in death, the "great things" he sought.

Notes

Preface

1. My publications resulting from this research include *The Cosmography of the Greek Apocalypse of Baruch and its Affinities,* Ph.D. diss., Brandeis University, 1992; "Baruch: An Ideal Sage," in *"Go to the Land I Will Show You": Studies in Honor of Dwight W. Young,* ed. Joseph P. Coleson and Victor Matthews (Winona Lake, Ind.: Eisenbrauns, 1996), 193–210; "The Social Setting of the Syriac Apocalypse of Baruch," *JSP* 16 (1997): 83–98; "Baruch: His Evolution from Scribe to Apocalyptic Seer," in *Biblical Figures outside the Bible,* ed. Michael E. Stone and Theodore A. Bergren (Harrisburg, Pa.: Trinity Press International, 1998), 264–89; and "Books of Baruch," *Dictionary of New Testament Background,* ed. Craig A. Evans and Stanley E. Porter (Downers Grove, Ill./Leicester: InterVarsity Press, 2000), 148–51.

Chapter 1

1. Various forms of the name are widely attested in the biblical and Second Temple periods. See Martin Noth, *Die israelitschen Personennamen in Rahmen der gemeinsemitischen Namengebung* (Hildesheim: Georg Olms Verlagsbuchhandlung, 1966), 183; Michael David Coogan, *West Semitic Personal Names in the Murashu Documents,* HSM 7 (Missoula, Mont.: Scholars Press, 1976), 12, 16–19, 69–70; Ran Zadok, *The Jews in Babylonia during the Chaldean and Achaemenian Periods according to the Babylonian Sources* (Haifa: University of Haifa, 1979); Michael H. Silverman, *Religious Values in the Jewish Proper Names at Elephantine* (Kevelaer: Verlag Butzon & Bereker, 1985), 73, 138–39, 259; Jeaneane D. Fowler, *Theophoric Personal Names in Ancient Hebrew,* JSOTSup 49 (Sheffield: Sheffield Academic Press, 1988), 90, 152, 213, 339; and Nahman Avigad, *Corpus of West Semitic Stamp Seals,* rev. and completed by Benjamin Sass (Jerusalem: Israel Academy of Sciences, Israel Exploration Society, and Institute of Archaeology, Hebrew University of Jerusalem, 1997), 111, 417, 464, cf. 779, 863, 926, 943, 1108.

2. This movement is aptly described by Moshe Weinfeld in *Deuteronomy and the Deuteronomic School* (Oxford: Clarendon Press, 1972). The accounts of Josiah's reign are found in 2 Kgs 22:1–23:30 and 2 Chron 34:1–35:27.

3. Note Nadav Na'aman's discussion of the historicity of the biblical account of similar reforms under Hezekiah: "The Debated Historicity of Hezekiah's Reform in the Light of Historical and Archaeological Research," *ZAW* 107 (1995): 181–95.

4. See 2 Kgs 23:30–34; 2 Chron 36:1–4.

5. For a survey of the Neo-Babylonian period, see H. W. F. Saggs, *The Babylonians,* Peoples of the Past 1 (Norman: University of Oklahoma Press, 1995), 163–75.

6. See 2 Kgs 24:8–16, 25:27–30; 2 Chron 36:9–10.

7. For ancient Near Eastern scribes and scribalism, see Peter T. Daniels, "Scribes and Scribal Techniques," *OEANE,* 4.500–502; and Philip R. Davies, *Scribes and Schools: The Canonization of the Hebrew Scriptures,* Library of Ancient Israel (Louisville, Ky.: Westminster/John Knox Press, 1998), 17–30, 74–88. Note also the following essays in *Civilizations of the Ancient Near East,* 4 vols., ed. Jack M. Sasson (New York: Charles Scribner's Sons, 1995): "Archives and Libraries in the Ancient Near East," by J. A. Black and W. J. Tait (4.2197–2209), "The Scribes of Egypt," by Edward F. Wente (4.2211–21), and "The Scribes and Scholars of Ancient Mesopotamia," by Laurie E. Pearce (4.2265–78).

8. Albright quoted from a discussion of "Scribal Concepts of Education," recorded in *City Invincible: A Symposium on Urbanization and Cultural Development in the Ancient Near East Held at the Oriental Institute of the University of Chicago, December 4–7, 1958,* ed. Carl H. Kraeling and Robert M. Adams (Chicago: University of Chicago Press, 1960), 123.

9. The familial and professional settings for learning are nicely surveyed by James L. Crenshaw in *Education in Ancient Israel: Across the Deadening Silence,* ABRL (New York: Doubleday, 1998). Note also E. Lipinski, "Royal and State Scribes in Ancient Jerusalem," in *Congress Volume, Jerusalem, 1986,* VTSup 40, ed. J. A. Emerton (Leiden: E. J. Brill, 1988), 157–64; and Nili S. Fox, *In the Service of the King: Officialdom in Ancient Israel and Judah,* Monographs of the Hebrew Union College 23 (Cincinnati: Hebrew Union College Press, 2000).

10. On the side supporting the existence of an organized school system are, among others, André Lemaire, *Les écoles et la formation de la Bible dans l'ancien Israël,* OBO 39 (Fribourg: Éditions Universitaires/Göttingen: Vandenhoeck & Ruprecht, 1981); E. W. Heaton, *The School Tradition of the Old Testament* (Oxford: Oxford University Press, 1994); and to an extent, Emile Puech, "Les écoles dans l'Israël préexilique: Donées épigraphiques," *Congress Volume, Jerusalem, 1986,* ed. J. A. Emerton, 189–203. Among the many scholars who doubt the existence of a widespread educational system are Graham I. Davies, in "Were There Schools in Ancient Israel?" in *Wisdom in Ancient Israel: Essays in*

Honour of J. A. Emerton, ed. John Day, Robert P. Gordon, and H. G. M. Williamson (Cambridge: Cambridge University Press, 1995), 199–211; Menahem Haran, "On the Diffusion of Literacy and Schools in Ancient Israel," in *Congress Volume, Jerusalem, 1986,* ed. J. A. Emerton, 81–95; Crenshaw, "Education in Ancient Israel," *JBL* 104 (1985): 601–15; Crenshaw, *Education in Ancient Israel,* 85–113; Davies, *Scribes and Schools,* 74–88; and Stuart Weeks, *Early Israelite Wisdom,* Oxford Theological Monographs (Oxford: Clarendon Press/ New York: Oxford University Press, 1994), 132–56. Lemaire, in *Les écoles,* 93n. 70, and Crenshaw, in *Education in Ancient Israel,* 2–5n. 6, provide thorough lists of previous studies on this topic.

11. Lachish Letter III. See Harry Torczyner, *Lachish I: The Lachish Letters* (London: Oxford University Press, 1938), 45–73, and F. M. Cross, "A Literate Soldier: Lachish Letter III," in *Biblical and Related Studies Presented to Samuel Iwry,* ed. A. Kort and S. Morschauser (Winona Lake, Ind.: Eisenbrauns, 1985), 41–47.

12. William G. Dever, "Iron Age Epigraphic Material from the Area of Khirbet el-Kôm," *HUCA* 40–41 (1969–70): 139–204; Ze'ev Meshel, "Kuntillet Ájrud—An Israelite Site from the Monarchical Period on the Sinai Border," *Qadmoniot* 9 (1976):118–24 [Hebrew].

13. See Avigad, *Corpus of West Semitic Stamp Seals.*

14. The debate over the extent of literacy in ancient Israel has raged for decades. Note the following: Alan R. Millard, "The Practice of Writing in Ancient Israel," *BA* 35 (1972): 98–111; Millard, "An Assessment of the Evidence for Writing in Ancient Israel," in *Biblical Archaeology Today: Proceedings of the International Congress on Biblical Archaeology, Jerusalem, April 1984,* ed. Janet Amitai (Jerusalem: Israel Exploration Society, 1985), 301–12; and Joseph Naveh, "A Paleographic Note on the Distribution of the Hebrew Script," *HTR* 61 (1968): 68–74. More recently William M. Schniedewind, in *Society and the Promise to David* (Oxford and New York: Oxford University Press, 1999), 74–77, has suggested that "literacy had spread well beyond the narrow confines of scribal schools," and that "[r]eading and writing were accessible to all classes" (75). His are some of the strongest statements in favor of widespread literacy in the on-going debate over the extent of literacy in ancient Israel and Judah. David W. Jamieson-Drake, in *Scribes and Schools in Monarchic Judah: A Socio-Archaeological Approach,* JSOTSup 109, Social World of Biblical Antiquity Series 9 (Sheffield: Almond Press, 1991), concludes that "schools"—a place outside the home where potential administrators were trained in reading and writing by a paid teacher—existed only in the late monarchic period.

15. Note Aaron Demsky, "Writing in Ancient Israel and Early Judaism, Part

One: The Biblical Period," in *Mikra: Text, Translation, Reading and Interpretation of the Hebrew Bible in Ancient Judaism and Early Christianity,* ed. Martin J. Mulder; CRIANT 2.1 (Assen: Van Gorcum/Philadelphia: Fortress Press, 1988) 1–20; Haran, "Diffusion of Literacy," 91–95; and Gerhard von Rad, *Wisdom in Ancient Israel,* 15–23. The fine study of state officials by Tryggve N. D. Mettinger, *Solomonic State Officials: A Study of the Civil Government Officials of the Israelite Monarchy,* ConBOT 5 (Lund: Gleerups Forlag, 1971), overemphasizes the influence of Egyptian bureaucracy on its Israelite counterpart.

16. The first part of the excerpt, through the line "than a tomb in the west," is taken from Papyrus Lansing, quoted from Miriam Lichtheim, *Ancient Egyptian Literature: A Book of Readings,* 3 vols. (Berkeley: University of California Press, 1973–80), 2.168; the remainder of the excerpt is from Chester Beatty Papyrus IV, quoted from Lichtheim, *Ancient Egyptian Literature,* 2.175.

17. Alan H. Gardiner, "Ramesside Texts Relating to the Taxation and Transport of Corn," *Journal of Egyptian Archaeology* 27 (1941): 19–20; cf. Lichtheim, *Ancient Egyptian Literature,* 2.170.

18. Davies, *Scribes and Schools,* 74–75; cf. A. Leo Oppenheim, *Ancient Mesopotamia: Portrait of a Dead Civilization* (Chicago: University of Chicago Press, 1964), 235–49.

19. For the Hebrew Bible note for example:1 Kgs 21:8; Esth 3:10, 12, 8:6, 8, 10; Neh 10:1–2; Job 9:7, 14:17, 41:15; Song 8:6; Isa 8:16, 29:11; Jer 32:10–11, 14, 44; Ezek 28:12; Dan 6:18, 8:26, 9:24, 12:4, 9. See also Avigad, "Hebrew Seals and Sealings and Their Significance for Biblical Research," in *Congress Volume: Jerusalem 1986,* 7–16, and "The Contribution of Hebrew Seals to an Understanding of Israelite Religion and Society," in *Ancient Israelite Religion: Essays in Honor of Frank Moore Cross,* ed. P. D. Miller, P. D. Hanson, and S. D. McBride (Philadelphia: Fortress Press), 195–208.

20. Avigad, *West Semitic Stamp Seals,* 18; Vaughn, "Palaeographic Dating of Judean Seals and Its Significance for Biblical Research," *BASOR* 313 (1999): 43–64. Bob Becking's skepticism as to the value of these artifacts for biblical studies seems excessive. See Becking "Inscribed Seals as Evidence for Biblical Israel? Jeremiah 40:7–41:15 *par example,*" in *Can a "History of Israel" Be Written?,* ed. Lester L. Grabbe, JSOTSup 245 (Sheffield: Sheffield Academic Press, 1997), 65–83. Larry Herr, *The Scripts of Ancient Northwest Semitic Seals,* HSM 18 (Missoula, Mont.: Scholars Press, 1978); cf. Herr, "Paleography and the Identification of Seal Owners," *BASOR* 254 (1980): 67–70.

21. Avigad, "Baruch the Scribe and Jerahmeel the King's Son," *IEJ* 28:1–2 (1978): 52–56; Avigad, "Jerahmeel & Baruch: King's Son and Scribe," *BA* 42:2 (1979): 114–18; and Avigad, *Hebrew Bullae from the Time of Jeremiah: Remnants*

of a Burnt Archive (Jerusalem: Israel Exploration Society, 1986). See also Tsvi Schneider, "Six Biblical Signatures: Seals and Seal Impressions of Six Biblical Personages Recovered," *BARev* 17:4 (July/August 1991): 26–33; Hershel Shanks, "Jeremiah's Scribe and Confidant Speaks from a Hoard of Clay Bullae," *BARev* 13:5 (1987): 58–65, and "Fingerprint of Jeremiah's Scribe," *BARev* 22:2 (March/April 1996): 36–38; and Philip J. King, *Jeremiah: An Archaeological Companion* (Louisville, Ky.: Westminster/John Knox Press, 1993), 85–101.

22. While N. P. Lemche questions the authenticity of these seals—see *BARev* 23:4 (July/August 1997): 37–38—Shmuel Ahituv concludes that the identification with Jeremiah's scribe Baruch "appears certain" (נראה כוודאי)—*Handbook of Ancient Hebrew Inscriptions: From the First Temple Period to the Beginning of the Second Temple Period* (Jerusalem: Bialik, 1992), 129 [Hebrew].

23. On Baruch and the social standing of scribes, see J. R. Lundbom, "Baruch, Seraiah, and Expanded Colophons in the Book of Jeremiah," *JSOT* 36 (1986): 107–8.

24. Similarly, Jer 36:1–4 notes that God told Jeremiah to compose a written account of all the messages he had given to him through the years. Jeremiah, rather than compose this document himself, immediately summoned Baruch and "Baruch wrote on the scroll at Jeremiah's dictation everything Yahweh had said to him" (36:4). God explicitly told Jeremiah to "take a scroll and write on it" (36:1), yet the prophet had Baruch do this. Although it may be that Jeremiah was not adequately literate to compose such a long document, it seems most likely that he asked Baruch to do this because writing was Baruch's profession and he knew all the formal protocols. Karel van der Toorn, "From the Oral to the Written: The Case of Old Babylonian Prophecy," in *Writings and Speech in Israelite and Ancient Near Eastern Prophecy*, ed. Ehud Ben Zvi and Michael H. Floyd; SBL Symposium Series 10 (Atlanta, Ga.: Society of Biblical Literature, 2000), 228–32, notes that, like Jeremiah, some Babylonian prophets used scribes to do the actual writing. The final written record, therefore, would have been influenced by the work of the scribe. "Since a scribe in antiquity is also an editor, the letters by prophets cannot be regarded, without qualification, as the transcript of the *ipsissima verba* of the prophet. Nor do the revelation of the message and its dictation coincide; the few days that lay between them may have erased or added certain details in the memory of the prophet" (Ibid., 229). The same obviously obtains, *mutatis mutandi*, with regard to the biblical prophecies.

25. Hebrew text can be found in Yohanan Aharoni, *Arad Inscriptions*, trans. Judith Ben-Or; ed. and rev. Anson Rainey (Jerusalem: Israel Exploration Society, 1981), 32–34.

26. See Yigael Yadin, *Bar-Kochba: The Rediscovery of the Legendary Hero of the Last Jewish Revolt against Imperial Rome* (London: Weidenfeld and Nicolson, 1971).

27. The phrase "in the hearing of" indicates that the text was read aloud, and in a public context this may suggest that the text being read is in some way important or authoritative. On this use of the phrase, see Harry M. Orlinsky, *Essays in Biblical Culture and Bible Translation* (New York: KTAV, 1974), 258–61; and Orlinsky, "The Septuagint as Holy Writ and the Philosophy of the Translators," *HUCA* 46 (1975): 94–96.

28. The principle texts with transcriptions and translations are published in Jean-Marie Durand, *Archives Épistolaires de Mari I/1,* ARM XXVI (Paris: Editions Recherche sur Civilisations, 1988), and Dominique Charpin, Francis Joannès, Sylvie Lackenbacher, and Bertrand Lafont, *Archives Épistolaires de Mari I/2,* ARM XXVI (Paris: Editions Recherche sur Civilisations, 1988). Note also Georges Dossin, *La correspondance féminine: transcrite et traduite,* ARM X (Paris: Librairie Orientaliste Paul Geuthner, 1978).

29. The literature on prophecy and divination at Mari is considerable, but the following, albeit early articles, are particularly valuable: Abraham Malamat, "Prophetic Revelations in New Documents from Mari and the Bible," *Volume du congrès, Genève 1965,* ed. G. W. Anderson, et al.; VTSup 15 (Leiden: E. J. Brill, 1966), 207–27; and William L. Moran, "New Evidence from Mari on the History of Prophecy," *Biblica* 50 (1969): 15–56. More recently, the Mari and other Mesopotamian evidence for "prophetic" activity continues to be studied, and in this regard the following collections are particularly noteworthy: Martti Nissinen and Simo Parpola, eds., *References to Prophecy in Neo-Assyrian Sources,* State Archives of Assyria Studies 7 (Helsinki: Neo-Assyrian Text Corpus Project, 1998); and Martti Nissinen, ed., *Prophecy in Its Ancient Near Eastern Context: Mesopotamian, Biblical, and Arabian Perspectives,* SBL Symposium Series 13 (Atlanta, Ga.: Society of Biblical Literature, 2000).

30. van der Toorn, "From the Oral to the Written," 225–33, describes the process of transmitting prophecies to Babylonian kings, and this process has many features in common with the events described in Jer 36. Thus, the Israelite protocols appear to have been part of a larger ancient Near Eastern cultural complex about how divine messages are passed-on to the king.

31. See also Moran, "New Evidence," 29–31.

32. The *apilum* is one of the higher ranks of diviners. Note also Huffmon's descriptions the various prophetic professionals—"A Company of Prophets: Mari, Assyria, Israel," Nissinen, *Prophecy in Its Ancient Near Eastern Context,* 47–70; cf. *CAD* 1:A, 2.170.

33. See also Moshe Anbar, "Mari and the Origin of Prophecy," *Kinattūtu ša*

dārâti: Raphael Kutscher Memorial Volume, ed. A. F. Rainey (Tel Aviv: Tel Aviv University Institute of Archaeology, 1993), 3–5.

34. See William H. Holladay, "The Identification of the Two Scrolls of Jeremiah," *VT* 30 (1980): 452–67. But does this passage provide an accurate model for how the Jeremianic corpus was compiled? Discounting the traditional views of Baruch's role in the production of this book, Robert P. Carroll, *Jeremiah,* OTL (London: SCM Press, 1986), 44–45, 61, and Carroll, "Arguing about Jeremiah: Recent Studies and the Nature of a Prophetic Book," *Congress Volume: Leuven 1989,* ed. J. A. Emerton, VTSup 43 (Leiden: E. J. Brill, 1991), 222–35, argues that this passage cannot be used to identify who wrote any part of Jeremiah. See also Gunther Wanke, *Untersuchungen zur sogenannten Baruchschrift,* BZAW 122 (Berlin: Walter de Gruyter, 1971). For a more traditional approach to this question, see J. Muilenburg, "Baruch the Scribe," *Proclamation and Presence,* ed. John I. Durham and J. R. Porter (Richmond, Va.: John Knox Press, 1970), 232–38. Richard Elliott Friedman, *Who Wrote the Bible* (New York: Summit Books, 1987), 146–49, proposes that Baruch may also have had a hand in the composition of the Deuteronomistic History, thereby becoming one of the authors/editors of a major portion of the Hebrew Bible. Friedman's opinion clearly grows out of the long-held but unverifiable thesis that Baruch composed the book of Jeremiah.

35. See also Martin Kessler, "Form-Critical Suggestions on Jer. 36," *CBQ* 28 (1966): 389–401; and Christopher R. Seitz, "The Prophet Moses and the Canonical Shape of Jeremiah," *ZAW* 101 (1989): 13–14.

36. See the related Akkadian term nabū, meaning "to name, summon, appoint, or cause to perform"; *CAD* 11:N, 1.32–39.

37. Davies, *Scribes and Schools,* 18–19, notes the characteristically detached nature of the scribal profession.

38. For additional detail about the traditions regarding Baruch's fate, see chapter four: "Baruch in Later Jewish, Christian, and Islamic Tradition."

39. This is pointed out also by Walter Brueggemann, "The 'Baruch Connection': Reflections on Jer 43:1–7," *JBL* 113:3 (1994): 408–9. Brueggemann focuses on the fictional aspects of the story, although he has not dismissed its potential historicity as thoroughly as Carroll has. I prefer to view the potential historicity of the Baruch pericopes more positively than does Carroll. A similar historical approach can be found in J. Andrew Dearman, "My Servants the Scribes: Composition and Context in Jeremiah 36," *JBL* 109:3 (1990): 403–21.

40. The early history of Egyptian Jewry can be found in Joseph Mélèze Modrzejewski, *The Jews of Egypt: From Rameses II to Emperor Hadrian,* trans. Robert Cornman (Philadelphia: Jewish Publication Society, 1995).

41. Brueggemann, "Baruch Connection," 409–12.

42. The opening line of 45:1 repeats the exact dating formula of 36:1, thus connecting the chapter on Jeremiah's scroll of disaster and Baruch's oracle. There are several other verbal similarities between 45:1 and 36:4, further indicating the editor's clear intention to link these two stories to one another. On the use of repetitive resumption as a linking device in the Hebrew Bible, see Shemaryahu Talmon, "The Presentation of Synchroneity and Simultaneity in Biblical Narrative," in *Studies in Hebrew Narrative Art through the Ages*, ed. Joseph Heinemann and S. Werses, Scripta Hierosolymitana 27 (Jerusalem: Magnes Press, 1978), 9–26.

43. Note that the verbal root here connoting labor or growing weary, יגע, appears also in Jeremiah 45:3, and this is a further indication that Jeremiah is purposefully alluding to these texts.

44. Compare, for example, Hans W. Wolff, *Joel and Amos: A Commentary on the Books of the Prophets Joel and Amos*, Hermeneia (Philadelphia: Fortress Press, 1977), 350–55; Francis I. Andersen and David Noel Freedman, *Amos: A New Translation with Introduction and Commentary*, AB 24A (New York: Doubleday, 1989), 141–44, 893, 919–26; and Shalom M. Paul, *Amos: A Commentary on the Book of Amos*, Hermeneia (Minneapolis: Fortress Press, 1991), 288–95.

45. On Baruch's alleged prophetic status, see "Baruch the Prophet" in chapter 4 below.

46. Similar conclusions were reached by Hannelis Schulte, "Baruch und Ebedmelech—Persönliche Heilsorakel im Jeremiabuche," *BZ* 32:2 (1988): 257–65.

47. Brueggemann, "Baruch Connection," 415; Marion Ann Taylor, "Jeremiah 45: The Problem of Placement," *JSOT* 37 (1987): 92–94.

48. Duhm, *Das Buch Jeremia*, Kurzer Hand-Commentar zum Alten Testament 11 (Tübingen: J. C. B. Mohr [P. Siebeck]), 1901.

49. Sigmund Mowinckel, *Zur Komposition des Buches Jeremia* (Kristiania: J. Dybwad, 1914). Mowinckel added another category of material, "D," which consists of material with characteristically deuteronomistic phraseology. Most scholars have treated Mowinckel's "D" material as part of "C."

50. William L. Holladay, *Jeremiah: A Commentary on the Book of the Prophet Jeremiah*, 2 vols., Hermeneia (Minneapolis: Fortress Press, 1986/1989), note especially 1.1–10 and 2.1–95; John Bright, *Jeremiah*, AB (Garden City, N.Y.: Doubleday & Co., 1965). Of particular value are two reviews of these Jeremiah commentaries: Walter Brueggemann, "Jeremiah: Intense Criticism/Thin Interpretation," *Int* 42 (1988): 268–80, and Robert P. Carroll, "Radical Clashes of Will and Style: Recent Commentary Writing on the Book of Jeremiah," *JSOT* 45 (1989): 99–114.

51. Among his many contributions in this area, see Carroll, *From Chaos to*

Covenant: Uses of Prophecy in the Book of Jeremiah (London: SCM/New York: Crossroad, 1981), 5–30, Carroll, *Jeremiah,* OTL (London: SCM Press, 1986). See Carroll's surveys of the issues in "Surplus Meaning and the Conflict of Interpretations: A Dodecade of Jeremiah Studies (1984–95)," *CRBS* 4 (1996): 115–59, and "Century's End: Jeremiah Studies at the Beginning of the Third Millennium," *CRBS* 8 (2000): 18–58. See also J. M. Ward, "The Eclipse of the Prophet in Contemporary Prophetic Studies," *USQR* 42 (1988): 97–104; and Seitz, "Canonical Shape of Jeremiah."

52. In a similar fashion E. W. Nicholson, *Preaching to the Exiles: A Study of the Prose Tradition in the Book of Jeremiah* (Oxford: Blackwell, 1970), 111–13, finds that although Baruch neither composed the book of Jeremiah nor created the prophet's persona, he did record the prophet's words and deeds, and it was in part from Baruch's records that later authors and editors fashioned the prophet's persona as well as the book as we have it.

53. Dearman, "My Servants the Scribes," 418. In a similar manner David A. Glatt-Gilad, "The Personal Names in Jeremiah as a Source for the History of the Period," *Hebrew Studies* 41 (2000): 31–45, uses onomastic evidence to support the essential historical reliability of the prose material in Jeremiah.

54. William McKane, *A Critical and Exegetical Commentary on Jeremiah,* 2 vols., ICC (Edinburgh: T. & T. Clark, 1986/1996); see Brueggemann, "Baruch Connection," and *A Commentary on Jeremiah: Exile and Homecoming* (Grand Rapids, Mich.: Eerdmans, 1998), 338–417. Note also the perceptive linkages between prophetic literature and history proposed by Robert R. Wilson, *Prophecy and Society in Ancient Israel* (Philadelphia: Fortress Press, 1980), 231–51, and Wilson, "Historicizing the Prophets: History and Literature in the Book of Jeremiah," in *On the Way to Nineveh: Studies in Honor of George M. Landes* (Atlanta, Ga.: ASOR/Scholars Press, 1999), 136–54.

55. See Dearman, "My Servants the Scribes," 418–21. Dearman proposes that the authors/editors of the Deuteronomistic History are also to be found among such a group of scribes. Alexander Rofé, "Studies in the Composition of the Book of Jeremiah," *Tarbitz* 44 (1974–75): 1–29 [Hebrew], likewise locates the composition of the book among Jeremiah's disciples and scribes. Note also Stephen A. Kaufman, "Rhetoric, Redaction, and Message in Jeremiah," in *Judaic Perspectives on Ancient Israel,* ed. Jacob Neusner, Baruch A. Levine, and Ernest S. Frerichs (Philadelphia: Fortress Press, 1987), 63–74, who by examining structure and ideology attempts to trace how Jeremiah and his disciples shaped and reshaped the materials in this book.

56. For background on the Septuagint, see Sidney Jellicoe, *The Septuagint and Modern Study* (Oxford: Clarendon Press, 1968); Emanuel Tov, "The Septuagint,"

in *Mikra: Text, Translation, Reading and Interpretation of the Hebrew Bible in Ancient Judaism and Early Christianity*, ed. M. J. Mulder (Assen/Philadelphia: Van Gorcum/Fortress Press, 1988), 161–88; and M. K. H. Peters, "Septuagint," *ABD*, 5.1093–1104.

57. On the complicated relations between these two versions of the book of Jeremiah, see the following: Emanuel Tov, *The Septuagint Translation of Jeremiah and Baruch: A Discussion of an Early Revision of Jeremiah 29–52 and Baruch 1:1–3:8*, HSM 8 (Missoula, Mont.: Scholars Press, 1976), Tov, "L'incidence de la critique textuelle sur la critique littéraire dans le livre de Jérémie," *RB* 79 (1972): 189–99, and Tov, *Textual Criticism of the Hebrew Bible* (Minneapolis/Assen: Fortress/van Gorcum, 1992), 319–27; Jerald G. Janzen, *Studies in the Text of Jeremiah*, HSM 6 (Cambridge: Harvard University Press, 1973), 1–9; and Louis Stulman, *The Other Text of Jeremiah: A Reconstruction of the Hebrew Text Underlying the Greek Version of the Prose Sections of Jeremiah with English Translation* (Lanham, Md.: University Press of America, 1985), and Stulman, "Some Theological and Lexical Differences Between the Old Greek and the MT of the Jeremiah Prose Discourses," *Hebrew Studies* 25 (1984): 18–23. Janzen, *Studies*, 2–9 provides a succinct overview of the history of research on this problem. Winfried Thiel, *Die deuteronomistische Redaktion von Jeremia 1–25*, WMANT 41 (Neukirchen-Vluyn: Neukirchener Verlag, 1973) and *Die deuteronomistische Redaktion von Jeremia 26–45*, WMANT 52 (Neukirchen-Vluyn: Neukirchener Verlag, 1981) prefers the priority of the LXX. Sven Soderlund, *The Greek Text of Jeremiah: A Revised Hypothesis*, JSOTSup 47 (Sheffield: JSOT Press, 1985) takes a more traditional approach to the issues and finds that two translators produced the present Greek text, that is, he disagrees with Tov's translator and reviser theory. Moreover, Soderlund maintains that Janzen's—and others—theory that the LXX preserves a superior textual witness than the MT is to facile to account for the many and varied differences between these two witnesses to the text of Jeremiah. While Soderlund's work is meticulous and thorough, his critiques of Tov's and Janzen's works are inconsequential and rarely offer any direct refutation but only alternate perspectives on the issues. Soderlund's book represents a return to older theories in Jeremiah studies.

58. In both versions chapter 52, the final chapter of the book, is a narrative account of the fall of Jerusalem.

59. Martin Kessler, "Jeremiah Chapters 26–45 Reconsidered," *JNES* 27:2 (1968): 86–87, views Baruch as "the next link in the Jeremiah-tradition." P.-M. Bogaert, "De Baruch à Jérémie: Les deux rédactions conservées du livre de Jérémie," *Le livre de Jérémie: Le prophète et son milieu, les oracles et leur transmission*, ed. P.-M. Bogaert, BETL 54 (Leuven: Leuven University Press, 1981),

168–73, notes that the order in the LXX suggests that Baruch will witness both the proclamation of Jeremiah's oracles and their ultimate fulfillment.

60. So Bogaert, "De Baruch à Jérémie," 173; cf. Bogaert, "Le personnage de Baruch et l'histoire du livre de Jérémie: Aux origines du livre de Baruch," *Bulletin of the International Organization for Septuagint and Cognate Studies* 7 (1974): 19 where he says: "The historical function of Baruch is more apparent when it is put back in the original order of the LXX; it is that of a notary who has also included in his responsibilities the act of ascertaining the fulfillment of Jeremiah's prophecies." In Lundbom's opinion, *Jeremiah: A Study in Ancient Hebrew Rhetoric* (Missoula, Mont.: Society of Biblical Literature and Scholars Press, 1975), 25–27, 111, 118–20, and "Baruch, Seraiah, and Expanded Colophons," 99–101, the Hebrew and Greek versions of the book of Jeremiah were edited respectively by Baruch in Egypt and by Baruch's brother Seraiah in Babylon. While the tradition that Baruch went into and remained in Egypt with Jeremiah cannot be fully substantiated (see chapter 4: "Baruch in Later Jewish, Christian, and Islamic Tradition"), it is nonetheless interesting to note that the two versions of Jeremiah close with their alleged editors being addressed in the fifty-first chapter of each of the two versions, Baruch in the Greek version and Seriah in the Masoretic version. See also Wanke, *Baruchschrift*, 133–43; and Axel Graupner, "Jeremia 45 als 'Schlußwort' des Jeremiabuches," in *Altes Testament und christliche Verkündigung: Festschrift für Antnius H. J. Gunneweg zum 65. Geburtstag,* ed. Manfred Oeming and Axel Graupner (Stuttgart: Kohlhammer, 1987), 287–308. In a somewhat similar fashion, Artur Weiser, "Das Gotteswort für Baruch: Jer. 45 und die sogenannte Baruchbiographie," in *Glaube und Geschichte im Alten Testament und andere ausgewählte Schriften,* ed. A. Weiser (Göttingen: Vandenhoeck & Ruprecht, 1961), 321–29, claimed that Baruch himself placed his oracle here in order to show that prophetic statements are always realized and that God favored him.

61. For a survey of the various explanations regarding the placement of chapter 45 in Masoretic Jeremiah, see Taylor, "Jeremiah 45," 79–98. Seitz prefers the priority of the Masoretic version and explains the placement of chapter 45 as the link or transition to the oracles against the nations; see Seitz, "Canonical Shape of Jeremiah," 18–27. Rather than focusing on the placement of the oracles against the nations alone as the motivating factor in this arrangement, I prefer to address the portrayal of Baruch as an important factor. In my view what was at issue was whether or not Baruch should be regarded as the Jeremiah's prophetic successor. As the following chapters will indicate, not only the two versions of Jeremiah but also many Jewish and Christian scholars throughout history have disputed this matter. Bogaert, "De Baruch à Jérémie," 170–71,

notes how the Masoretic version reads "Baruch the scribe and Jeremiah the prophet" at Jer 36:26, while the same passage in the Greek version (Jer 43:26 in LXX) reads "Baruch and Jeremiah." Although Tov and Janzen identify this as an example of the expansionistic tendencies of the Masoretic version of Jeremiah (see Tov, *Septuagint Translation,* and "L'incidence"; and Janzen, *Studies,* 72, 149), I would suggest that the motivation behind this "expansionistic tendency" in the Masoretic version is in part the editor's wish to denigrate the role of Baruch to Jeremiah, or at least to differentiate their roles. Thus, Baruch was merely the well-trained scribe, while Jeremiah was the divinely-inspired prophet. Note also Bogaert, "De Baruch à Jérémie," 171–72, where he details other differences between the Masoretic and the Greek versions of Jeremiah which may have some bearing on the portrayal of Baruch and Jeremiah.

62. James L. Crenshaw, "Transmitting Prophecy across Generations," in *Writings and Speech in Israelite and Ancient Near Eastern Prophecy,* ed. Ehud Ben Zvi and Michael H. Floyd; SBL Symposium Series 10 (Atlanta, Ga.: Society of Biblical Literature, 2000), 37, identifies six components that characterize prophetic activity: "(1) the putative revelatory moment during which an enigmatic vision or word captures the imagination; (2) a period of reflection about the meaning of this captivating message; (3) the articulation of the message in terms of a religious tradition deemed authoritative; (4) the refining of that word or vision by means of poetic language and/or rhetorical style; (5) the addition of supportive arguments, either threatening or comforting; and (6) the actual proclamation, complete with gestures and tone of voice, and occasionally accompanied by symbolic actions." I would add that this sixth step is eventually and obviously followed by the (7) writing, (8) editing, (9) transmitting, and (10) interpretation of these putative divine revelations.

63. In this regard, see David L. Petersen, "Rethinking the Nature of Prophetic Literature," in *Prophecy and Prophets: The Diversity of Contemporary Issues in Scholarship,* ed. Yehoshua Gitay, Society of Biblical Literature Semeia Studies (Atlanta, Ga.: Scholars Press, 1997), 23–40.

64. See Bogaert, *Apocalypse de Baruch: Introduction, traduction du syriaque et commentaire,* Sources Chrétiennes 144–145 (Paris: Le Cerf, 1969), 1.104–8. Note also the following: *b. Meg* 14b and *Sifre Num* §78 (ed. Horowitz, 74) list Baruch, along with his father Neriah and brother Seraiah, as prophet and priests descended from Rahab the harlot; *S. Olam Rab.* 20 (ed. Ratner, 87) lists Baruch as one who prophesied in the days of the destruction of the temple under Nebuchadnezzar. *Mekhilta d'Rabbi Ishmael* Bô (ed. Horowitz-Rabin, 5–6; Lauterbach, 1.14–15) expresses doubts as to Baruch's status as a prophet: "You will also find it with regard to Baruch ben Neriah who was complaining before God.

'You said, *woe is me for the Lord has added sorrow to my pain . . .*' (Jer 45:3). I have been treated differently than the other disciples of the prophets. Joshua served Moses, and the Holy Spirit rested upon him. Elisha served Elijah, and the Holy Spirit rested upon him. But I, why have I been treated differently than the other disciples of the prophets? *I am weary with my groaning and I find no rest* (Jer 45:3). *Rest* here is nothing other than prophecy, as it was said 'and the spirit rested upon them . . . and they prophesied' (Num 11:26). And it says, 'The spirit of Elijah *has rested* upon Elisha' (2 Kgs 2:15). And it says, 'and the spirit of the Lord will rest upon him' (Isa 11:2). Come and see what God replies to him: 'thus you shall say to him, thus says the Lord, behold, that which I have built I will tear down . . . but you seek great things for yourself? Do not seek them' (Jer 45:4–5). The *great things* mentioned here is none other than prophecy as it is said, 'Please tell me all the *great things* that Elisha has done' (2 Kgs 8:4). It also says, 'call to me and I will answer you, and will tell you *great things* and hidden things that you do not know' (Jer 33:3). He said, 'Baruch ben Neriah, there is no vineyard. What need is there for a fence? There is no flock. What need is there for a shepherd? Why? Because, behold, I am bringing evil on all flesh, says the Lord. But your life I will give you as booty wherever you go' (Jer 45:5). Thus you find everywhere that the prophets prophesy only for the sake of Israel." This passage indicates that Baruch sought the prophetic mantle in vane. His error was seeking the prophetic mantle (the *great things*) for his benefit and not Israel's.

Chapter 2

1. Note Michael E. Stone, "Ideal Figures and Social Context: Priest and Sage in the Early Second Temple Period," in *Ancient Israelite Religion: Essays in Honor of Frank Moore Cross,* ed., Patrick D. Miller, et al. (Philadelphia: Fortress Press, 1987), 575–86; John J. Collins, "The Sage in the Apocalyptic and Pseudepigraphic Literature," in *The Sage in Israel and the Ancient Near East,* ed. John G. Gammie and Leo Perdue (Winona Lake, Ind.: Eisenbrauns, 1990), 343–54; and Jacob Neusner, "Sage, Priest, Messiah: Three Types of Judaism in the Age of Jesus," in his *Judaism in the Beginning of Christianity* (Philadelphia: Fortress Press, 1984), 35–44.

2. Christine Schams, *Jewish Scribes in the Second-Temple Period,* JSOTSup 291 (Sheffield: Sheffield Academic Press, 1998) focuses on texts that present Jewish images of scribes in this era. Her study indicates the variety of roles "scribes" played in early Jewish societies. These roles include among others secretary, sage, philosopher, lawyer, and biblical interpreter.

3. Due to standard phonetic principles, the Babylonian term *kašdû* is realized as *kaldû* in Assyrian, i.e., the *šd* becomes *ld*; see *GAG,* 30g.

4. See W. Lee Humphreys, "A Lifestyle for the Diaspora: A Study of the Tales of Esther and Daniel," *JBL* 92 (1973): 211–23; Robert Gnuse, "The Jewish Dream Interpreter in a Foreign Court: The Recurring Use of a Theme in Jewish Literature," *JSP* 7 (1990): 29–53.

5. A. Leo Oppenheim, *The Interpretation of Dreams in the Ancient Near East, with a Translation of an Assyrian Dream-Book,* TAPS 46:3 (Philadelphia: American Philosophical Society, 1956). The ancient Israelites also used standard dream report and interpretation formulae. For details on biblical dream interpretation, see Michael Fishbane, *Biblical Interpretation in Ancient Israel* (Oxford: Clarendon Press, 1985), 447–57.

6. Edited excerpts from dream texts in Oppenheim, *Interpretation of Dreams,* 259–69.

7. This material is discussed by Tzvi Abusch, "Some Reflections on Mesopotamian Witchcraft," in *Religion and Politics in the Ancient Near East,* ed. Adele Berlin (Bethesda: University Press of Maryland, 1996), 21–33. See also Walter Farber, "Witchcraft, Magic, and Divination in Ancient Mesopotamia," *CANE,* 3.1895–1909.

8. The classic treatments of ancient Israelite wisdom traditions are still Gerhard von Rad, *Wisdom in Israel* (Nashville, Tenn.: Abingdon Press, 1972), and James L. Crenshaw, *Old Testament Wisdom: An Introduction,* rev. and enlarged ed. (Louisville, Ky.: Westminster/John Knox Press, 1998). See also Crenshaw, "The Contemplative Life in the Ancient Near East," *CANE,* 4.2445–57; and Lester L. Grabbe, *Priests, Prophets, Diviners, Sages: A Socio-Historical Study of Religious Specialists in Ancient Israel* (Valley Forge, Pa.: Trinity Press International, 1995), 152–80.

9. Crenshaw, *Education in Ancient Israel: Across the Deadening Silence,* ABRL (New York: Doubleday, 1998). One of the major publications on sages, *Sages in Israel and the Ancient Near East,* ed. John G. Gammie and Leo G. Perdue (Winona Lake, Ind.: Eisenbrauns, 1990), addresses the issue from a cross-cultural perspective. Crenshaw, however, (*Education,* 178–79n. 52) identifies critical flaws in the theoretical orientation and the lack of a clear definition in this study.

10. Note the several excellent, up-to-date introductory essays in *The Parallel Apocrypha,* ed. John R. Kohlenberger III (New York/Oxford: Oxford University Press, 1997). Another excellent introduction is that of Daniel J. Harrington, *Invitation to the Apocrypha* (Grand Rapids, Mich.: Eerdmans, 1999). Dated, but still valuable introductions are, among others, Bruce M. Metzger, *An Introduction to*

the Apocrypha (New York/Oxford: Oxford University Press, 1957), and Edgar J. Goodspeed, *The Story of the Apocrypha* (Chicago: University of Chicago Press, 1939).

11. English translations of many of these texts are readily available: *The Apocrypha and Pseudepigrapha of the Old Testament,* 2 vols., ed. James H. Charlesworth (Garden City, N.Y.: Doubleday & Company, Inc., 1983, 1985); *The Apocrypha and Pseudepigrapha of the Old Testament,* 2 vols., ed. R. H. Charles (Oxford: Clarendon Press, 1913); and *The Apocryphal Old Testament,* ed. H. F. D. Sparks (Oxford: Clarendon Press, 1984).

12. See James H. Charlesworth, "A History of Pseudepigrapha Research: The Re-emerging Importance of the Pseudepigrapha," *ANRW* II:19:1 (1979): 54–88; Michael E. Stone, "Why Study the Pseudepigrapha?" *BA* 46:4 (1983): 235–43; and Geza Vermes, "Jewish Studies and New Testament Interpretation," *JJS* 21:1 (1980): 1–17.

13. See Sidney Jellicoe, *The Septuagint and Modern Study* (Oxford: Clarendon Press, 1968), and Emanuel Tov, "The Septuagint," in *Mikra: Text, Translation, Reading and Interpretation of the Hebrew Bible in Ancient Judaism and Early Christianity,* ed. M. J. Mulder, CRIANT (Assen/Philadelphia: Van Gorcum/Fortress Press, 1988), 161–88.

14. P.-M. Bogaert, "Le nom de Baruch dans la littérature pseudépigraphique: L'apocalypse syriaque et le livre deutérocanonique," in *La littérature juive entre Tenach et Mischna: Quelques problèmes,* ed. W. C. Van Unnik, Recherches Bibliques IX (Leiden: E. J. Brill, 1974), 61–72; cf. H. Schmid and W. Speyer, "Baruch," *Jahrbuch für Antike und Christentum,* 17 (Münster: Aschendorffsche Verlagsbuchhandlung, 1974), 185–87.

15. Bogaert, "Nom de Baruch," 65–66. Cf. R. R. Harwell, "The Principal Versions of Baruch" (Ph.D. diss., Yale University, 1915), 60–61.

16. Note that NRSV 1:8 reads ". . . Baruch took the vessels. . . ." The proper name does not appear in the manuscripts but has been added by the translators in an attempt to interpret the admittedly difficult verse. Bogaert, "Le personnage de Baruch," 20, notes that even with the introduction the work is better associated with Jeremiah and not Baruch because the οὗτοι οἱ λόγοι of Bar 1:1 refers back to Jeremiah, the book immediately preceding this one in the Greek Bible, or perhaps the book of which it is a part. Bogaert, "Le personnage de Baruch," 20, dates the work between 63 B.C.E. and 70 C.E.

17. Tov, ed., *Book of Baruch,* and Tov, *The Septuagint Translation of Jeremiah and Baruch: A Discussion of an Early Revision of Jeremiah 29–52 and Baruch 1:1–3:8,* HSM 8 (Missoula, Mont.: Scholars Press, 1976), presents the evidence for the Hebrew *Vorlage* of 1:1–3:8. Harwell, "Principal Versions," 63, and David G.

Burke, *The Poetry of Baruch: A Reconstruction and Analysis of Baruch 3:9–5:9,* SBLSCS 10 (Chico, Calif.: Scholars Press, 1982) present evidence for a Hebrew original for the entire book.

18. In addition to the standard introductions, see B. N. Wambacq, "L'unité du livre de Baruch," *Biblica* 46 (1966): 574–76; Carey Moore, "Toward the Dating of the Book of Baruch," *CBQ* 36 (1974): 312–20; and P.-M. Bogaert, "Le personnage de Baruch et l'histoire du livre de Jérémie: Aux origines du Livre deutérocanonique de Baruch," in *Studia Evangelica, vol. VII: Papers Presented to the Fifth International Congress on Biblical Studies held at Oxford, 1973,* ed. Elizabeth A. Livingstone (Berlin: Akademie Verlag, 1982), 73–81.

19. Bar 1:1—καὶ οὗτοι οἱ λόγοι τοῦ βιβλίου οὓς ἔγραψεν Βαρουχ—draws on the Greek translation of Jeremiah 29:1 (LXX 36:1)—καὶ οὗτοι οἱ λόγοι τῆς βίβλου οὓς ἀπέστειλεν Ιερεμιας.

20. Harry M. Orlinsky, *Essays in Biblical Culture and Bible Translation* (New York: KTAV, 1974), 258–61; "The Septuagint as Holy Writ and the Philosophy of the Translators," *HUCA* 46 (1975): 94–96.

21. Note Humphreys, "Lifestyle for the Diaspora."

22. Like Persian king Cyrus, Baruch sought the restoration of the Temple's cultic vessels that had been plundered by the Babylonians (cf. Ezra 1:7–10; Bar 1:8–9; 2 Kgs 24:13, 25:13–17).

23. In an interesting indication of dependence on the text of Daniel 5 or at least on the same tradition appearing there, Bar 1:11–12 also confuses the relationship of the last Babylonian kings. This passage identifies Belshazzar as Nebuchadnezzar's son when in fact Nebuchadnezzar's son, the one who served as his vice-regent, was Nabonidus.

24. For the links with Daniel in this prayer, see the notes in *The Book of Baruch,* ed. and trans. Emanuel Tov, Texts and Translations 8 (Missoula, Mont.: Scholars Press, 1975), 15–27; Wambacq, "Les prieres de Baruch 1,15–2,19 et de Daniel 9,5–19," *Biblica* 40 (1959): 463–75; and L. E. Tony André, *Les Apocryphes de l'Ancien Testament* (Florence: Osvaldo Paggi, 1903), 251–52. On the question of the possible relationships between the Book of Baruch and the Theodotion translation of Daniel, see Tov, "The Relations Between the Greek Versions of Baruch and Daniel," in *Armenian and Biblical Studies,* ed. Michael E. Stone (Jerusalem: St. James Press, 1976), 27–34.

25. See Moshe Weinfeld, *Deuteronomy and the Deuteronomic School* (Oxford: Clarendon Press, 1972).

26. Thus the original composition of this prayer was made sometime after the composition of the book of Daniel in the Maccabbean period. See J. Schreiner, *Baruch,* Die Neue Echter Bibel Altes Testament 14 (Würzburg: Echter Verlag, 1986).

Tov, *Septuagint Translation,* 165–67, dates the translation into Greek of Jeremiah and the Book of Baruch to some time before 116 B.C.E. based on evidence from ben Sira. Moreover, he dates the revision of this Old Greek translation of these books to the latter part of the second or early part of the first century B.C.E. Moore's dating this prayer as early as the fourth century B.C.E. is rather too early; see Moore, "Toward the Dating," 316–17.

27. Penitent prayers of similar tone are offered by Ezra, another "scribe" and leader of the people, in Ezra 9:5–15 and by Nehemiah in Neh 1:4–11 (note also the communal prayer in Neh 9).

28. Note the study of this material by Burke, *Poetry of Baruch.* See also Crenshaw, *Old Testament Wisdom,* 176–77, who notes a possible dependence on Ben Sira and therefore dates this text to the first century B.C.E.

29. Werner Jaeger's classic, *Paideia: The Ideals of Greek Culture,* 3 vols., trans. Gilbert Highet (New York/Oxford: Oxford University Press, 1939–44), traces how social, moral, and intellectual values were transmitted in Classical Greece. See also Jaeger, *Early Christianity and Greek Paideia* (Cambridge: Belknap/Harvard University Press, 1985).

30. This equation of Wisdom with Torah-obedience is also made by Ben Sira (24:23) and is part of the process of the growing centrality of the Torah as the focal point in the Jewish community. On this, see John J. Collins, *Jewish Wisdom in the Hellenistic Age,* OTL (Louisville: Westminster/John Knox Press, 1997), 1–20, 42–61; Daniel J. Harrington, "The Wisdom of the Scribe According to Ben Sira," in *Ideal Figures in Ancient Judaism,* ed. G. W. E. Nickelsburg and John J. Collins, SCS 12 (Chico, Calif.: Scholars Press, 1980), 181–89, and Crenshaw, *Old Testament Wisdom,* 143–47.

31. Crenshaw, *Education in Ancient Israel,* 253; Ibid., 71.

32. On the character and social functions of Israelite and early Jewish sages and accompanying Wisdom traditions, in addition to Crenshaw, *Education in Ancient Israel,* see Joseph Blenkinsopp, *Sage, Priest, Prophet: Religious and Intellectual Leadership in Ancient Israel,* Library of Ancient Israel (Louisville, Ky.: Westminster/John Knox Press, 1995), 9–65.

33. I treat this issue at length in *The Early History of Heaven* (Oxford/New York: Oxford University Press, 2000).

34. See J. T. Milik, *The Books of Enoch: Aramaic Fragments of Qumran Cave 4* (Oxford: Clarendon Press, 1976), 273–74, and Michael E. Stone, "The Book of Enoch and Judaism in the Third Century B.C.E.," *CBQ* 40 (1978): 479–92.

35. For additional information on the antiquity of the traditions about Enoch's astronomical knowledge, see Milik, *Books of Enoch,* 8–10; James C. VanderKam, *Enoch: A Man for All Generations,* Studies on Personalities of the Old

Testament (Columbia: University of South Carolina Press, 1995); and Christ-fried Böttrich, "Astrologie in der Henochtradition," *ZAW* 109:2 (1997): 222–45.

36. Schreiner, *Baruch*, 47, dates this section to circa 200 B.C.E.

37. See von Rad, *Wisdom in Israel* (New York: Abingdon Press, 1972), 240–62.

38. This unit has several phrases that have close parallels in the *Psalms of Solomon*. It seems likely that the two are depending on another now lost text. See also Moore, "Toward the Dating," 317–19, and R. B. Wright, *"Psalms of Solomon," OTP*, 2.647–49. Because of the apparent connection to the Psalms of Solomon, Schreiner, *Baruch*, 47, dates this text to the middle of the first century B.C.E.

39. The second letter is addressed to "Shemaiah the Nehelamite." In this let-ter Jeremiah rebuffs Shemaiah for sending a letter condemning Jeremiah as a false prophet to a priest in Jerusalem. This letter, whether actual or not, indi-cates the level of hostility that must have existed among prophets with com-peting theological or political views. On this hostility, see Crenshaw, *Prophetic Conflict: Its Effect upon Israelite Religion*, BZAW 124 (Berlin: Walter de Gruyter, 1971). *2 Baruch* ends with Baruch writing letters to two exilic communities (2 Bar. 77:11–87:1). The editor of *2 Maccabees* also used the literary device of let-ters to encourage exiles to remain faithful to Jewish traditions and practices (*2 Macc* 1:1–2:18). The idea of sending letters encouraging exiles seems to have its origin with Jeremiah. A historical event of such letter writing occurred in the fifth century. A Jewish leader working for the Persian administration in Egypt sent a letter in 419 B.C.E. to the Jewish exiles living in the military colony on the island of Elephantine on the Upper Nile and encouraged them to observe the customs of Passover. For texts and translations of what has become known as the "Passover Papyrus," see Bezalel Porten and Ada Yardeni, *Textbook of Ara-maic Documents from Ancient Egypt: 1 Letters*, The Hebrew University Depart-ment of the History of the Jewish People, Texts and Studies for Students (Winona Lake, Ind.: Eisenbrauns, 1986), 54–55, and James M. Lindenberger, *Ancient Aramaic and Hebrew Letters*, ed. Kent H. Richards, *SBL Writings from the Ancient World*, vol. 4 (Atlanta, Ga.: Scholars Press, 1994), 56–58.

40. Lists and details regarding possible biblical allusions in this final section of the book can be found in André, *Apocryphes*, 252, and Burke, *Poetry of Baruch*, 223–58. Quotations or allusions to the *Psalms of Solomon* appear in 5:5,7,8; see Wright, *"Psalms of Solomon," OTP*, 2.647–8.

41. Schreiner, *Baruch*, dates this section to after 63 B.C.E. Moore, "Toward the Dating," 318–19 dates the section 4:4–5:4 to 200–150 B.C.E. and the section 5:5–9 to the first century B.C.E. Moore here as elsewhere pushes the dates back too early based largely on (1) what thematic elements the prayers do not

contain and (2) his claim that the prayers existed prior to their appearance in the written form of the book. Dating these anonymous prayers based on thematic elements is very unreliable since these are common themes indeed and not necessarily restricted to any specific time between 586 B.C.E. and the Herodian period. Moreover, while it is likely that these otherwise anonymous prayers existed prior to their incorporation into this book, this reality does not help date the book itself.

42. *2 Baruch* ends with Baruch giving similar exhortations to the exiles in Babylon (2 Bar 77–87).

43. Note also Bogaert, *Apocalypse de Baruch,* 2.453.

44. For the various traditions on the fates of Baruch and Jeremiah, see chapter 4.

45. Note that according to a "Coptic Jeremiah Apocryphon" edited by Kuhn, Jeremiah hid from king Zedekiah by sitting in a tomb; see K. H. Kuhn, "A Coptic Jeremiah Apocryphon," *Le Muséon* 83:1–2 (1970): 116. This same text later suggests that after arriving in Babylon, Jeremiah sat in a tomb and prayed (Ibid., 308, 315). It is clear that the Coptic text has borrowed and confused the tradition about Baruch sitting in a tomb as mentioned in the *Paraleipomena of Jeremiah*. In this "Coptic Jeremiah Apocryphon" Jeremiah retains his prominence over Baruch. In fact, Baruch is even eclipsed in the narrative by Abimelech.

46. Compare *3 Bar.,* prologue 2, and Kuhn, "Coptic Jeremiah Apocryphon," 112–13, 122–24, 293–94, 320–23.

47. Although some scholars have argued that the Paraleipomena of Jeremiah is a Christian text, the consensus is that this is an originally Jewish text that has undergone some Christian revision, especially 9:10–32. See for example Gerhard Delling, *Jüdische Lehre und Frömmigkeit in den Paralipomena Jeremiae,* BZAW 100 (Berlin: Töpelmann, 1967), 4–17, 34–36, 71–75; Albert-Marie Denis, *Introduction aux pseudépigraphis grecs d'Ancien Testament,* SVTP 1 (Leiden: E. J. Brill, 1970), 74–75; J. Rendel Harris, *The Rest of the Words of Baruch* (London: Clay, 1889), 33–34; S. E. Robinson, "4 Baruch," *OTP* 2.414–15; and Michael E. Stone, "Baruch, Rest of the Words of," *Encyclopedia Judaica,* 16 vols. (Jerusalem/New York: Encyclopaedia Judaica/Macmillan, 1971–72), 4.276–77.

48. Agrippa I was made "king" first of regions to the east and north of the Sea of Galilee by Emperor Caligula in 37 C.E., and then Emperor Claudius added all of Judea, Samaria, and the Galilee to his kingdom, which he then ruled from 41–44 C.E. The reference to "the vineyard of Agrippa" is a clear indication that this text dates to sometime after this period.

49. See Bogaert, *Apocalypse de Baruch,* 177–221; Robinson, "4 Baruch," *OTP* 2.414–17; Harris, *Rest of the Words of Baruch,* 33–34.

50. See George W. E. Nickelsburg, "Narrative Traditions in the Paraleipomena of Jeremiah and 2 Baruch," *CBQ* 35 (1973): 60–68, and Nickelsburg, "Stories of Biblical and Early Post-Biblical Times," *Jewish Writings of the Second Temple Period,* ed. Michael E. Stone, CRIANT 2.2 (Van Gorcum/Philadelphia: Assen/Fortress Press, 1984), 72–75.

51. See *2 Bar.* 10:5; *3 Bar.* Introduction.

52. Greek text here according to *Paraleipomena Jeremiou,* ed. Robert A. Kraft and Ann-Elizabeth Purintun, Texts and Translations 1 (Missoula, Mont.: Society of Biblical Literature, 1972). For an English translation of *2 Baruch,* see A. F. J. Klijn, "2 (Syriac Apocalypse of) Baruch," *OTP,* 1.615–52.

53. The personal pronouns indicate that several people are being referred to here and not just Jeremiah or Baruch, i.e., the plural ὑμῶν is used in *Paraleipomena of Jeremiah* 1:2 and not the singular σοῦ, while in *2 Bar.* 2:1 it is the plural ʿbdykwn and not the singular ʿbdyk. One would expect to see the singular form of the personal pronouns in each of these cases if the author intended to refer to either Jeremiah or Baruch alone.

54. Nickelsburg, "Narrative Traditions," 60–68, convincingly demonstrates that *2 Bar.* and Par. Jer. depended on a common source. Compare Bogaert, *Apocalypse de Baruch,* 1.177–221, who argues for the dependence of Par. Jer. on 2 Bar.

55. For the words used to describe Baruch and Jeremiah in the *Paraleipomena of Jeremiah* and what these terms indicate about this text's images of Baruch and Jeremiah and their relationship to one another, see Delling, *Jüdische Lehre,* 18–29, and Jean Riaud, "La figure de Jérémie dans les *Paralipomena Jeremiae,*" *Mélanges bibliques et orientaux en l'honneur de M. Henri Cazelles,* AOAT 212 (Kevelaer/Neukirchen-Vluyn: Verlag Butzon & Bercker/Neukirchener Verlag, 1981), 373–85.

56. Note *2 Bar.* 33:1–3 where the people in Jerusalem quote a command Jeremiah gave to Baruch to remain in Jerusalem to care for the people in Jeremiah's absence. This passage indicates that Baruch was Jeremiah's successor, but it also suggests that Jeremiah remained superior to Baruch until he left for Babylon. The command quoted by the people occurs nowhere in *2 Bar.,* or elsewhere in the Baruch literature to my knowledge.

57. The traditions represented in Par. Jer. may view both Baruch and Abimelech (i.e., the Ebed-Melech mentioned in Jer 38:1–13, 39:15–18) as Jeremiah's successors. Whenever Jeremiah addresses Baruch in this book he speaks to both Baruch and Abimelech, apparently viewing the two as equally his disciples or successors while he is in Babylon (see Par. Jer. 7:16, 32; 8:7; 9:7–8, 26, 29, 32). Par. Jer. 9:23–29 is of particular importance because here Jeremiah delivers to both Baruch and Abimelech "all the mysteries which he had seen." Although this chapter evidences clear Christian editorial activity, this does not mean that

the entire work is a Christian production, see Harris, *Rest of the Words of Baruch*, 13–17, and Delling, *Jüdische Lehre*, 34–36, 68–74.

Chapter 3

1. For the issues and texts relating to apocalyptic literature and movements in early Judaism and Christianity, see John J. Collins, *The Apocalyptic Imagination: An Introduction to the Jewish Matrix of Christianity* (New York: Crossroad, 1984); Michael E. Stone, "Apocalyptic Literature," in *Jewish Writings of the Second Temple Period*, ed. Michael E. Stone, CRIANT 2.2 (Assen/Philadelphia: Van Gorcum/Fortress, 1984), 433–35; George W. E. Nickelsburg, "Social Aspects of Palestinian Jewish Apocalypticism," in *Apocalypticism in the Mediterranean World and the Near East: Proceedings of the International Colloquium on Apocalypticism, Uppsala, August 12–17, 1979,* ed. David Hellholm, 2d ed. (Tübingen: J. C. B. Mohr [Paul Siebeck], 1989), 641–50; and Paul D. Hanson, "Apocalypse, Genre," and "Apocalypticism," in *Interpreter's Dictionary of the Bible, Supplementary Volume* (Nashville, Tenn.: Abingdon Press, 1976), 27–34.

2. Note John J. Collins, "Apocalyptic Eschatology as the Transcendence of Death," *CBQ* 44 (1982): 91–111.

3. See Adolfo Roitman, *A Day at Qumran: The Dead Sea Sect and Its Scrolls* (Jerusalem: The Israel Museum, 1997).

4. Devorah Dimant, "Men as Angels: The Self-Image of the Qumran Community," in *Religion and Politics in the Ancient Near East,* ed. Adele Berlin (Bethesda: University Press of Maryland, 1996), 93–103.

5. Adela Yarbro Collins, "Introduction," in *Early Christian Apocalypticism: Genre and Social Setting,* ed. Adela Yarbro Collins, Semeia 36 (Decatur, Ga.: Scholars Press/Society of Biblical Literature, 1986), 7. The latter part of this definition was crafted at a scholarly conference that took place after the publication of Semeia 14 and was then added to John J. Collins, "Introduction: Towards the Morphology of a Genre," in *Apocalypse: The Morphology of a Genre,* ed. John J. Collins, Semeia 14 (Missoula, Mont.: Scholars Press, 1979), 9. This volume represents the work of the Society of Biblical Literature's Apocalypse Group which was charged with surveying all the apocalypses from the period 250 B.C.E.–250 C.E.

6. Michael E. Stone, "The Books of Enoch and Judaism in the Third Century B.C.E.," *CBQ* 40 (1978): 479–92.

7. Notable studies on the issue of pseudepigraphy include the following: Norbert Brox, ed. *Pseudepigraphie in der heidnischen und jüdisch-christlichen Antike* (Darmstadt: Wissenschaftliche Buchgesellschaft, 1977); Bruce Metzger, "Literary Forgeries and Canonical Pseudepigrapha," *JBL* 91 (1972): 3–24; and

Wolfgang Speyer, *Die literarische Fälschung im heidenischen und christlichen Altertum: Ein Versuch ihrer Deutung,* HAW 1.2 (Munich: Beck, 1971).

8. The literature on theodicy is vast but note the following studies: *Theodicy in the Old Testament,* ed. James L. Crenshaw, *Issues in Religion and Theology,* vol. 4 (Philadelphia: Fortress Press, 1983); Crenshaw, "Theodicy," *ABD,* 6.444–47; Crenshaw, *Urgent Advice and Probing Questions: Collected Writings on Old Testament Wisdom* (Macon, Ga.: Mercer University Press, 1995); and Crenshaw, "The Sojourner Has Come to Play the Judge: Theodicy on Trial," in *God in the Fray: A Tribute to Walter Brueggemann,* ed. Tod Linafelt and Timothy K. Beal (Minneapolis: Fortress Press, 1998). This issue continues to vex the human soul and is treated well by Harold S. Kushner, *When Bad Things Happen to Good People* (New York: Schocken Books, 1981).

9. For introduction and commentary, see P.-M. Bogaert, *Apocalypse de Baruch: Introduction, traduction du syriaque et commentaire,* SC 144–145 (Paris: Le Cerf, 1969). Note also A. F. J. Klijn, "Recent Developments in the Study of the Syriac Apocalypse of Baruch," *JSP* 4 (1989): 3–17.

10. For the current state of the debate over the dating of and relationship between these two apocalypses, see Michael E. Stone, *Fourth Ezra: A Commentary on the Book of Fourth Ezra* (Minneapolis: Fortress Press, 1990), 9–10, 39–40.

11. Compare *2 Bar.* 32:8–9; 33:33–41; 44:1–3; 46:1–6; 77:11–16; 84:1–11. In this regard John J. Collins, "The Sage in the Apocalyptic and Pseudepigraphic Literature," in *The Sage in Israel and the Ancient Near East,* ed. John G. Gammie and Leo Perdue (Winona Lake, Ind.: Eisenbrauns, 1990), 353, notes that "there is no opposition between the law and these (eschatological) expectations, but the law alone is no longer sufficient for the pastoral needs of the people."

12. So Stone, *Fourth Ezra,* 28–33, 304–42.

13. Unless otherwise noted, all translations of the Syriac text are mine and are based on the text in S. Dedering, "Apocalypse of Baruch," in *The Old Testament in Syriac According to the Peshitta Version,* Part IV, Fascicle 3 (Peshitta Institute. Leiden: E. J. Brill, 1973). For conveniently available English translations, see Klijn, "2 (Syriac Apocalypse of) Baruch," *OTP* 1.615–52; R. H. Charles, *The Apocalypse of Baruch: Translated from the Syriac* (London: Adam and Charles Black, 1896), and Charles, "The Apocalypse of Baruch," *APOT* 2.470–526. Note also the revision of Charles's translation by L. J. Brockington, "The Syriac Apocalypse of Baruch," *AOT* 835–95.

14. The Syriac term b'š/bîš is the equivalent of and commonly translates the Hebrew term rᶜ "evil" in the Bible; see Robert Payne Smith, *Thesaurus Syriacus,* 2 vols. (Oxford: Clarendon Press, 1879–1901), 1.438–41. Thus the author of *2 Baruch* makes an unmistakable connection with biblical terminology.

15. The phrase was coined by Morton Smith, *Palestinian Parties and Politics*

That Shaped the Old Testament (New York: Columbia University Press, 1971). The movement and its ideology are discussed in detail in Moshe Weinfeld, *Deuteronomy and the Deuteronomic School* (Oxford: Clarendon Press, 1972), and *Those Elusive Deuteronomists: The Phenomenon of Pan-Deuteronomism,* ed. Linda S. Schearing and Steven L. McKenzie, JSOTSup 268 (Sheffield: Sheffield Academic Press, 1999). Note also Richard E. Friedman, *Who Wrote the Bible?* (New York: Summit Books, 1987), 101–49.

16. Jer 4:3–9; 6:1–2,19; 7:30–34; 11:6–17; 18:11–17; 19:3–9; 21:10; 35:17; 39:16; 44:2–3, 11; 45:5.

17. Jer 13:10, 16:10–13, 44:22–23; cf. Deut 4:25, 28:20, 31:18, 29.

18. See Marc Z. Brettler, "The Book of Judges: Literature as Politics," *JBL* 108 (1989): 405–28.

19. This theme occurs also in Jer 4:3–29.

20. Isaiah 10:5–34 addresses the same issue of the just suffering at the hands of the wicked. The answer proffered there is that in due time God will punish the wicked Assyrians for their arrogance and for their excessive malevolence against Israel.

21. For the tactics and techniques of warfare in the ancient Near East, see Yigael Yadin, *The Art of Warfare in Biblical Lands: In the Light of Archaeological Study,* 2 vols. (New York: McGraw-Hill, 1963).

22. This issue is treated insightfully by Daniel Merkur, "The Visionary Practices of the Jewish Apocalypticists," in *The Psychoanalytic Study of Society,* vol. 14, ed. L. Bryce Boyer and Simon A. Grolnick (Hillsdale, N.J.: Analytic Press, 1989), 119–48. See also Stone, *Fourth Ezra,* 23–33.

23. As discussed in chapter two, the tradition that Baruch wrote words of comfort and instruction for the exilic community appears also in Baruch 1:1 and appears to draw on Jer 29:1 and the letter Jeremiah sent to the exiles.

24. I discuss this further in *The Early History of Heaven* (Oxford/New York: Oxford University Press, 2000).

25. Translation of this passage is based on Syriac text in Charles, *Apocalypse of Baruch,* 161–63.

26. See Robert R. Wilson, *Prophecy and Society in Ancient Israel* (Philadelphia: Fortress Press, 1980), 141–46, 253–63, and Gerhard von Rad, *The Message of the Prophets* (New York: Harper and Row Publishers, 1965), 66–67.

27. The use of this technique in the Bible is detailed by Michael Fishbane, *Biblical Interpretation in Ancient Israel* (Oxford: Clarendon Press, 1985), 372–79.

28. This has already been observed by Frederick James Murphy, *The Structure and Meaning of Second Baruch* (Atlanta, Ga.: Scholars Press, 1985), 117–34.

29. According to Sifre Deut. 357 (ed. Finkelstein, 426), God showed the events of the "end of time" to Moses.

30. See Murphy, *Structure and Meaning*, 23.

31. See S. E. Loewenstamm, "The Death of Moses," in *Studies on the Testament of Abraham*, ed. G. W. E. Nickelsburg, SCS 6 (Missoula, Mont.: Scholars Press, 1976), 185–217. Compare *2 Bar.* 84:1–11.

32. Murphy, *Structure and Meaning*, 25, cf. 117–33, entitles chapter 84 "Baruch renews the covenant which Moses established."

33. The link with Moses is also evident in other ways. Note the verbal association with Moses in the words "Hear, O children of Israel" (*2 Bar.* 77:2, cf. Deut 6:4).

34. This draws on the words of Moses in Deuteronomy 30:11–20 (cf. *2 Bar.* 19:1–4).

35. On the role of charisma in leadership, see S. N. Eisenstadt, *Max Weber on Charisma and Institution Building: Selected Papers* (Chicago: University of Chicago Press, 1968); and Ronald E. Clements, "Max Weber, Charisma and Biblical Prophecy," in *Prophecy and Prophets: The Diversity of Contemporary Issues in Scholarship*, ed. Yehoshua Gitay, Society of Biblical Literature Semeia Studies (Atlanta, Ga.: Scholars Press, 1997), 89–108.

36. Contra Benjamin D. Sommer, "Did Prophecy Cease: Evaluating a Reevaluation," *JBL* 115 (1996) 31–47. For the variety of "prophetic" activity in postbiblical and Second Temple periods, see David E. Aune, *Prophecy in Early Christianity and the Ancient Mediterranean World* (Grand Rapids, Mich.: Eerdmans, 1983), and Frederick E. Greenspahn, "Why Prophecy Ceased," *JBL* 108 (1989): 37–49.

37. Nahum M. Sarna, "The Authority and Interpretation of Scripture in Jewish Tradition," in *Understanding Scripture: Explorations of Jewish and Christian Traditions of Interpretation*, ed. Clemens Thoma and Michael Wyschogrod (Mahwah, N.J.: Paulist Press, 1987), 9–10.

38. In this regard, see Crenshaw, *Education in Ancient Israel*, 139–85.

39. The teachings of Ezra in 4 Ezra likewise enable people to achieve salvation in the last days (4 Ezra 14:22). A latter-day descendent of Enoch will proclaim Enoch's teaching to those living in the last days according to *2 Enoch* 35. Similarly, Jesus is said to have appointed select followers to proclaim his teachings after his death (Matt 28:16–20).

40. According to *2 Bar.* 59:1–2 the "lamp" is the Law which was promulgated by Moses, Aaron, Miriam, Joshua and Caleb. Speaking to the seer Ezra in 4 Ezra 14, God promises to "light in your heart the lamp of understanding." This inspiration is for the purpose of writing the twenty-four books of Scripture which Ezra discloses to the public, as well as seventy esoteric books which are meant only for a select community. These seventy books can be disclosed to these initiates because "in them is the spring of understanding, the fountain of

wisdom, and the river of knowledge." Moreover, the terminology equating fountains with teachers of the Law is part of a larger complex of ongoing transformations of the biblical well motif. See Michael Fishbane, "The Well of Living Water: A Biblical Motif and Its Ancient Transformations," in *"Shar'arei Talmon": Studies in the Bible, Qumran, and the Ancient Near East Presented to Shemaryahu Talmon,* ed. Michael Fishbane and Emanuel Tov (Winona Lake, Ind.: Eisenbrauns, 1992), 3–16.

41. The role of inspired interpreter also figures in Michael E. Stone's description of the figure of the wise in "Ideal Figures and Social Context: Priest and Sage in the Early Second Temple Period," in *Ancient Israelite Religion: Essays in Honor of Frank Moore Cross,* ed., Patrick D. Miller, et al. (Philadelphia: Fortress Press, 1987), 575–86.

42. See also Gwendolyn B. Sayler, *Have the Promises Failed? A Literary Analysis of 2 Baruch,* SBLDS 72 (Chico, Calif.: Scholars Press, 1984), 79–85, 110–18.

43. A similar social setting may obtain for the Ascension of Isaiah. Robert G. Hall, "The *Ascension of Isaiah:* Community Situation, Date, and Place in Early Christianity," *JBL* 109:2 (1990): 289–306, observes that the Ascension of Isaiah originated in an early Christian prophetic school centered on an inspired prophet.

44. In the "Book of the Heavenly Luminaries," *1 Enoch 72–82,* a book devoted to cosmological speculations, Enoch is portrayed as the one who provided subsequent generations with information he received by divine revelation. He instructed Methuselah to write down his revelations and pass them on to his "children" who would then pass it on to all subsequent generations (82:1–3). This cosmological information would enable people to follow the correct calendar. This passage, like those in *2 Baruch,* provides us with information regarding the groups passing on the revelations allegedly given to the ancient seers. Their authors created the fiction that their revelations originated from an ancient person of renown. This revelation was transmitted to the modern author who now fulfills his responsibility by passing it on to his generation.

45. Fishbane, "From Scribalism to Rabbinism: Perspectives on the Emergence of Classical Judaism," in *The Sage in Israel and the Ancient Near East,* ed. John G. Gammie and Leo Perdue (Winona Lake, Ind.: Eisenbrauns, 1990), 440.

46. See Siegfried Bergler, *Joel als Schriftinterpret,* Beiträge zur Erforschung des Alten Testaments und des antiken Judentums, vol. 16 (Frankfurt am Main: P. Lang, 1988), and Crenshaw, *Joel: A New Translation with Introduction and Commentary,* AB 24C (New York: Doubleday, 1995), 26–28, 36–37, and passim.

47. Cf. CD 7:4–5, 20:13; Hodayot 2:9–10. Note also Bilhah Nitzan, *Pesher Habakkuk: A Scroll from the Wilderness of Judaea (1QpHab). Text, Translation and Commentary* (Jerusalem: Bialik Institute, 1986), 176 [Hebrew].

48. For the debate on whether the Teacher wrote any of the Qumran texts compare J. T. Milik, *Ten Years of Discovery in the Wilderness of Judaea*, SBT 26 (London: SCM Press Ltd., 1959), 37; Frank Moore Cross, *The Ancient Library of Qumran* 3rd ed., Biblical Seminar 30 (Sheffield: Sheffield Academic Press, 1995), 90–93; Maurya P. Horgan, *Pesharim: Qumran Interpretations of Biblical Books*, CBQMS 8 (Washington, D.C.: The Catholic Biblical Association of America, 1979), 3; and James VanderKam and Peter Flint, *The Meaning of the Dead Sea Scrolls: Their Significance for Understanding the Bible, Judaism, Jesus, and Christianity* (New York: HarperCollins, 2002), 282–85.

49. Hebrew text in Chaim Rabin, *The Zadokite Documents* (Oxford: Clarendon Press, 1954) 2, 5.

50. Translation based on Hebrew text in *The Dead Sea Scrolls: Study Edition*, 2 vols., ed. Florentino García Martínez and Eibert J. C. Tigchelaar (Leiden: E. J. Brill, 1997–98)1.162. For English translations of the Qumran documents, see Geza Vermes, *The Complete Dead Sea Scrolls in English* (New York/London: Penguin Press, 1997), and Michael Wise, Martin Abegg Jr., and Edward Cook, *The Dead Sea Scrolls: A New Translation* (New York: HarperCollins, 1996).

51. The term "Yahad," Hebrew יחד, means "community" and is the term the people of Qumran used to refer to their organization, "The Community."

52. The phrase "preparing the way in the desert" clearly draws on Isa 40:3.

53. On the place of the Hebrew Bible and the interpretation of it by the Teacher of Righteousness within the social structure of the Qumran community, see Fishbane, "Use, Authority and Interpretation of Mikra at Qumran," in *Miqra*, ed. M. J. Mulder, CRIANT I. 2 (Assen: Van Gorcum/ Philadelphia: Fortress Press, 1989), 341–79. Fishbane notes (340), that at Qumran there was ". . . both Mikra and its Interpretation, as guided by the head teacher and those authorized to interpret under his guidance (or the exegetical principles laid down by him)." Compare 1QS 8:11–16 where it is said regarding specially qualified men within the Qumran community that "When these have been confirmed on the foundation of the Yahad for two full years in perfection of behavior, they shall become set apart as holy in the midst of the Council of the members of the Yahad. And every matter hidden from Israel but which has been discovered by the Interpreter, he shall not conceal from these men out of fear of a spirit of apostasy. . . . And when these become [members of the Yahad] in Israel [according to these stipulations], they shall become set apart from the habitation of men of iniquity in order to go into the wilderness to prepare the way of that person just as it is written, 'in the wilderness prepare the way of . . . in the desert make straight a path for our God' (Isa 40:3). This [path] is the interpretation of the Torah which he (God) commanded through Moses so that they

act according to all that has been revealed from age to age and according to what the prophets have revealed by his [God's] Holy Spirit."

54. Heinz Feltes, *Die Gattung des Habakukkommentars von Qumran (1QpHab): Eine Studie zum frühen jüdischen Midrasch,* Forschung zur Bibel 58 (Würzburg: Echter Verlag, 1986).

55. For definitions and descriptions, see John J. Collins, ed., *Apocalypse: Morphology of a Genre.*

56. See Collins, "The Sage in the Apocalyptic and Pseudepigraphic Literature," 343–54. What is happening in Judaism is part of broader cultural transformations vis-à-vis sages in the hellenistic world. Each community or philosophical school in the hellenistic world had its own image of the ideal sage; see George B. Kerferd, "The Sage in Hellenistic Philosophical Literature," in *The Sage,* ed. Gammie and Perdue, 319–28. Different Jewish groups were likewise imagining their sages in new ways, and the evolution of Baruch's persona reflects one of these new images.

57. See Klaas Spronk, *Beatific Afterlife in Ancient Israel and in the Ancient Near East* (Neukirchen-Vluyn: Neukirchener Verlag/Kevelaer: Butzon & Bercker, 1986), 315–16, 327–28, 334–40.

58. Note Michael Fishbane, *Text and Texture: Close Readings of Selected Biblical Texts* (New York: Schocken Books, 1979), 34–38.

59. See also Karel van der Toorn, "Funerary Rituals and Beatific Afterlife in Ugaritic Texts and the Bible," *BO* 48 (1991): 66.

60. See C. L. Seow, "Linguistic Evidence and the Dating of Qohelet," *JBL* 115:4 (1996): 643–66. For a detailed discussion of the pertinent issues regarding the date of Daniel, see John J. Collins, *Daniel: A Commentary on the Book of Daniel,* Hermenia (Minneapolis: Fortress Press, 1993), 1–71.

61. See Plato, Phaedo, 85E-86D; 91C-95A; 115C-D; and 246E-249D; and Wilhelm Bousset, "Die Himmelsreise der Seele," *Archiv für Religionswissenschaft* 4 (1901): 136–69, 229–73.

62. 10, 614A-621D.

63. Cicero, *De re publica, De legibus* (tr. Keyes) 265, 279, 283. The Roman poet Vergil (70–19 B.C.E.) describes ancient Greek beliefs about netherworldly punishments that purify a soul so that it might be reincarnated into a physical body; see *Aeneid,* book 6.

64. I developed these matters more fully in *The Early History of Heaven.*

65. Introduction and English translation by Peter Alexander in *OTP* 2.223–302.

66. In this regard, see Jacob Neusner, "Religious Authority in Judaism: Modern and Classical Modes," *Int* 39:4 (1985): 373–87. Neusner concludes by saying: "Judaism as we know it means to provide for the faithful an enduring and

ever present encounter with the living God. The meeting is through the medium of revelation contained in the Torah learned through rabbinical modes of exegesis" (387).

67. Thomas B. Dozeman, "Masking Moses and Mosaic Authority in Torah," *JBL* 119:1 (2000): 21–45, discusses how Moses' glowing face and his veil symbolize his divine authority.

68. The Targums report that they saw "the glory of the God of Israel," while the rabbis generally prefer to say that they saw the divine presence in a prophetic vision like Ezekiel and others.

69. See above and Wilson, *Prophecy and Society,* 141–46, 253–63.

70. See Fishbane, *Biblical Interpretation,* 479–485.

71. On this transition, see Fishbane, "From Scribalism to Rabbinism," 439–56, and Neusner, "Religious Authority in Judaism," 374.

72. Introductions and English translations of *3 Baruch* are available in *OTP* 2.653–79, *AOT* 897–914, and *APOT* 2.527–41. A critical edition of the Greek text is found in *Apocalypsis Baruchi Graece,* ed. J.-C. Picard, PVTG 2 (Leiden: E. J. Brill, 1967), 61–96.

73. See Picard, "Observations sur l'Apocalypse greque de Baruch I: Cadre historique fictif et efficacité symbolique," *Semitica* 20 (1970): 77–103.

74. Greek text in *Daniel, Susanna, Bel et Draco,* ed. Joseph Ziegler, Septuaginta Vetus Testamentum Graecum 16.2 (Göttingen: Vandenhoeck & Ruprecht, 1954), 189, 193.

75. This topic is treated fully by James C. VanderKam, *Enoch: A Man for All Generations,* Studies on the Personalities of the Old Testament (Columbia: University of South Carolina Press, 1995).

76. See Michael E. Stone, "Lists of Revealed Things in Apocalyptic Literature," in *Magnalia Dei: The Mighty Acts of God,* ed. F. M. Cross, et al. (Garden City, N.Y.: Doubleday, 1976), 414–52.

77. Daniel C. Harlow, *The Greek Apocalypse of Baruch (3 Baruch) in Hellenistic Judaism and Early Christianity,* SVTP 12 (Leiden: E. J. Brill, 1996), following a common approach to the cosmology of this text, supposes that the appearance in only the fifth of an alleged seven heavens is part of a polemic against heavenly ascent.

Chapter 4

1. M. R. James, *Apocrypha Anecdota II,* ed. J. Armitage Robinson, Texts and Studies 5:1 (Cambridge: Cambridge University Press, 1897), liv; James, *The Lost Apocrypha of the Old Testament: Their Titles and Fragments* (London/New York: SPCK/Macmillan, 1936), 77. Note also P.-M. Bogaert, *Apocalypse de Baruch:*

Introduction, traduction du syriaque et commentaire, 2 vols., SC 144–145 (Paris: Le Cerf, 1969), 1.457, and Albert-Marie Denis, *Introduction aux Pseudépigraphes Grecs d'Ancien Testament*, SVTP 1 (Leiden: E. J. Brill, 1970), 83.

2. Hippolytus, *Refutatio omnium haeresium*, ed. Paul Wendland, GCS 26:3 (Hildesheim/New York: Georg Olms Verlag, 1977), 127–34. For an English translation, see "The Refutation of All Heresies," in *The Ante-Nicene Fathers: Translations of the Fathers Down to A. D. 325*, 10 vols., ed. Alexander Roberts et al., rev. A. Cleveland Coxe (New York: Charles Scribner's Sons, 1926), 5.69–73.

3. See J. Montserrat-Torrents, "La philosophie du *Livre de Baruch* de Justin," in *Studia Patristica XVIII: Papers of the 1983 Oxford Patristics Conference*, ed. Elizabeth A. Livingstone (Kalamazoo, Mich.: Cistercian Publications, 1985), 253–61.

4. Daniel C. Harlow, *The Greek Apocalypse of Baruch (3 Baruch) in Hellenistic Judaism and Early Christianity*, SVTP 12 (Leiden: E. J. Brill, 1996), 18n. 67.

5. *b. Meg.* 14b, *Sifre Num* 78 (ed. Horovitz, 74), *Sifre Zuta* 29 on Num 10:29 (ed. Horovitz, 263), *y. Sota* 9, 24b and *S. Ōlam Rab.* 20 (ed. Ratner, 87) list him as one of the prophets. Cf. *Encyclopedia of Biblical Personalities: As Seen by the Sages of the Talmud and Midrash*, ed. Israel Yitzhaq Hasidah (Jerusalem: Rueven Mas, 1995), 85, 403 [Hebrew].

6. Eusebius, *Praeparatio Evangelica*, 10.14.6 (Migne, *PG* xxi, cols. 837–38; *La Préparation Évangélique*, ed. Guy Schroeder and Edouard des Places, SC 369 [Paris: Éditions du Cerf, 1991], 468–69) reports that during the reign of Josiah, προφητευουσιν Ἱερεμίας Βαροὺχ Ὀλδᾶ καὶ ἄλλοι προφῆται. Cf. Origen, *Homilies on Jeremiah*, 8.5 (Migne, *PG*, xiii, cols. 341–44; *Origéne, Homélies sur Jérémie*, ed. Pierre Husson and Pierre Nautin, SC 232:1 [Paris: Éditions du Cerf, 1976], 366, 367).

7. Michael E. Stone, *Armenian Apocrypha Relating to the Patriarchs and Prophets* (Jerusalem: Israel Academy of Sciences and Humanities, 1982), 163.

8. *Prophetarum vitae fabulosae: indices apostolorum discipulorumque domini Dorotheo, Epiphanio, Hippolyto aliisque vindicata*, ed. T. Schermann (Leipzig: Teubner, 1907), 2. Baruch is occasionally identified as one of the prophets in the iconography and hagiography of the medieval eastern churches; see *Lexikon der Christlichen Iknographie*, 8 vols., ed. Engelbert Kirschbaum (Freiburg: Herder, 1968–1976), 5.336. As a saint he has a feast day, September 29th; see Albert Ehrhard, *Überlieferung und Bestand der hagiographischen und homiletischen Literatur der Griechischen Kirche: Von den Anfängen bis zum Ende des 16. Jahrhunderts*, vol. 1, ed. Erich Klostermann and Carl Schmidt, TU 50:1 (Leipzig: Hinrichs, 1937), 461.

9. Bo', 1 (ed. Horovitz-Rabin, 5–6; Lauterbach, 1.13–15).

10. Susan Niditch, "Merits, Martyrs, and 'Your Life as Booty': An Exegesis of *Mekilta, Pisha 1*," *JSJ* 13:1–2 (1988): 170–71, points out that Baruch became a

mediator on behalf of Israel not by becoming a prophet, but by becoming a righteous sufferer.

11. See Joseph Bidez and Franz Cumont, *Les mages hellénisés: Zoroastre, Ostanès et Hystaspe d'après la tradition greque,* 2 vols. (Paris: Société d'Edition "Les belles Lettres," 1973): 1.49–50; 2.131–32.

12. For an introduction and translation, see Wolf Leslau, *Falasha Anthology,* Yale Judaica Series 6 (New Haven/London: Yale University Press, 1951), 57–76. Martha Himmelfarb, *Tours of Hell: An Apocalyptic Form in Jewish and Christian Literature* (Philadelphia: Fortress, 1983), 21–23, places the book in a schema describing the origin and development of the ascent motif in Jewish and Christian literature.

13. The following texts identify Baruch as a priest: *b. Meg.* 14b; *Sifre Num.* 78 (ed. Horovitz, 74); and *Sifre Zuta* 29 on Num 10:29 (ed. Horovitz, 263). On Baruch's possible priestly lineage, see Bogaert, *Apocalypse de Baruch,* 1.108–110.

14. For the pertinent passages from Ishodad of Merv, Gregory Abul Faradj (Bar Hebraeus), Solomon of Basrah, and Bar Bahloul, see Bidez and Cumont, *Les mages hellénisés,* 1.49–50; 2.129, 131, 134–35.

15. Jacob Neusner, "Note on Barukh ben Neriah and Zoroaster," *Numen* 12:1 (1965): 66–69. Note also Louis Ginzberg, "Baruch," in *The Jewish Encyclopedia,* 12 vols., ed. Isidore Singer and Cyrus Adler (New York/London: Funk & Wagnall's Company, 1901–1906), 1.548–49, and James, *The Lost Apocrypha,* 79.

16. See the introductions to the various Baruch pseudepigrapha for data on the Christian interpolations in these texts. The Baruch quotation in *Altercatio Simonis Judaei et Theophili Christiani* 17, in which Baruch prophesies about the birth, life and death of Jesus, appears to be such a Christian addition to the Book of Baruch. See James, *The Lost Apocrypha,* 78–79; James, *Apocrypha Anecdota II,* liii–liv; and Denis, *Introduction,* 83. The passage attributed to Baruch by Cyprian (*Testimonies* iii.29) has affinities with *2 Baruch,* but may be either an addition to one of the extant Baruch pseudepigrapha or a fragment from an otherwise unknown Baruch pseudepigraphon. See Bogaert, *Apocalypse de Baruch,* 1.259–69; James, *The Lost Apocrypha,* 77–79, idem, *Apocrypha Anecdota II,* liv; and Denis, *Introduction,* 83–84.

17. See *Sifre Num* 99 (ed. Horovitz, 99) and *Pirqe R. El.* 53 (Friedlander, 430–31). According to a Coptic Jeremiah apocryphon sometimes entitled "The History of the Captivity in Babylon," Baruch betrayed Jeremiah and was responsible for the prophet's imprisonment; see K. H. Kuhn, "A Coptic Jeremiah Apocryphon," *Le Muséon* 83:1–2 (1970): 116–17.

18. *Sifre Num* 99 (ed. Horovitz, 99); *Pirqe R. El.* 53 (Friedlander, 430–31); *Pesiq. R.* 26 (ed. Friedmann, 130b; Braude, 2.532); *2 'Abot R. Nat.* 43 (ed. Schechter, 122; Saldarini, 269); *b. Der. Er. Zut.* 1.

19. See Hannelis Schulte, "Baruch und Ebedmelech—Persönliche Heilso-rakel im Jeremiabuche," *BZ* 32:2 (1988): 257–65; Christopher R. Seitz, "The Prophet Moses and the Canonical Shape of Jeremiah," 16–23; and K. Kohler, "The Pre-Talmudic Haggada, I," *JQR* 5 (1893): 414–19.

20. Ebed-Melech is identified with Zedekiah in Targum Pseudo-Jonathan to Jer 38:7, *b. Mo'ed Qat.* 16b, and *Midr. Ps.* 7,18 (ed. Buber, 72, Braude, 1.117–18); cf. *Midr. Ps.* 7,14 (ed. Buber, 70, Braude, 1.112–13). Note also Par. Jer. 9:29, where Jeremiah reveals to both Baruch and Abimelech (read Ebed-Melech) "all the mysteries which he had seen."

21. Similarly, see Bogaert, *Apocalypse de Baruch*, 1.113–18.

22. "Jeremiah [dwelt] in the land of Tahpanhes which is in the land of Eg[ypt]"; "[Je]remiah son of Hilkiah from the land of Egy[pt]."

23. *Seder Olam* 26, *Shir HaShirim Rabba* 5 and *b. Megillot* 16b

24. *The Travels of Rabbi Petachia of Ratisbon,* trans. and ed. A. Benisch (London: Trubner and Co., 1856), 21–23, 35, 49–51.

25. Compare Josephus, *Antiquities* 10.179, 182 and *Midrash Eser Galuyot* (text in *Bet HaMidrash,* ed. Adolph Jellinek [Jerusalem: Wahrmann, 1967], 135).

26. For Hebrew text and English translation, see *The Travels of Rabbi Petachia of Ratisbon,* 20–23, 34–35, 50–51. See Joshua Prawer, *The History of the Jews in the Latin Kingdom of Jerusalem* (Oxford: Clarendon, 1988) 206–15, for details on the composition and transmission of this text.

27. For the social and anthropological significance of pilgrimage, see E. Alan Morinis, *Sacred Journeys: The Anthropology of Pilgrimage* (New York: Greenwood Press, 1992); Robert G. Ousterhout, *The Blessings of Pilgrimage* (Urbana: University of Illinois Press, 1990); and Ian Reader and Tony Walter, *Pilgrimage in Popular Culture* (Basingstoke: Macmillan, 1993).

Epilogue

1. The phrase "pseudepigraphic imagination" is inspired by John J. Collins's "apocalyptic imagination" (see Collins, *The Apocalyptic Imagination: An Introduction to the Jewish Matrix of Christianity* [New York: Crossroad, 1984]) and Michael Fishbane's "exegetical imagination" (see Fishbane, *The Exegetical Imagination: On Jewish Thought and Theology* [Cambridge: Harvard University Press, 1998]). Both of these works are certainly relevant to the activity of the "pseudepigraphic imagination."

Bibliography

Abusch, Tzvi. "Some Reflections on Mesopotamian Witchcraft." In *Religion and Politics in the Ancient Near East,* edited by Adele Berlin, 21–33. Bethesda: University Press of Maryland, 1996.

Aḥituv, Shmuel. *Handbook of Ancient Hebrew Inscriptions: From the First Temple Period to the Beginning of the Second Temple Period.* Jerusalem: Bialik, 1992 [Hebrew].

Anbar, Moshe. "Mari and the Origin of Prophecy." In *Kinattūtu ša dārâti: Raphael Kutscher Memorial Volume,* edited by A. F. Rainey, 1–5. Tel Aviv: Tel Aviv University Institute of Archaeology, 1993.

Andersen, Francis I., and David Noel Freedman. *Amos: A New Translation, with Introduction and Commentary.* AB 24A. New York: Doubleday, 1989.

André, L. E. Tony. *Les Apocryphes de l'Ancien Testament.* Florence: Osvaldo Paggi, 1903.

The Assyrian Dictionary of the Oriental Institute of the University of Chicago. Chicago: Oriental Institute, 1956–.

Aune, David E. *Prophecy in Early Christianity and the Ancient Mediterranean World.* Grand Rapids, Mich.: Eerdmans, 1983.

Avigad, Nahman. "Baruch the Scribe and Jerahmeel the King's Son." *IEJ* 28:1–2 (1978): 52–56.

———. "The Contribution of Hebrew Seals to an Understanding of Israelite Religion and Society." In *Ancient Israelite Religion: Essays in Honor of Frank Moore Cross,* edited by P. D. Miller, P. D. Hanson, and S. D. McBride, 195–208. Philadelphia: Fortress Press, 1987.

———. *Corpus of West Semitic Stamp Seals.* Revised and completed by Benjamin Sass. Jerusalem: Israel Academy of Sciences, Israel Exploration Society, and Institute of Archaeology, Hebrew University of Jerusalem, 1997.

———. *Hebrew Bullae from the Time of Jeremiah: Remnants of a Burnt Archive.* Jerusalem: Israel Exploration Society, 1986.

———. "Hebrew Seals and Sealings and Their Significance for Biblical Research." In *Congress Volume, Jerusalem, 1986,* edited by J. A. Emerton, 7–16. VTSup 40. Leiden: E. J. Brill, 1988.

———. "Jerahmeel and Baruch: King's Son and Scribe." *BA* 42:2 (1979): 114–18.

Benisch, A., trans. and ed. *The Travels of Rabbi Petachia of Ratisbon.* London: Trubner and Co., 1856.

Bergler, Siegfried. *Joel als Schriftinterpret*. Beiträge zur Erforschung des Alten Testaments und des antiken Judentums 16. Frankfurt am Main: P. Lang, 1988.

Bidez, Joseph, and Franz Cumont. *Les mages hellénisés: Zoroastre, Ostanès et Hystaspe d'après la tradition grecque*. 2 vols. Paris: Société d'Edition "Les belles Lettres," 1973.

Black, J. A., and W. J. Tait. "Archives and Libraries in the Ancient Near East." In *Civilizations of the Ancient Near East*, 4 vols., edited by Jack M. Sasson, 4.2197–209. New York: Charles Scribner's Sons, 1995.

Blenkinsopp, Joseph. *Sage, Priest, Prophet: Religious and Intellectual Leadership in Ancient Israel*. Library of Ancient Israel. Louisville, Ky.: Westminster/John Knox Press, 1995.

Bogaert, Pierre-Maurice. *Apocalypse de Baruch: Introduction, traduction du syriaque et commentaire*. 2 vols. SC 144–45. Paris: Le Cerf, 1969.

———. "De Baruch à Jérémie: Les deux rédactions conservées du livre de Jérémie" In *Le livre de Jérémie: Le prophète et son milieu, les oracles et leur transmission*, edited by P.-M. Bogaert, 168–73. BETL 54. Leuven: Leuven University Press, 1981.

———. "Le nom de Baruch dans la littérature pseudépigraphique: L'apocalypse syriaque et le livre deutérocanonique." In *La littérature juive entre Tenach et Mischna: Quelques problèmes*, edited by W. C. Van Unnik, 61–72. Recherches bibliques 9. Leiden: E. J. Brill, 1974.

———. "Le personnage de Baruch et l'histoire du livre de Jérémie: Aux origines du livre de Baruch." *Bulletin of the International Organization for Septuagint and Cognate Studies* 7 (1974): 19–21.

———. "Le personnage de Baruch et l'histoire du livre de Jérémie: Aux origines du Livre deutérocanonique de Baruch." In *Studia Evangelica*, vol. 7: *Papers Presented to the Fifth International Congress on Biblical Studies Held at Oxford, 1973*, edited by Elizabeth A. Livingstone, 73–81. Texte und Untersuchungen zur Geschichte der altchristlichen Literatur 126. Berlin: Akademie Verlag, 1982.

Böttrich, Christfried. "Astrologie in der Henochtradition." *ZAW* 109:2 (1997): 222–45.

Bousset, Wilhelm. "Die Himmelsreise der Seele." *Archiv für Religionswissenschaft* 4 (1901): 136–69, 229–73.

Brettler, Marc Z. "The Book of Judges: Literature as Politics," *JBL* 108 (1989): 405–28.

Bright, John. *Jeremiah*. AB. Garden City, N.Y.: Doubleday, 1965.

Brockington, L. J. "The Syriac Apocalypse of Baruch." In *AOT*, 835–95.

Brox, Norbert, ed. *Pseudepigraphie in der Heidnischen and jüdisch-christlichen Antike*. Darmstadt: Wissenschaftliche Buchgesellschaft, 1977.

Brueggemann, Walter. "The 'Baruch Connection': Reflections on Jer 43:1–7." *JBL* 113:3 (1994): 405–20.

———. *A Commentary on Jeremiah: Exile and Homecoming.* Grand Rapids, Mich.: Eerdmans, 1998.

———. "Jeremiah: Intense Criticism/Thin Interpretation." *Int* 42 (1988): 268–80.

Burke, David G. *The Poetry of Baruch: A Reconstruction and Analysis of Baruch 3:9–5:9.* SBLSCS 10. Chico, Calif.: Scholars Press, 1982.

Carroll, Robert P. "Arguing about Jeremiah: Recent Studies and the Nature of a Prophetic Book." In *Congress Volume: Leuven 1989,* edited by J. A. Emerton, 222–35. VTSup 43. Leiden: E. J. Brill, 1991.

———. "Century's End: Jeremiah Studies at the Beginning of the Third Millennium." *CRBS* 8 (2000): 18–58.

———. *From Chaos to Covenant: Uses of Prophecy in the Book of Jeremiah.* London: SCM/New York: Crossroad, 1981.

———. *Jeremiah.* OTL. London: SCM Press, 1986.

———. "Radical Clashes of Will and Style: Recent Commentary Writing on the Book of Jeremiah." *JSOT* 45 (1989): 99–114.

———. "Surplus Meaning and the Conflict of Interpretations: A Dodecade of Jeremiah Studies, 1984–95." *CRBS* 4 (1996): 115–59.

Charles, R. H. "The Apocalypse of Baruch." *APOT* 2.470–526.

———. *The Apocalypse of Baruch: Translated from the Syriac.* London: Adam and Charles Black, 1896.

———, ed. *The Apocrypha and Pseudepigrapha of the Old Testament.* 2 vols. Oxford: Clarendon Press, 1913.

Charlesworth, James H. "A History of Pseudepigrapha Research: The Re-emerging Importance of the Pseudepigrapha." *ANRW* II:19:1 (1979): 54–88.

Charlesworth, James H., ed. *The Apocrypha and Pseudepigrapha of the Old Testament.* 2 Vols. Garden City, N.Y.: Doubleday, 1983–85.

Charpin, Dominique, Francis Joannès, Sylvie Lackenbacher, and Bertrand Lafont. *Archives Épistolaires de Mari I/2,* ARM XXVI. Paris: Editions Recherche sur Civilisations, 1988.

Clements, Ronald E. "Max Weber, Charisma and Biblical Prophecy." In *Prophecy and Prophets: The Diversity of Contemporary Issues in Scholarship,* edited by Yehoshua Gitay, 89–108. Society of Biblical Literature Semeia Studies. Atlanta, Ga.: Scholars Press, 1997.

Collins, John J. "Apocalyptic Eschatology as the Transcendence of Death." *CBQ* 44 (1982): 91–111.

———. *The Apocalyptic Imagination: An Introduction to the Jewish Matrix of Christianity.* New York: Crossroad, 1984.

———. *Daniel: A Commentary on the Book of Daniel.* Hermenia. Minneapolis: Fortress Press, 1993.

———. "Introduction: Towards the Morphology of a Genre." In *Apocalypse: The Morphology of a Genre.* Semeia 14, edited by John J. Collins, 1–20. Missoula, Mont.: Society of Biblical Literature, 1979.

———. *Jewish Wisdom in the Hellenistic Age.* OTL. Louisville, Ky.: Westminster/John Knox Press, 1997.

———. "The Sage in the Apocalyptic and Pseudepigraphic Literature." In *The Sage in Israel and the Ancient Near East,* edited by John G. Gammie and Leo Perdue, 343–54. Winona Lake, Ind.: Eisenbrauns, 1990.

———. ed. *Apocalypse: The Morphology of a Genre.* Semeia 14. Missoula, Mont.: Society of Biblical Literature, 1979.

Coogan, Michael David. *West Semitic Personal Names in the Murashu Documents.* HSM 7. Missoula, Mont.: Scholars Press, 1976.

Crenshaw, James L. "The Contemplative Life in the Ancient Near East." In *CANE,* 4.2445–57.

———. "Education in Ancient Israel." *JBL* 104 (1985): 601–15.

———. *Education in Ancient Israel: Across the Deadening Silence.* ABRL. New York: Doubleday, 1998.

———. *Joel: A New Translation with Introduction and Commentary.* AB 24C. New York: Doubleday, 1995.

———. *Old Testament Wisdom: An Introduction.* Revised and Enlarged Edition. Louisville, Ky.: Westminster/John Knox Press, 1998.

———. *Prophetic Conflict: Its Effect upon Israelite Religion.* BZAW 124. Berlin: Walter de Gruyter, 1971.

———. "The Sojourner Has Come to Play the Judge: Theodicy on Trial." In *God in the Fray: A Tribute to Walter Brueggemann,* edited by Tod Linafelt and Timothy K. Beal. Minneapolis: Fortress Press, 1998.

———. "Theodicy." *ABD* 6.444–47.

———. *Theodicy in the Old Testament.* Issues in Religion and Theology 4. Philadelphia: Fortress Press, 1983.

———. "Transmitting Prophecy across Generations." In *Writings and Speech in Israelite and Ancient Near Eastern Prophecy,* edited by Ehud Ben Zvi and Michael H. Floyd, 31–44. SBL Symposium Series 10. Atlanta, Ga.: Society of Biblical Literature, 2000.

———. *Urgent Advice and Probing Questions: Collected Writings on Old Testament Wisdom.* Macon, Ga.: Mercer University Press, 1995.

Cross, Frank Moore. *The Ancient Library of Qumran.* 3rd Edition. Biblical Seminar 30. Sheffield: Sheffield Academic Press, 1995.

———. "A Literate Soldier: Lachish Letter III." In *Biblical and Related Studies Presented to Samuel Iwry,* edited by A. Kort and S. Morschauser, 41–47. Winona Lake, Ind.: Eisenbrauns, 1985.

Daniels, Peter T. "Scribes and Scribal Techniques." In *OEANE,* 4.500–502.

Davies, Graham I. "Were There Schools in Ancient Israel?" In *Wisdom in Ancient Israel: Essays in Honour of J. A. Emerton,* edited by John Day, Robert P. Gordon, and H. G. M. Williamson, 199–211. Cambridge: Cambridge University Press, 1995.

Davies, Philip R. *Scribes and Schools: The Canonization of the Hebrew Scriptures.* Library of Ancient Israel. Louisville, Ky.: Westminster/John Knox Press, 1998.

Dearman, J. Andrew. "My Servants the Scribes: Composition and Context in Jeremiah 36." *JBL* 109:3 (1990): 403–21.

Dedering, Sven "Apocalypse of Baruch." In *The Old Testament in Syriac According to the Peshitta Version,* Part IV, Fascicle 3. Peshitta Institute. Leiden: E. J. Brill, 1973.

Delling, Gerhard. *Jüdische Lehre und Frömmigkeit in den Paralipomena Jeremiae.* BZAW 100. Berlin: Töpelmann, 1967.

Denis, Albert-Marie. *Introduction aux pseudépigraphis grecs d'Ancien Testament.* SVTP 1. Leiden: E. J. Brill, 1970.

Dimant, Devorah. "Men as Angels: The Self-Image of the Qumran Community." In *Religion and Politics in the Ancient Near East,* edited by Adele Berlin, 93–103. Bethesda: University Press of Maryland, 1996.

Doré, Gustave. *The Doré Bible Illustrations.* New York: Dover Publications, 1974.

———. *Pictures of the Bible: The New Testament and the Apocrypha.* Cambridge, Mass.: Harbour Press, 1988.

———. *Pictures of the Bible: The Old Testament and the Book of Maccabees.* Cambridge, Mass.: Harbour Press, 1988.

Dossin, Georges. *La correspondance féminine: transcrite et traduite,* ARM X. Paris: Librairie Orientaliste Paul Geuthner, 1978.

Dozeman, Thomas B. "Masking Moses and Mosaic Authority in Torah." *JBL* 119:1 (2000): 21–45.

Duhm, Bernhard, *Das Buch Jeremia.* Kurzer Hand-Commentar zum Alten Testament, vol. 11. Tübingen: J. C. B. Mohr (P. Siebeck), 1901.

Durand, Jean-Marie. *Archives Épistolaires de Mari I/1.* ARM XXVI. Paris: Editions Recherche sur Civilisations, 1988.

Ehrhard, Albert. *Überlieferung und Bestand der hagiographischen und homiletischen Literatur der griechischen Kirche: Von den Anfängen bis zum Ende des 16. Jahrhunderts,* edited by Erich Klostermann and Carl Schmidt. TU 50:1. Leipzig: Hinrichs, 1937.

Eisenstadt, S. N. *Max Weber on Charisma and Institution Building: Selected Papers.* Chicago: University of Chicago Press, 1968.

Farber, Walter. "Witchcraft, Magic, and Divination in Ancient Mesopotamia." In *CANE,* 3.1895–1909.

Feltes, Heinz. *Die Gattung des Habakukkommentars von Qumran (1QpHab): Eine Studie zum frühen jüdischen Midrasch.* Forschung zur Bibel 58. Würzburg: Echter Verlag, 1986.

Fishbane, Michael. *Biblical Interpretation in Ancient Israel.* Oxford: Clarendon Press, 1985.

———. *The Exegetical Imagination: On Jewish Thought and Theology.* Cambridge: Harvard University Press, 1998.

———. "From Scribalism to Rabbinism: Perspectives on the Emergence of Classical Judaism." In *The Sage in Israel and the Ancient Near East,* edited by John G. Gammie and Leo Perdue, 439–56. Winona Lake, Ind.: Eisenbrauns, 1990.

———. *Text and Texture: Close Readings of Selected Biblical Texts.* New York: Schocken Books, 1979.

———. "Use, Authority and Interpretation of Mikra at Qumran." In *Miqra,* edited by M. J. Mulder, 341–79. CRIANT I. 2. Assen: Van Gorcum/Philadelphia: Fortress Press, 1989.

———. "The Well of Living Water: A Biblical Motif and Its Ancient Transformations." In *"Shar'arei Talmon": Studies in the Bible, Qumran, and the Ancient Near East Presented to Shemaryahu Talmon,* edited by Michael Fishbane and Emanuel Tov, 3–16. Winona Lake, Ind.: Eisenbrauns, 1992.

Fowler, Jeaneane D. *Theophoric Personal Names in Ancient Hebrew.* JSOTSup 49. Sheffield: Sheffield Academic Press, 1988.

Fox, Nili S. *In the Service of the King: Officialdom in Ancient Israel and Judah.* Monographs of the Hebrew Union College 23. Cincinnati: Hebrew Union College Press, 2000.

Friedman, Richard E. *Who Wrote the Bible?* New York: Summit Books, 1987.

Gammie, John G., and Leo G. Perdue, eds. *Sages in Israel and the Ancient Near East.* Winona Lake, Ind.: Eisenbrauns, 1990.

Gardiner, A. "Ramesside Texts Relating to the Taxation and Transport of Corn." *Journal of Egyptian Archaeology* 27 (1941): 19–73.

Ginzberg, Louis. "Baruch." In *The Jewish Encyclopedia.* 12 vols, edited by Isidore Singer and Cyrus Adler, 1.548–49. New York/London: Funk & Wagnall's Company, 1901–1906.

Glatt-Gilad, David A. "The Personal Names in Jeremiah as a Source for the History of the Period," *Hebrew Studies* 41 (2000): 31–45.

Gnuse, Robert. "The Jewish Dream Interpreter in a Foreign Court: The Recurring Use of a Theme in Jewish Literature." *JSP* 7 (1990): 29–53.

Goodspeed, Edgar J. *The Story of the Apocrypha*. Chicago: University of Chicago Press, 1939.

Grabbe, Lester L. *Priests, Prophets, Diviners, Sages: A Socio-Historical Study of Religious Specialists in Ancient Israel*. Valley Forge, Pa.: Trinity Press International, 1995.

Graupner, Axel. "Jeremia 45 als 'Schlußwort' des Jeremiabuches." In *Altes Testament und christliche Verkündigung: Festschrift für Antnius H. J. Gunneweg zum 65. Geburtstag*, edited by Manfred Oeming and Axel Graupner, 287–308. Stuttgart: Kohlhammer, 1987.

Greenspahn, Frederick E. "Why Prophecy Ceased." *JBL* 108 (1989): 37–49.

Hall, Robert G. "The *Ascension of Isaiah:* Community Situation, Date, and Place in Early Christianity." *JBL* 109:2 (1990): 289–306.

Hanson, Paul D. "Apocalypse, Genre," and "Apocalypticism." In *Interpreter's Dictionary of the Bible, Supplementary Volume*, 27–34. Nashville, Tenn.: Abingdon Press, 1976.

Haran, Menahem. "On the Diffusion of Literacy and Schools in Ancient Israel." In *Congress Volume, Jerusalem, 1986*, edited by J. A. Emerton, 81–95. VTSup 40. Leiden: E. J. Brill, 1988.

Harlow, Daniel C. *The Greek Apocalypse of Baruch (3 Baruch) in Hellenistic Judaism and Early Christianity*. SVTP 12. Leiden: E. J. Brill, 1996.

Harrington, Daniel J. *Invitation to the Apocrypha*. Grand Rapids, Mich.: Eerdmans, 1999.

———. "The Wisdom of the Scribe According to Ben Sira." In *Ideal Figures in Ancient Judaism*, edited by G. W. E. Nickelsburg and John J. Collins, 181–89. SCS 12. Chico, Calif.: Scholars Press, 1980.

Harris, J. Rendel. *The Rest of the Words of Baruch*. London: Clay, 1889.

Harwell, R. R. "The Principal Versions of Baruch." Ph.D. diss., Yale University, 1915.

Hasidah, Israel Yitzhaq, ed. *Encyclopedia of Biblical Personalities: As Seen by the Sages of the Talmud and Midrash*. Jerusalem: Rueven Mas, 1995 [Hebrew].

Heaton, E. W. *The School Tradition of the Old Testament*. Oxford: Oxford University Press, 1994.

Hellholm, David, ed. *Apocalypticism in the Mediterranean World and the Near East: Proceedings of the International Colloquium on Apocalypticism, Uppsala, August 12–17, 1979*. 2d Edition. Tübingen: J. C. B. Mohr (Paul Siebeck), 1989.

Herr, Larry G. "Paleography and the Identification of Seal Owners." *BASOR* 254 (1980): 67–70.

———. *The Scripts of Ancient Northwest Semitic Seals*. HSM 18. Missoula, Mont.: Scholars Press, 1978.

Himmelfarb, Martha. *Tours of Hell: An Apocalyptic Form in Jewish and Christian Literature*. Philadelphia: Fortress, 1983.

Hippolytus. *Refutatio omnium haeresium.* Edited by Paul Wendland. GCS 26:3. Hildesheim/New York: Georg Olms Verlag, 1977.

———. "The Refutation of All Heresies." In *The Ante-Nicene Fathers: Translations of the Fathers Down to* A.D. 325. 10 vols., edited by Alexander Roberts, et al., and revised by A. Cleveland Coxe, 5.69–73. New York: Charles Scribner's Sons, 1899–1926.

Holladay, William H. "The Identification of the Two Scrolls of Jeremiah." *VT* 30 (1980): 452–67.

Holladay, William L. *Jeremiah: A Commentary on the Book of the Prophet Jeremiah.* 2 vols. Hermeneia. Minneapolis: Fortress Press, 1986/1989.

Horgan, Maurya P. *Pesharim: Qumran Interpretations of Biblical Books.* CBQMS 8. Washington, D.C.: The Catholic Biblical Association of America, 1979.

Humphreys, W. Lee. "A Lifestyle for the Diaspora: A Study of the Tales of Esther and Daniel." *JBL* 92 (1973): 211–23.

Jaeger, Werner W. *Early Christianity and Greek Paideia.* Cambridge: Belknap/Harvard University Press, 1985.

———. *Paideia: The Ideals of Greek Culture.* 3 vols. Translated by Gilbert Highet. New York/Oxford: Oxford University Press, 1939–44.

James, Montague Rhodes. *Apocrypha Anecdota II,* edited by J. Armitage Robinson. Texts and Studies 5:1. Cambridge: Cambridge University Press, 1897.

———. *The Lost Apocrypha of the Old Testament: Their Titles and Fragments.* London/New York: SPCK/Macmillan, 1936.

Jamieson-Drake, David W. *Scribes and Schools in Monarchic Judah: A Socio-Archaeological Approach.* JSOTSup109. Social World of Biblical Antiquity Series 9. Sheffield: Almond Press, 1991.

Janzen, Jerald G. *Studies in the Text of Jeremiah.* HSM 6. Cambridge: Harvard University Press, 1973.

Jellicoe, Sidney. *The Septuagint and Modern Study.* Oxford: Clarendon Press, 1968.

Jellinek, Adolph, ed. *Bet HaMidrash.* Jerusalem: Wahrmann, 1967.

Kaufman, Stephen A. "Rhetoric, Redaction, and Message in Jeremiah." In *Judaic Perspectives on Ancient Israel,* edited by Jacob Neusner, Baruch A. Levine, and Ernest S. Frerichs, 63–74. Philadelphia: Fortress Press, 1987.

Kerferd, George B. "The Sage in Hellenistic Philosophical Literature." In *The Sage in Israel and the Ancient Near East,* edited by John G. Gammie and Leo Perdue, 319–28. Winona Lake, Ind.: Eisenbrauns, 1990.

Kessler, Martin. "Form-Critical Suggestions on Jer. 36." *CBQ* 28 (1966): 389–401.

———. "Jeremiah Chapters 26–45 Reconsidered," *JNES* 27:2 (1968): 81–88.

King, Philip J. *Jeremiah: An Archaeological Companion*. Louisville, Ky.: Westminster/John Knox Press, 1993.

Kirschbaum, Engelbert, ed. *Lexikon der Christlichen Ikonographie*. 8 vols. Freiburg: Herder, 1968–1976.

Klijn, A. F. J. "2 (Syriac Apocalypse of) Baruch." In *OTP* 1.615–52.

———. "Recent Developments in the Study of the Syriac Apocalypse of Baruch." *JSP* 4 (1989): 3–17.

Kohlenberger, John R. III, *The Parallel Apocrypha*. New York/Oxford: Oxford University Press, 1997.

Kohler, K. "The Pre-Talmudic Haggada, I." *JQR* 5 (1893): 414–19.

Kraeling, Carl H., and Robert M. Adams, eds. *City Invincible: A Symposium on Urbanization and Cultural Development in the Ancient Near East Held at the Oriental Institute of the University of Chicago, December 4–7, 1958*. Chicago: University of Chicago Press, 1960.

Kraft, Robert A., and Ann-Elizabeth Purintun, eds. *Paraleipomena Jeremiou*. Texts and Translations 1. Missoula, Mont.: Society of Biblical Literature, 1972.

Kuhn, K. H. "A Coptic Jeremiah Apocryphon," *Le Muséon* 83:1–2 (1970): 95–135; *Le Muséon* 83:3–4 (1970): 291–350.

Kushner, Harold S. *When Bad Things Happen to Good People*. New York: Schocken Books, 1981.

Lemaire, André. *Les écoles et la formation de la Bible dans l'ancien Israël*. OBO 39. Fribourg: Éditions Universitaires/Göttingen: Vandenhoeck & Ruprecht, 1981.

Leslau, Wolf. *Falasha Anthology*. Yale Judaica Series 6. New Haven/London: Yale University Press, 1951.

Lindenberger, James M. *Ancient Aramaic and Hebrew Letters*. SBL Writings from the Ancient World, vol. 4. Atlanta, Ga.: Scholars Press, 1994.

Lipinski, E. "Royal and State Scribes in Ancient Jerusalem." In *Congress Volume, Jerusalem, 1986*, edited by J. A. Emerton, 157–64. VTSup 40. Leiden: E. J. Brill, 1988.

Loewenstamm, S. E. "The Death of Moses." In *Studies on the Testament of Abraham*, edited by G. W. E. Nickelsburg, 185–217. SCS 6. Missoula, Mont.: Scholars Press, 1976.

Lundbom, J. R. "Baruch, Seraiah, and Expanded Colophons in the Book of Jeremiah." *JSOT* 36 (1986): 89–114.

———. *Jeremiah: A Study in Ancient Hebrew Rhetoric*. Missoula, Mont.: Society of Biblical Literature and Scholars Press, 1975.

Malamat, Abraham. "Prophetic Revelations in New Documents from Mari and the Bible." In *Volume du congrès, Genève 1965*, edited by G. W. Anderson et al., 207–27. VTSup 15. Leiden: E. J. Brill, 1966.

Martínez, Florentino García, and Eibert J. C. Tigchelaar, eds. *The Dead Sea Scrolls: Study Edition*. 2 vols. Leiden: E. J. Brill, 1997–98.

McKane, William. *A Critical and Exegetical Commentary on Jeremiah*. 2 vols. ICC. Edinburgh: T. & T. Clark, 1986/1996.

Merkur, Daniel. "The Visionary Practices of the Jewish Apocalypticists." *The Psychoanalytic Study of Society*, vol. 14, edited by L. Bryce Boyer and Simon A. Grolnick, 119–48. Hillsdale, N.J.: Analytic Press, 1989.

Meshel, Zeëv. "Kuntillet Ájrud—An Israelite Site from the Monarchical Period on the Sinai Border." *Qadmoniot* 9 (1976):118–24 [Hebrew].

Metzger, Bruce. *An Introduction to the Apocrypha*. New York/Oxford: Oxford University Press, 1957.

———. "Literary Forgeries and Canonical Pseudepigrapha." *JBL* 91 (1972): 3–24.

Milik, J. T. *The Books of Enoch: Aramaic Fragments of Qumran Cave 4*. Oxford: Clarendon Press, 1976.

———. *Ten Years of Discovery in the Wilderness of Judaea*. SBT 26. London: SCM Press Ltd., 1959.

Millard, Alan R. "An Assessment of the Evidence for Writing in Ancient Israel." In *Biblical Archaeology Today: Proceedings of the International Congress on Biblical Archaeology, Jerusalem, April 1984*, edited by Janet Amitai, 301–12. Jerusalem: Israel Exploration Society, 1985.

———. "The Practice of Writing in Ancient Israel," *BA* 35 (1972): 98–111.

Modrzejewski, Joseph Mélèze. *The Jews of Egypt: From Rameses II to Emperor Hadrian*. Translated by Robert Cornman. Philadelphia: Jewish Publication Society, 1995.

Moore, Carey. "Toward the Dating of the Book of Baruch." *CBQ* 36 (1974): 312–20.

Montserrat-Torrents, J. "La philosophie du *Livre de Baruch* de Justin." In *Studia Patristica XVIII: Papers of the 1983 Oxford Patristics Conference*, edited by Elizabeth A. Livingstone, 253–61. Kalamazoo, Mich.: Cistercian Publications, 1985.

Moran, William L. "New Evidence from Mari on the History of Prophecy." *Biblica* 50 (1969): 15–56.

Morinis, E. Alan. *Sacred Journeys: The Anthropology of Pilgrimage*. New York: Greenwood Press, 1992.

Mowinckel, Sigmund. *Zur Komposition des Buches Jeremia*. Kristiania: J. Dybwad, 1914.

Muilenburg, James. "Baruch the Scribe." In *Proclamation and Presence*, edited by John I. Durham and J. R. Porter, 232–38. Richmond: John Knox Press, 1970.

Murphy, Frederick James. *The Structure and Meaning of Second Baruch*. Atlanta, Ga.: Scholars Press, 1985.

Na'aman, Nadav. "The Debated Historicity of Hezekiah's Reform in the Light of Historical and Archaeological Research." *ZAW* 107 (1995): 181–95.

Naveh, Joseph. "A Paleographic Note on the Distribution of the Hebrew Script." *HTR* 61 (1968): 68–74.

Neusner, Jacob. *Judaism in the Beginning of Christianity.* Philadelphia: Fortress Press, 1984.

———. "Note on Barukh ben Neriah and Zoroaster." *Numen* 12:1 (1965): 66–69.

———. "Religious Authority in Judaism: Modern and Classical Modes." *Int* 39:4 (1985): 373–87.

Nicholson, E. W. *Preaching to the Exiles: A Study of the Prose Tradition in the Book of Jeremiah.* Oxford: Blackwell, 1970.

Nickelsburg, George, W. E. "Narrative Traditions in the Paraleipomena of Jeremiah and 2 Baruch." *CBQ* 35 (1973): 60–68.

———. "Social Aspects of Palestinian Jewish Apocalypticism." In *Apocalypticism in the Mediterranean World and the Near East: Proceedings of the International Colloquium on Apocalypticism, Uppsala, August 12–17, 1979,* edited by David Hellholm, 641–50. 2d edition. Tübingen: J. C. B. Mohr (Paul Siebeck), 1989.

———. "Stories of Biblical and Early Post-Biblical Times." In *Jewish Writings of the Second Temple Period,* edited by Michael E. Stone, 33–87. CRIANT 2.2. Van Gorcum/Philadelphia: Assen/Fortress Press, 1984.

Niditch, Susan. "Merits, Martyrs, and 'Your Life as Booty': An Exegesis of *Mekilta, Pisha 1.*" *JSJ* 13:1–2 (1988): 160–71.

Nissinen, Martti, ed. *Prophecy in its Ancient Near Eastern Context: Mesopotamian, Biblical, and Arabian Perspectives.* SBL Symposium Series 13. Atlanta, Ga.: Society of Biblical Literature, 2000.

Nissinen, Martti, and Simo Parpola, eds. *References to Prophecy in Neo-Assyrian Sources.* State Archives of Assyria Studies 7. Helsinki: Neo-Assyrian Text Corpus Project, 1998.

Nitzan, Bilhah. *Pesher Habakkuk: A Scroll from the Wilderness of Judaea (1QpHab). Text, Translation and Commentary.* Jerusalem: Bialik Institute, 1986 [Hebrew].

Noth, Martin. *Die israelitschen Personennamen in Rahmen der gemeinsemitischen Namengebung.* Hildesheim: Georg Olms Verlagsbuchhandlung, 1966.

Oppenheim, A. Leo. *Ancient Mesopotamia: Portrait of a Dead Civilization.* Chicago: University of Chicago Press, 1964.

———. *The Interpretation of Dreams in the Ancient Near East, with a Translation of an Assyrian Dream-Book.* TAPS 46:3. Philadelphia: American Philosophical Society, 1956.

Orlinsky, Harry M. *Essays in Biblical Culture and Bible Translation.* New York: KTAV, 1974.

———. "The Septuagint as Holy Writ and the Philosophy of the Translators." *HUCA* 46 (1975): 89–114.

Ousterhout, Robert G. *The Blessings of Pilgrimage*. Urbana: University of Illinois Press, 1990.

Paul, Shalom M. *Amos: A Commentary on the Book of Amos*. Hermeneia. Minneapolis: Fortress Press, 1991.

Pearce, Laurie E. "The Scribes and Scholars of Ancient Mesopotamia." In *Civilizations of the Ancient Near East*, 4 vols., edited by Jack M. Sasson, 4.2265–78. New York: Charles Scribner's Sons, 1995.

Peters, M. K. H. "Septuagint." In *ABD*, 5.1093–104.

Petersen, David L. "Rethinking the Nature of Prophetic Literature." In *Prophecy and Prophets: The Diversity of Contemporary Issues in Scholarship*, edited by Yehoshua Gitay, 23–40. Society of Biblical Literature Semeia Studies. Atlanta, Ga.: Scholars Press, 1997.

Picard, J.-C., ed. *Apocalypsis Baruchi Graece*. PVTG 2. Leiden: E. J. Brill, 1967.

———. "Observations sur l'Apocalypse greque de Baruch I: Cadre historique fictif et efficacité symbolique." *Semitica* 20 (1970): 77–103.

Porten, Bezalel, and Ada Yardeni. *Textbook of Aramaic Documents from Ancient Egypt: 1 Letters*. Hebrew University Department of the History of the Jewish People, Texts and Studies for Students. Winona Lake, Ind.: Eisenbrauns, 1986, 54–55.

Prawer, Joshua. *The History of the Jews in the Latin Kingdom of Jerusalem*. Oxford: Clarendon, 1988.

Puech, Emile. "Les écoles dans l'Israël préexilique: Donées épigraphiques." In *Congress Volume, Jerusalem, 1986*, edited by J. A. Emerton, 189–203. VTSup 40. Leiden: E. J. Brill, 1988.

Rabin, Chaim. *The Zadokite Documents*. Oxford: Clarendon Press, 1954.

Rad, Gerhard von. *The Message of the Prophets*. New York: Harper and Row Publishers, 1965.

———. *Wisdom in Israel*. Nashville, Tenn.: Abingdon Press, 1972.

Reader, Ian, and Tony Walter. *Pilgrimage in Popular Culture*. Basingstoke: Macmillan, 1993.

Riaud, Jean. "La figure de Jérémie dans les *Paralipomena Jeremiae*." In *Mélanges bibliques et orientaux en l'honneur de M. Henri Cazelles*, edited by André Caquot and Mathias Delcor, 373–85. AOAT 212. Kevelaer/Neukirchen-Vluyn: Verlag Butzon & Bercker/Neukirchener Verlag, 1981.

Robinson, S. E. "4 Baruch." In *OTP* 2.414–15.

Rofé, Alexander. "Studies in the Composition of the Book of Jeremiah." *Tarbitz* 44 (1974–75): 1–29 [Hebrew].

Roitman, Adolfo. *A Day at Qumran: The Dead Sea Sect and Its Scrolls.* Jerusalem: The Israel Museum, 1997.

Saggs, H. W. F. *The Babylonians.* Peoples of the Past 1. Norman: University of Oklahoma Press, 1995.

Sarna, Nahum M. "The Authority and Interpretation of Scripture in Jewish Tradition." In *Understanding Scripture: Explorations of Jewish and Christian Traditions of Interpretation,* edited by Clemens Thoma and Michael Wyschogrod, 9–20. Studies in Judaism and Christianity. Mahwah, N.J.: Paulist Press, 1987.

Sasson, Jack M., ed. *Civilizations of the Ancient Near East.* 4 vols. New York: Charles Scribner's Sons, 1995.

Sayler, Gwendolyn B. *Have the Promises Failed? A Literary Analysis of 2 Baruch.* SBLDS 72. Chico, Calif.: Scholars Press, 1984.

Schams, Christine. *Jewish Scribes in the Second-Temple Period.* JSOTSup 291. Sheffield: Sheffield Academic Press, 1998.

Schearing, Linda S., and Steven L. McKenzie, eds. *Those Elusive Deuteronomists: The Phenomenon of Pan-Deuteronomism.* JSOTSup 268. Sheffield: Sheffield Academic Press, 1999.

Schermann, Theodor, ed. *Prophetarum vitae fabulosae: indices apostolorum discipulorumque domini Dorotheo, Epiphanio, Hippolyto aliisque vindicata.* Leipzig: Teubner, 1907.

Schmid, H., and W. Speyer. "Baruch." In *Jahrbuch für Antike und Christentum,* vol. 17, 177–90. Münster: Aschendorffsche Verlagsbuchhandlung, 1974.

Schneider, Tsvi. "Six Biblical Signatures: Seals and Seal Impressions of Six Biblical Personages Recovered." *BARev* 17:4 (July/August 1991): 26–33.

Schniedewind, William M. *Society and the Promise to David.* Oxford/New York: Oxford University Press, 1999.

Schreiner, J. *Baruch.* Die Neue Echter Bibel Altes Testament 14. Würzburg: Echter Verlag, 1986.

Schulte, Hannelis. "Baruch und Ebedmelech—Persönliche Heilsorakel im Jeremiabuche." *BZ* 32:2 (1988): 257–65.

Seitz, Christopher R. "The Prophet Moses and the Canonical Shape of Jeremiah." *ZAW* 101 (1989): 3–27.

Seow, C. L. "Linguistic Evidence and the Dating of Qohelet." *JBL* 115:4 (1996): 643–66.

Shanks, Hershel. "Jeremiah's Scribe and Confidant Speaks from a Hoard of Clay Bullae." *BARev* 13:5 (1987): 58–65.

———. "Fingerprint of Jeremiah's Scribe." *BARev* 22:2 (March/April 1996): 36–38.

Silverman, Michael H. *Religious Values in the Jewish Proper Names at Elephantine.* Kevelaer: Verlag Butzon and Bereker, 1985.

Smith, Morton. *Palestinian Parties and Politics That Shaped the Old Testament.* New York: Columbia University Press, 1971.

Smith, Robert Payne. *Thesaurus Syriacus,* 2 vols. Oxford: Clarendon Press, 1879–1901.

Soderlund, Sven. *The Greek Text of Jeremiah: A Revised Hypothesis.* JSOTSup 47. Sheffield: JSOT Press, 1985.

Sommer, Benjamin D. "Did Prophecy Cease: Evaluating a Reevaluation." *JBL* 115 (1996): 31–47.

Sparks, H. F. D., ed. *The Apocryphal Old Testament.* Oxford: Clarendon Press, 1984.

Speyer, Wolfgang. *Die literarische Fälschung im heidenischen und christlichen Altertum: Ein Versuch ihrer Deutung.* HAW 1.2. Munich: Beck, 1971.

Spronk, Klaas. *Beatific Afterlife in Ancient Israel and in the Ancient Near East.* Neukirchen-Vluyn: Neukirchener Verlag/Kevelaer: Butzon & Bercker, 1986.

Stone, Michael E. "Apocalyptic Literature." In *Jewish Writings of the Second Temple Period,* edited by Michael E. Stone, 383–441. CRIANT 2.2. Assen/Philadelphia: Van Gorcum/Fortress, 1984.

———. *Armenian Apocrypha Relating to the Patriarchs and Prophets.* Jerusalem: Israel Academy of Sciences and Humanities, 1982.

———. "Baruch, Rest of the Words of." In *Encyclopedia Judaica.* 16 vols., 4.276–77. Jerusalem/New York: Encyclopaedia Judaica/Macmillan, 1971–72.

———. "The Books of Enoch and Judaism in the Third Century B.C.E." *CBQ* 40 (1978): 479–92.

———. *Fourth Ezra: A Commentary on the Book of Fourth Ezra.* Hermeneia. Minneapolis: Fortress Press, 1990.

———. "Ideal Figures and Social Context: Priest and Sage in the Early Second Temple Period." In *Ancient Israelite Religion: Essays in Honor of Frank Moore Cross,* edited by Patrick D. Miller, et al., 575–86. Philadelphia: Fortress Press, 1987.

———. "Lists of Revealed Things in Apocalyptic Literature." In *Magnalia Dei: The Mighty Acts of God,* edited by F. M. Cross, W. E. Lemke, and P. D. Miller Jr., 414–52. Garden City, N.Y.: Doubleday, 1976.

———. "Why Study the Pseudepigrapha?" *BA* 46:4 (1983): 235–43.

Stone, Michael E., ed. *Jewish Writings of the Second Temple Period.* CRIANT 2.2. Assen/Philadelphia: Van Gorcum/Fortress, 1984.

Stulman, Louis. *The Other Text of Jeremiah: A Reconstruction of the Hebrew Text Underlying the Greek Version of the Prose Sections of Jeremiah with English Translation.* Lanham, Md.: University Press of America, 1985.

———. "Some Theological and Lexical Differences Between the Old Greek and the MT of the Jeremiah Prose Discourses." *Hebrew Studies* 25 (1984): 18–23.

Talmon, Shemaryahu. "The Presentation of Synchroneity and Simultaneity in Biblical Narrative." In *Studies in Hebrew Narrative Art through the Ages,* edited by Joseph Heinemann and S. Werses, 9–26. Scripta Hierosolymitana 27. Jerusalem: Magnes Press, 1978.

Taylor, Marion Ann. "Jeremiah 45: The Problem of Placement." *JSOT* 37 (1987): 79–98.

Thiel, Winfried. *Die deuteronomistische Redaktion von Jeremia 1–25.* WMANT 41. Neukirchen-Vluyn: Neukirchener Verlag, 1973.

———. *Die deuteronomistische Redaktion von Jeremia 26–45,* WMANT 52. Neukirchen-Vluyn: Neukirchener Verlag, 1981.

Toorn, Karel van der. "From the Oral to the Written: The Case of Old Babylonian Prophecy." In *Writings and Speech in Israelite and Ancient Near Eastern Prophecy,* edited by Ehud Ben Zvi and Michael H. Floyd, 219–34. SBL Symposium Series 10. Atlanta, Ga.: Society of Biblical Literature, 2000.

———. "Funerary Rituals and Beatific Afterlife in Ugaritic Texts and the Bible." *BO* 48 (1991): 40–66.

Torczyner, Harry. *Lachish I: The Lachish Letters.* London: Oxford University Press, 1938.

Tov, Emanuel. "L'incidence de la critique textuelle sur la critique littéraire dans le livre de Jérémie." *RB* 79 (1972): 189–99.

———. "The Relations between the Greek Versions of Baruch and Daniel." In *Armenian and Biblical Studies,* edited by Michael E. Stone, 27–34. Jerusalem: St. James Press, 1976.

———. "The Septuagint." In *Mikra: Text, Translation, Reading and Interpretation of the Hebrew Bible in Ancient Judaism and Early Christianity,* edited by M. J. Mulder, 161–88. CRIANT. Assen/Philadelphia: Van Gorcum/Fortress Press, 1988.

———. *The Septuagint Translation of Jeremiah and Baruch: A Discussion of an Early Revision of Jeremiah 29–52 and Baruch 1:1–3:8.* HSM 8. Missoula, Mont.: Scholars Press, 1976.

———. *Textual Criticism of the Hebrew Bible.* Minneapolis/Assen: Fortress/van Gorcum, 1992.

Tov, Emanuel, ed. and trans. *The Book of Baruch.* Texts and Translations 8. Missoula, Mont.: Scholars Press, 1975.

VanderKam, James C. *Enoch: A Man for All Generations.* Studies on the Personalities of the Old Testament. Columbia: University of South Carolina Press, 1995.

VanderKam, James C., and Peter Flint. *The Meaning of the Dead Sea Scrolls: Their*

Significance for Understanding the Bible, Judaism, Jesus, and Christianity. New York: HarperCollins, 2002.

Vaughn, Andrew G. "Palaeographic Dating of Judean Seals and Its Significance for Biblical Research." *BASOR* 313 (1999): 43–64.

Vermes, Geza. *The Complete Dead Sea Scrolls in English.* New York/London: Penguin Press, 1997.

⸺. "Jewish Studies and New Testament Interpretation." *JJS* 21:1 (1980): 1–17.

Wambacq, B. N. "Les prieres de Baruch 1:15–2–19 et de Daniel 9:5–19." *Biblica* 40:2 (1959): 463–75.

⸺. "L'unité du livre de Baruch." *Biblica* 46 (1966): 574–76.

Wanke, Gunther. *Untersuchungen zur sogenannten Baruchschrift.* BZAW 122. Berlin: Walter de Gruyter, 1971.

Ward, J. M. "The Eclipse of the Prophet in Contemporary Prophetic Studies." *USQR* 42 (1988): 97–104.

Weeks, Stuart. *Early Israelite Wisdom.* Oxford Theological Monographs. Oxford/ New York: Clarendon Press/Oxford University Press, 1994.

Weinfeld, Moshe. *Deuteronomy and the Deuteronomic School.* Oxford: Clarendon Press, 1972.

Weiser, Artur. "Das Gotteswort für Baruch: Jer. 45 und die sogenannte Baruch-biographie." In *Glaube und Geschichte im Alten Testament und andere ausgewählte Schriften,* edited by A. Weiser, 321–29. Göttingen: Vandenhoeck & Ruprecht, 1961.

Wente, Edward F. "The Scribes of Egypt." In *Civilizations of the Ancient Near East,* 4 vols., edited by Jack M. Sasson, 4.2211–21. New York: Charles Scribner's Sons, 1995.

Wilson, Robert R. "Historicizing the Prophets: History and Literature in the Book of Jeremiah." In *On the Way to Nineveh: Studies in Honor of George M. Landes,* 135–54. Atlanta, Ga.: ASOR/Scholars Press, 1999.

⸺. *Prophecy and Society in Ancient Israel.* Philadelphia: Fortress Press, 1980.

Wise, Michael, Martin Abegg Jr., and Edward Cook. *The Dead Sea Scrolls: A New Translation.* New York: HarperCollins, 1996.

Wolff, Hans W. *Joel and Amos: A Commentary on the Books of the Prophets Joel and Amos.* Hermeneia. Philadelphia: Fortress Press, 1977.

Wright, J. Edward. "Baruch: An Ideal Sage." In *"Go to the Land I Will Show You": Studies in Honor of Dwight W. Young,* edited by Joseph P. Coleson and Victor Matthews, 193–210. Winona Lake, Ind.: Eisenbrauns, 1996.

⸺. "Baruch: His Evolution from Scribe to Apocalyptic Seer." In *Biblical Figures Outside the Bible,* edited by Michael E. Stone and Theodore A. Bergren, 264–89. Harrisburg, Pa.: Trinity Press International, 1998.

———. "Books of Baruch." In *Dictionary of New Testament Background,* edited by Craig A. Evans and Stanley E. Porter, 148–51. Downers Grove, Ill./Leicester: InterVarsity Press, 2000.

———. *The Cosmography of the Greek Apocalypse of Baruch and Its Affinities.* Ph.D. diss., Brandeis University, 1992.

———. *The Early History of Heaven.* Oxford/New York: Oxford University Press, 2000.

———. "The Social Setting of the Syriac Apocalypse of Baruch." *JSP* 16 (1997): 83–98.

Wright, R. B. *"Psalms of Solomon."* In *OTP,* 2.647–49.

Yadin, Yigael. *The Art of Warfare in Biblical Lands: In the Light of Archaeological Study.* 2 vols. New York: McGraw-Hill, 1963.

Yarbro Collins, Adela, ed. *Early Christian Apocalypticism: Genre and Social Setting,* Semeia 36. Decatur, Ga.: Scholars Press/Society of Biblical Literature, 1986.

———. "Introduction." In *Early Christian Apocalypticism: Genre and Social Setting,* edited by Adela Yarbro Collins, 1–11. Semeia 36. Decatur, Ga.: Scholars Press/Society of Biblical Literature, 1986.

Zadok, Ran. *The Jews in Babylonia during the Chaldean and Achaemenian Periods According to the Babylonian Sources.* Haifa: University of Haifa, 1979.

Ziegler, Joseph, ed., *Daniel, Susanna, Bel et Draco.* Septuaginta Vetus Testamentum Graecum 16.2. Göttingen: Vandenhoeck & Ruprecht, 1954.

Index

Index of Biblical and Ancient Sources